A HISTORY OF
TRAVEL IN AMERICA

Sample of wall paper printed in 1825 in celebration of the completion of the Erie Canal. Often used in making band-boxes of the period. Printed by a stencil process, endlessly repeated. L. F. Amer.

ALLEGHENY COLLEGE LIBRARY

A History of Travel
in
America

Being an Outline of the Development in Modes of Travel from Archaic
Vehicles of Colonial Times to the Completion of the First Trans-
continental Railroad: the Influence of the Indians on the Free
Movement and Territorial Unity of the White Race: the
Part Played by Travel Methods in the Economic Conquest
of the Continent: and those Related Human Experiences,
Changing Social Conditions and Governmental Atti-
tudes which Accompanied the Growth of a
National Travel System

BY
SEYMOUR DUNBAR

With two maps, twelve colored plates and four hundred illustrations

VOLUME III

INDIANAPOLIS
THE BOBBS-MERRILL COMPANY
PUBLISHERS

PRINTED IN THE UNITED STATES OF AMERICA
BY THE CORNWALL PRESS, INC.

A HISTORY OF
TRAVEL IN AMERICA

A HISTORY OF
TRAVEL IN AMERICA

CHAPTER XXXIV

IMPORTANCE OF STAGE-COACH TRAVEL BETWEEN 1800 AND 1840 — SPEED AND RATES OF FARE — COMPETITION BETWEEN RIVAL NEW ENGLAND LINES — ITS EFFECT ON A BOSTON DANCING MASTER — WHEELED VEHICLES OF SMALL USE WEST OF THE ALLEGHANIES UNTIL AFTER 1820 — CHICAGO IN 1833 — DEVELOPMENT OF STAGE LINES IN THE MIDDLE WEST — THE STAGE DRIVER — ACCIDENTS — ADVENTURE OF HENRY CLAY — THE LOST SPEECH OF BLACK HAWK

IT is doubtful if any description written to-day could adequately portray the importance — in its relation to the affairs of the people — which stage-coach traffic assumed during the period between 1800 and 1840. During the years in question it was the only means by which a large part of the population could accomplish overland journeys, and even in those instances wherein rivers and canals were available for some portions of the expeditions to be undertaken, travellers often had to resort to the stage-coach for considerable parts of the distances traversed. There was no general thought[1] of the future possibility of more comfortable and rapid means of overland conveyance, and all those circumstances of progress

[1] Until about 1826.

by stage which now seem to us to be so archaic and remote were then esteemed as the height of travel luxury. It was seldom that complaints were made by the public about the uncomfortable and wearying conditions that inevitably attended stage-coach travel in those times. Whatever happened on a journey was accepted as a matter of course and endured with complaisance and fortitude. The foreign traveller Weld[1] gives an illuminating description of the spirit in which both passengers and stage-coach driver met, with mutual understanding, the difficulties of an expedition. He says: "The driver frequently had to call to the passengers in the stage to lean out of the carriage, first on one side, then on the other, to prevent it from oversetting in the deep ruts with which the road abounds. 'Now, gentlemen, to the right!' Upon which the passengers stretched their bodies half way out of the carriage to balance on that side. 'Now, gentlemen, to the left!' " and so on.

The speeds attained by the stage-coaches in those days were esteemed as little short of marvelous. Isaiah Thomas, Jr.,[2] had occasion in 1812 to travel from Washington to Baltimore. The trip required one and a half days for its completion in a coach drawn by three horses. He rode in a regular passenger conveyance. The much swifter mail coaches over the same route then left Washington at four o'clock in the morning and reached Baltimore, under favorable conditions, about an hour before midnight on the same day These rates of movement were typical of the speeds maintained throughout the East for many years. One of the best known stage-coach trips of the time was that between Provi-

---

[1] In his "Travels through the States of North America": Vol. i, pp. 37-38.
[2] The well-known Boston printer. His book is entitled "Reminiscences and Sketches."

dence and Boston. Travellers from New York to Boston usually left their destination by a steamboat which landed them in Providence in about twenty-three hours, and they then immediately embarked in stage-coaches to traverse the remaining forty miles to the Massachusetts metropolis. No less than fifteen or twenty, and sometimes twenty-five coaches a day plied between the two cities. In a letter written in 1822 in description of the trip, it was said: "We were rattled from Providence to Boston in four hours and fifty minutes. If any one wants to go faster he may send to Kentucky and charter a streak of lightning."

The fare for the Providence-Boston trip was ordinarily three dollars, but the price of a stage-coach ticket, either for that journey or any other, was by no means permanently fixed. Whenever a new stage line was established the older organizations whose field was thus invaded usually reduced their price of passage in the hope that the new company would thereby find its business unprofitable and be compelled to abandon its competition. If the new company met the lowered passenger tariff then the established lines would promptly make another reduction. When all parties to one of these rate-cutting controversies entered upon the struggle with a grim determination to win, the results were sometimes peculiar and also highly satisfactory to the travelling public. One of the most memorable of these fights for traffic was begun by the action of a new Boston-Providence line in reducing its charge to $2.50. The old lines retaliated by a still further cut to $2.00. By this time the people of the two cities became enthusiastic in their efforts to encourage the combatants, and so heartily did the warring New England companies enter into the spirit of the fray that the cost of tickets between the communities soon disappeared altogether, and every passenger by any of the competing lines was finally in receipt of a free dinner and a bottle of wine in payment for the privilege of transporting him over the road.

The people of the two towns — or as many of them as could possibly do so — arose to the occasion and for a brief interval the travel between the places assumed astonishing proportions. At this time one of the prominent dancing teachers of Boston was a man named Shaffer, very well known and famous for his wit. When the stage-coach lines had reached the point of carrying their patrons for nothing and giving them wine and food in addition, Shaffer could stand the strain no longer. He dismissed his classes; closed his academy; abandoned his profession; and spent his entire time for more than a week in being carried back and forth between Providence and his own home, pausing between trips to enjoy the hospitality of the company he had deigned to honor with his patronage. The inevitable truce between the competing proprietors, and its attendant restoration of rates, was the catastrophe which sent the dancing master and many other of his townsmen back to their ordinary vocations. It was Shaffer who responded one day when an extraordinarily fat man descended from the stage-coach in front of a tavern and inquired how much the establishment charged for its dinner. Shaffer walked slowly around the new arrival, then backed away a few steps in order to get a better view, cocked his head to one side and said: "For that size, four dollars."

Thurlow Weed,[1] in an account of a trip between Albany and Rochester, New York, in 1824, gives further

[1] In his "Autobiography"; vol. 1, pp. 139-140.

RAILROADS, AND RAILROAD CARS.

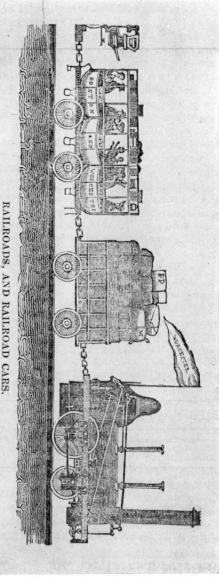

Here is a very good representation of the most common apparatus for travelling on railroads. First you see, on the right hand, the engine, as it is called—I mean the boiler—and place to put the fire and wood ; and the pipe or large tube for the smoke to escape out. Fastened to the hind part of this, by a chain, is a car in which they put the passengers' baggage ; and sometimes goods or merchandise. Attached to this last is a passenger car ; and to that another, and another, and so on.

Sometimes they have six or eight passenger cars, or even more. In the present instance I have shown you only one, with a small part of another ; just because I had not room enough for more.

What you see at the sides of the passenger cars, hanging down a little way, are steps or stirrups, much like those of coaches and chaises ; to assist the passengers in ascending and descending. The wheels of the cars are low, but very strong.

218.—A contemporary explanation of the new apparatus for travelling. Page from a book of the period. The consequences of linking the cars of a train together by means of chains are discussed in Chapter XLIII, in an account of the first railway of New York State.

insight into conditions encountered by stage-coach travellers. He says in his narrative:

"We left Albany at seven o'clock in the evening, and traveled diligently for seven nights and six days. The road from Albany to Schenectady, with the exception of two or three miles, was in a horrible condition, and that west of Schenectady, until we reached Tribe's Hill, still worse. For a few miles in the vicinity of Palatine Church there was a gravelly road over which the driver could raise a trot, but this was a luxury experienced in but few localities and those far between. Passengers walked to ease the coach every day and each night. Although they did not literally carry rails on their shoulders to pry the coach out of the ruts, they were frequently called upon to use rails for that purpose. Such snail-paced movements and such discomforts in travel would be regarded as unendurable now; and yet passengers were patient and some of them even cheerful, under all those ills and annoyances. That, however, was an exceptional passage. It was only when we had horrid bad roads that the stages dragged their slow length along."

Josiah Quincy[1] also left his observations of a stage journey from Philadelphia to Washington in February of 1826. The record was made in his diary and reads:

"At three o'clock this morning the light of a candle under the door and the rousing knock told me that it was time to depart, and shortly after I left Philadelphia by the Lancaster stage, otherwise a vast, illimitable wagon, with seats without backs, capable of holding some sixteen passengers with decent comfort to themselves, and actually encumbered with some dozen more. After riding until eight o'clock we reached the breakfast house, where we partook of a good meal, and took on Messrs. Storm and Wheaton. We then proceeded through a most beautiful tract of country with good fences and stone barns which proved the excellence of the farming. The roads seemed actually lined with Conestoga wagons each drawn by six stalwart horses and laden with farm produce."

On this trip Quincy went from Boston to New York in four days, from New York to Philadelphia in one day, and from Philadelphia to Washington in three days, making his entire time for the journey between Boston and Washington eight days. It was in the following year of 1827 that the work of building the Baltimore and Ohio

[1] His description of a trip from Boston to New York appears in Chapter XI.

219.—The *Baltimore and Ohio Railroad March*. Its publication was inspired by the interest and excitement attending the commencement of the road and the ceremonies of July 4, 1828, on which day the piece of music was offered for sale in Baltimore.

Railroad was proposed, and Quincy's trip, therefore, furnishes a fair illustration of conditions attending stagecoach travel and of the time consumed by it just before the commencement of the railroad era.

Quincy also tells a story of a Massachusetts traveller who, at about the same period, was dashing through the town of Andover on a Sabbath day in his carriage, in defiance of the laws of the commonwealth, when he was halted and threatened with arrest by an indignant church deacon. But the wayfarer was equal to the emergency. Checking his horses and assuming an appearance of profound anxiety, he cried to the deacon, "Tell the good people of Andover that you permitted me to pass because my mother is lying dead in Boston"; and as the deacon recoiled a step from the news thus shouted to him, the traveller gave his horses their heads again and called back to the deacon, "You may add also, if you please, that she has been lying dead there for some twenty years." The carriage then disappeared in a cloud of dust.

Owing to the lack of bridges across the rivers, except in a few thickly settled districts and the immediate neighborhood of cities, any extended journey by coach or wagon necessitated frequent recourse to ferries. Many of these were nothing but rickety scows whose pertinacity in holding together was often the marvel of those voyagers who sought their use, although they sometimes did fulfil expectations by collapsing or sinking under a too onerous burden. Nearly every passage of a river by ferry — except on a busy highway — was an hour of anxiety. An experience of the sort was apparently too familiar to the Americans for comment or chronicle, but a few visitors from other lands did leave accounts of such navigations.

One of these[1] wrote the following description of the manner in which he got his equipage across a stream:

"The next job was to ferry the baggage over; and this effected, the horse was towed across by the nose, an operation of some delicacy both to actors and spectators. Lastly came the transportation of the wagon, and here all my seamanship served only to show the hazard incurred of losing the whole conveyance. If the rope . . . old and much worn, had given way, as I fully expected it would, when the wagon was half-channel over and nothing in sight but four or five inches of railing above the water, we must have bivouac'd where we were. . . . Fortunately we succeeded in dragging the carriage across, and when the four wheels fairly touched the bank I thought of course that all our difficulties were over. But the united strength of all aboard, males and females, young and old combined, could not budge it more than a foot out of the water. I don't know what we should have done had we not spied near the landing place a fathom or two of chain, one end of which our active little commanding officer soon tied to the carriage, and the horse being hitched to the other we drew it triumphantly to land, with a cheer that made the forest ring."

During the second, third and fourth decades after 1800 nearly all the principal cities as far west as Pittsburgh were connected by several lines of stage-coaches. Certain of these lines carried the United States mails and made the quickest trips between the communities they served. The other lines maintained slower schedules. This phase of the varying land travel accommodations obtainable at that time is well illustrated in a volume dealing with the development of Pennsylvania.[2] In its discussion of the service existing between Pittsburgh and Philadelphia in 1831, the book says:

"The announcement was made in the Pittsburg papers of May, 1831, that Reeside, Slaymaker & Company had, with their usual enterprise and public spirit, established four lines of stage coaches to run through to Philadelphia; the first in two and a half days; the second in four days, both of them daily; the third to start tri-weekly, and the fourth to run daily in four days . . . . This was considered at the time a great

[1] Captain Basil Hall of the British Navy, in "Travels in North America": Vol. i, pp. 270-271.
[2] W. H. Wilson's "Notes on the Internal Improvements of Pennsylvania."

advance upon the previous traveling facilities. The writer well recollects the advent of the fast mail line to run through in two and a half days. The coaches were built as light as possible consistent with strength and carried but six passengers each. The four-horse teams were carefully selected, and changed every ten miles. As the sound of the horn announced the approach of the stage to the changing station the fresh horses were brought out, each in charge of a groom, and the change was effected and the coach rolling away before the passengers hardly realized what was being done. The contrast to the old order of things was so marked as to excite a good deal of wonder and remark along the road."([1])

By the year 1832 the trip between Boston and New York — in which Quincy but six years before had consumed four days — had been reduced to one of forty-one hours. In the last-named case, however, the passengers were not permitted to stop during the night at a tavern even for four or five hours of sleep, but were carried forward both day and night without intermission. At that time the swift-moving passenger between the two cities ordinarily paid a fare of eleven dollars. During the previous forty years the general improvements of roads throughout the East, coupled with competition, had resulted in a considerable reduction in the cost of stage-coach transportation. Whereas in 1832 a man could be conveyed from Boston to New York for eleven dollars, in 1783 and for some time thereafter the stage patron had been compelled to pay ten dollars for his passage between Boston and Hartford. Perhaps in a general way the decrease to the public in the cost of stage-coach travel amounted to about fifty per cent. during the generation immediately following 1800.

In the winter time — except in those regions where snow was not a serious impediment to travel — the stage-coach lines sometimes placed their vehicles on sled bodies instead of wheels and succeeded in maintaining their

[1] Stage tickets from Philadelphia to Pittsburgh, during the heyday of stage-coach travel, cost from $15.00 to $20.00.

service with but a small decrease in speed. On occasions when the ordinary stage-coach body would have been too heavy to be dragged through the snow its use was temporarily abandoned in favor of small, open, box-like structures, in which the travellers were exposed to all the in-

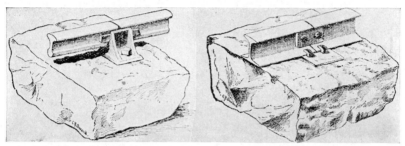

220.—Primitive American rails and tracks. The stone sleeper and rail at the left illustrate the track construction of the Portage railway, built by the state of Pennsylvania between Hollidaysburg and Johnstown in 1832. The block and rail at the right show the first track of the Camden and Amboy road, in 1831. From the National Museum's illustrations of its original specimens.

clemencies of the weather. The salient features of a winter trip to Philadelphia from New York in 1836 are thus stated:[1]

"On the fourteenth of February, 1836, I left Philadelphia at 5 p. m., and was fourteen hours going to New York with the Great Southern Mail, although the sleighing was good. We rode in an open sleigh or box on runners, and the passengers sat on the mail-bag. The fare from Philadelphia to New York was six dollars."

The conditions of land travel just previous to the introduction of the canal and railway were very far from being uniform throughout the whole extent of territory east of the Mississippi. It was only in the northern and eastern sections of the country, and as far west as Pittsburgh, Wheeling and Washington, that there existed so favorable a situation as has been described. Some of the

[1] S. W. Robert's "Address to the Pennsylvania Historical Society."

typical adventures to be expected by the man who journeyed west of Pittsburgh by stage, even at as late a day
as 1837, are suggested in an account of an overland trip
from Pittsburgh to the town of Erie, Pennsylvania, written
by a Scotch civil engineer[1] who travelled extensively
through the country in the year named for the purpose
of studying American public works. He said:

"On the road leading from Pittsburg on the Ohio to the town of
Erie, on the lake of that name, I saw all the varieties of forest road-
making in great perfection. Sometimes our road lay for miles through
extensive marshes, which we crossed by corduroy roads, formed of
trees. . . . cut in lengths of about ten or twelve feet and laid close
to each other across the road to prevent the vehicles from sinking; at
others the coach stuck fast in mud, from which it could be extricated
only by the combined efforts of the coachman and passengers; and at one
place we traveled for upward of a quarter of a mile through a forest
flooded with water which stood to the height of several feet on many
of the trees, and occasionally covered the naves of the coach-wheels.
The distance of the route from Pittsburg to Erie is one hundred and
twenty-eight miles, which was accomplished in forty-six hours, being
at the very slow rate of two miles and three-quarters an hour, although
the conveyance by which I traveled carried the mail, and stopped only
for breakfast, dinner and tea, but there was considerable delay caused
by the coach being once upset and several times mired."

In the South the roads suitable for vehicles were still
few and far between when compared with similar highways in the North, and much of the overland movement
of the people, except on north-and-south roads near the
coast, was still accomplished on horseback. During the
second war with Great Britain communication by sailing
packets between the north Atlantic states and the southern
seaboard was almost entirely cut off, and for commercial
purposes there remained no method of intercourse between those two sections of the country save that afforded
by the Conestoga wagons. Long trains of those land

[1] David Stevenson. The quotation here given is from his "Sketch of the Civil Engineering of North America, etc.," London: MDCCCXXXVIII, pp. 216-8.

frigates departed daily from the northern cities toward the South, laden with commodities desired by the people of that region. As a natural consequence of the time and expense incurred in making a journey by that means from the North to the South, the expense of conveying goods between the two regions was extraordinarily high. The freight rate by Conestoga wagon from Boston to Charleston was no less than forty cents a pound for goods of light weight, or eight hundred dollars a ton.

From ten to twenty overland wagons that had started from Baltimore, New Haven, New York, Philadelphia, Boston and Richmond arrived in Charleston every day during a considerable period of the War of 1812, so that if the various charges on the goods carried by them averaged but ten cents a pound, the aggregate freight costs for ten or twenty wagon loads of articles so transported from the North to that one city would have been between four thousand and eight thousand dollars a day. Not all this merchandise, of course, was destined for Charleston. Much of it went still farther south to other communities.

This long interruption of sea travel by means of the swift sailing packets that had hitherto united the northern and southern ports really proved a stimulus to the development of land movement between the two sections, for it forced the people to an increased use of stage-coaches and to the betterment of their roads. After the war the Atlantic sailing packets never wholly recovered their previous prestige as passenger carriers. Within a dozen years little steamboats appeared on the various bays and rivers, and in course of time those mechanical craft began running in close business connection with various southern stage lines. Thus was forming a new system that competed for and secured a large portion of the human traffic between North and South until railways supplanted the stage-coach part of the coalition.

Other conditions that retarded the development of travel facilities in the South between 1800 and 1830 have been outlined in those chapters dealing with the diplomatic conflict between the white and red races. Land travel from the South to the West — save on three or four roads leading through Virginia and North Carolina to Tennessee and Kentucky — was still a matter of considerable toil. Yet the communication facilities between the East and the Mississippi were showing a marked improvement when compared with the situation that had existed a few years before. An illustration of the progress made in bringing the East and the extreme West more closely together is that contained in the respective intervals of time which were required to carry the President's message from Washington to Little Rock, Arkansas, in 1819 and in 1829. The message of December 7, 1819, was seventy-eight days on its journey to Little Rock, and did not arrive in that town until February 22 of 1820. Jackson's annual message of December 8, 1829, in contrast, was hurried from Washington to Little Rock in the astonishing time of fourteen days. A local newspaper[1] commented on the prodigy in the following words: "Thus have the improvements which have been made in the expedition of our mails brought us, as it were, sixty-four days nearer the city of the General Government than we were ten years ago." Doubtless the editor who uttered this encomium on the progress of his day thought that the possibilities of development had about reached their limit.

The disabilities under which the people of the West

[1] "Little Rock Gazette," December 29.

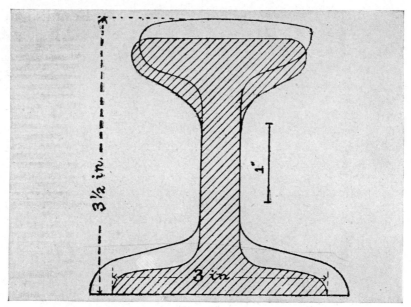

3½ in.

1"

3 in.

221.—The first T rail. Shaded section shows the design as originally whittled out of a pine stick by Stevens in 1830. Unshaded section shows rail as made in England for him in 1831. This is the Camden and Amboy rail depicted in the preceding. From the National Museum's illustration of its original specimen.

labored, from the beginning of the century until about 1825, are suggested by an observation of Christopher Schultz in his *Travels on an Inland Voyage*. Schultz remarks: "If the mud does not get quite over your boot tops when you sit in the saddle they call it a middling good road."

The observation here quoted is a humorous exaggeration, but it is nevertheless true that any human movement over the so-called roads of the Middle West was at certain times out of the question. In the rainy seasons, in fact, vehicle traffic was not even attempted throughout large districts of the country and travel was performed on horseback or not at all.

Another description of early western road conditions, somewhat more elaborate than that of Schultz, is contained in Charles Cleaver's *History of Chicago from 1833 to 1892; Describing the Difficulties of the Route from New York to Chicago.*[1] In his reminiscences of the conditions he encountered in the village of Chicago during 1833 and thereafter, Cleaver says:

"Parties informed us that in the spring we would find it almost impossible to get around for the mud—a truth very forcibly illustrated when a few months later I got into a wagon to go about one and a half miles northwest. . . . It was with the greatest difficulty that two good horses could pull the empty wagon through the two feet of mud and water across the prairie we had to cross. I once heard Mr. Elston's place called 'the mud farm,' not an inappropriate name for it at that time. A year or two later I saw many teams stuck fast in the streets of the village. I remember once a stage coach got mired in Clark Street opposite the Sherman House, where it remained several days with a board driven into the mud at the side of it bearing this inscription: 'No bottom here.' I once saw a lady stuck in the mud in the middle of Randolph Street at the crossing of La Salle. She was evidently in need of help, as every time she moved she sank deeper and deeper. An old gentleman from the country, seeing the situation, offered to help her, which had such an effect upon her modesty that with one desperate effort she drew her feet out minus her shoes, which were afterward found over a foot in the mire, and reached the sidewalk in her stockings."

At the time Henry Clay was making his appeal for a national highway between the East and the West, it usually required about three or four weeks to travel from New York or Washington to Cincinnati, Corydon,[2] or St. Louis. In a copy of the *Western Censor and Emigrant's Guide,* published in Indianapolis on January 19, 1824, appeared a little paragraph indicating that the latest news from the state capital was dated January tenth. Eight days, therefore, had been required to span the distance between Corydon and Indianapolis. In the same issue of the *Western Censor* appeared another item in-

[1] Page 50.
[2] Then the capital of Indiana; a small town in the southern part of the state.

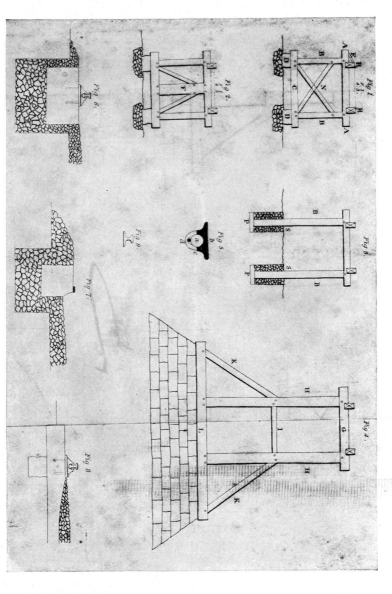

222.—Figures 1 to 4 show early American methods of railroad track building across low regions. The three lower figures show the track of the road built by Pennsylvania between Philadelphia and Columbia in 1832-4. Discussed in Chapter XLII. From Wood's "A Practical Treatise on Rail-Roads: Philadelphia, 1832."

dicating that the most recent information received from Washington was dated December twenty-seventh. More than three weeks had elapsed between the departure of the letters from the national capital and their arrival at Indianapolis.

The first number of the *Western Censor*—that of March 7, 1823—contains a communication describing an overland trip between Indianapolis and Fort Armstrong, four hundred miles north of St. Louis. It was made by Israel Mitchell and a small party of Indiana people. They were twenty-three days on the way. In telling of the journey Mitchell said: "We suffered more than can well be imagined from wet, cold and hunger, being wet to the knees and often to the neck. The streams through Illinois were all high, and had no timber on them to make rafts, and we had no alternative left but to swim. Had it not been for honey we must have nearly perished. We had not a full meal of meat for thirteen days, and for four days nothing but honey. . . . Fasting and fatigue have weakened us very much." Mitchell also mentioned that a steamboat named *Virginia* had recently reached Fort Armstrong from Wheeling, in Virginia, after a voyage of three weeks. This was the first steamboat to penetrate so far up the Mississippi River.

It was not until the year 1820 that the upper part of the Mississippi valley found itself in fairly reliable and regular communication with the eastern states. Even then the new era in overland rapid transit was at first mainly concerned with the delivery of the mails. The routes used were the old roads — and their later continuations — which extended westward through the mountains and into Tennessee and Kentucky. A St. Louis newspaper of 1820[1] mentions the revolution in the speed of the mails in the following paragraph:

"After the vexatious delays which we have been long subjected to in our mail communication with the Atlantic states it is a matter of agreeable satisfaction to find a line established on which dependence can be placed. On the Vincennes route we now have regular arrivals from the principal towns in Kentucky and Ohio in six days, from Washington to Baltimore in twenty, Philadelphia twenty-one, New York twenty-two, and Boston twenty-four."

From this it will be seen that by special effort a man might, at that date, proceed overland from New York to St. Louis in but little more than three weeks, and that only six days were required to go from Cincinnati or Louisville to the town on the western bank of the Mississippi. Passenger stage-coaches appeared on the western part of this route a few months later. An Indiana newspaper of 1820[2] announced certain new facilities for travel then impending in a paragraph which read:

"We are gratified in seeing it announced that a line of stages is established to run from Louisville through Vincennes to St. Louis. This will be an invaluable accommodation to travelers to the West, who have hitherto been obliged to resort to tedious and vexatious means of conveyance. We are glad also to see the progress of public improvement. Comfortable houses and good farms are creating on the St. Louis road, and a stage coach with passengers will soon be humming across those vast and cheerless prairies, where, but a short time since, the wolf and deer were the principal inhabitants, or men in savage attire, as ferocious and wild as they. The benefits of the enterprise of Mr. Foyles will be felt and acknowledged by many a grateful traveler, and we hope it will receive the particular attention of the Postmaster-General."

This overland movement to the West, aided by Mr. Foyles, followed the earlier Kentucky roads to Louisville. There the travellers crossed to the north side of the Ohio, and by means of the old Vincennes trail — recently widened and improved — they proceeded to the second

[1] "The Enquirer," Feb. 12.
[2] "The Indiana Centinel" of Sept. 2.

capital of Indiana territory and then swung westward across Illinois.[1] On this and some other of the early roads of the West the pioneer stage-coach companies adopted a rule which caused a considerable fluctuation in the rates of fare which passengers were charged for their transportation. A traveller was arbitrarily considered to weigh one hundred pounds. As the "Mail Stage

223.—The road-bed, stone foundations, stone stringers and flat iron rails used in laying part of the Baltimore and Ohio Railroad in 1833. Numerous experiments and methods in track-making were tried by the Baltimore and Ohio during the first years of its existence. From the National Museum's illustrations of its original rails and stone blocks.

Rules" of the Emison and McClure Company put it, "one hundred pounds weight will constitute a passenger, and to be paid for accordingly, and a greater or less weight in proportion."[2] So it will be seen that if a traveller had the misfortune to weigh one hundred and fifty pounds he would, according to the regulations, constitute a passenger and a half, and would be compelled to pay for himself on that basis; and if he tipped the scales at two hundred pounds he then represented two

[1] On another page will be found a photographic reproduction of a stage-coach "way bill" used by one of the stage companies which operated over this road shortly after 1820. It will be noticed that the distances along the road are reckoned in almost every instance in the number of miles between two taverns. Only four settlements are recorded on the way bill, in contrast to the names of sixteen taverns at which the coaches stopped for food or a change of horses. One of the taverns—that of Joshua Piles—was owned by the proprietor of the stage line.
[2] This is rule number three contained on the Emison and McClure broadside of stage-travel regulations, a photographic reproduction of which is shown elsewhere.

persons, as far as the price of his ticket was concerned. He was, however, allowed to carry fifteen pounds of excess weight in the stage, provided the said fifteen pounds was baggage and not a component part of his own person. Rule number nineteen of the Emison and McClure Company disclaimed responsibility for the loss of any trunks or other baggage carried by coach. Aside from these features of administration, which were doubtless common to all or nearly all the early stage companies of the interior, their rules indicated a real and business-like desire to satisfy their patrons. The employees of the companies were forbidden to indulge in language or conduct that was unseemly, and were instructed to treat passengers with "the utmost politeness."

Although by this time there were numerous stage routes in the eastern states on which travellers went forward toward their destinations both by day and night without intermission, the newer roads in the interior did not permit a like procedure, and the speed attained by the pioneer stage lines of the Middle West was but a fraction of that accomplished by the eastern lines of the same years. The schedules of the first coaches running over the road between Louisville and Vincennes were announced to the public by means of advertisements when the service was projected, and one of these announcements[1] read:

"The Vincennes stage to Louisville leaves Francis Cunningham's in Market Street, Vincennes, on Wednesday mornings at six o'clock, arrives in Louisville at three o'clock P. M. on the Friday following— leaves Louisville on Saturday morning at six o'clock and returns to Vincennes on the Monday following at three o'clock P. M.—distance to Louisville one hundred and twenty-six miles."

Including the two nights spent on the road between

[1] From the "Indiana Centinel and Public Advertiser" of May 13, 1820.

761

the cities named, it consequently appears that the traveller proceeded at an average rate of less than two and one-fourth miles an hour. The running schedule for that part of the journey between Vincennes and St. Louis[1] was as follows:

"The Union Line of stages, in conjunction with the Louisville Line, will commence on the fifth day of September, inst., to run regular from Vincennes, Ia., to St. Louis, Mo., to leave Vincennes every Tuesday at two o'clock P. M., arrive at St. Louis on Friday by two o'clock P. M. Leave St. Louis on every Saturday at half past four A. M. and arrive at Vincennes on Monday by six P. M."

Similar advertisements, published during the next few years in the same parts of the country, showed that an average rate of movement not exceeding three miles an hour was all that could be expected by stage-coach during any extended journey which required one or more nights on the road. A man journeying from Vincennes to St. Louis by the road and in the manner here outlined spent three days in crossing the state of Illinois.[2]

A considerable traffic soon appeared on this first of the "through routes" of the Middle West, and two other necessary conveniences of travel — in addition to the stage-coaches themselves — speedily multiplied. These were the taverns and the ferries. Innkeepers and ferry proprietors competed almost as actively for traffic as did the coach lines themselves, and their representatives always met the incoming stages, distributing to the passengers printed handbills which called to their attention

[1] As announced by Proprietor Foyle in the "Indiana Centinel" of September 2, 1820. Regular service between Vincennes and St. Louis was not established until some months after the coaches were put in operation between Louisville and Vincennes.

[2] After writing the above paragraphs relating to the beginning of periodic stage-coach travel in the Middle West, the author, in an endeavor to fix the precise date of this event, came upon an advertisement reading as follows: "SPECIAL NOTICE. The U. S. Mail Stage from Vincennes to Louisville will commence its regular running on the twentieth April. The St. Louis Union Line from Vincennes to St. Louis will also start at the same time. Travelers from Louisville to St. Louis by this conveyance will be but five days on the road. THE PROPRIETORS." From the "Western Sun," of Vincennes, April 7, 1821.

the excellencies or conveniences of the institutions whose interests they advocated.[1] Although it often happened that a stage-coach company owned, or had an interest in, several of the taverns along its route, and although the coaches of any given line always stopped at one particular inn, there was no obligation on the part of the travellers themselves to patronize taverns with which their convey-

224.—Sectional View and side view of the roadbed and track structure adopted by the Boston and Lowell road in 1834-1835. The rails rested on stone blocks, which in turn stood on deep foundations of broken stone. From Stevenson's "Sketches of the Civil Engineering of North America": 1838.

ances were affiliated, and constant efforts were made by rival landlords and ferrymen to secure patronage. A steady stream of westward-bound emigrants also moved through the country either in their own canvas-covered wagons or on horseback, and these were likewise the legitimate prey of all those who represented any feature of the new transportation facilities that were so rapidly coming into existence.

The position held by a stage-coach driver of the old days, in the estimation of his acquaintances and the general public, was very similar to that of the captain of a steamboat. Some famous drivers, indeed, stood on so lofty a plane in the eyes of the world that they can only be likened to the commanders of the ocean steamships of the present time. By virtue of their duties they came into constant contact with all the prominent political, social and

[1] A number of these early western handbills, issued in advertisement of hostelries and ferries along the Louisville-St. Louis road, are elsewhere shown.

commercial figures of the country. Their attention and favorable opinion were also always sought by that large — though less consequential — part of the public which was so deeply impressed by the measure of their responsibility and the majestic demeanor of their professional attitude. The high place occupied by a famous stage driver in the eyes of the youth of the country during the heyday of stage travel is suggested by the words of one who was familiar with the life of those days. He said:

"My earliest recollections are intimately associated with coaches, teams and drivers, and, like most boys raised in an old stage tavern, I longed to be a man, when I could aspire to the greatness and dignity of a professional stage driver. In my boyish eyes no position in life had so many attractions as that of driving a stage team. A Judge, a Congressman, even Henry Clay or President Jackson did not measure up to the character of John Mills or Charley Howell in my juvenile fancy."[1]

Nor was this estimate of the coach driver confined exclusively to people other than the driver himself. There is a record that one of the fraternity once remarked, "While I drive this coach I am the whole United States of America." Yet the ordinary wage of a driver was only twelve dollars a month, exclusive of his board and lodging. While on duty he took his meals at the taverns along the road in company with his passengers — though he did not sit at the head of the table — and he was always sure of a bed to himself, no matter how urgently and vainly some belated traveller might plead for a like accommodation.

It was a time in which the free use of intoxicating drinks — especially of brandy and whisky — was more common than it is to-day, and stage-coach drivers, like a large majority of other men, drank whenever they had the opportunity and the inclination, yet it should be said

[1] Searight's "The Old Pike": p. 182.

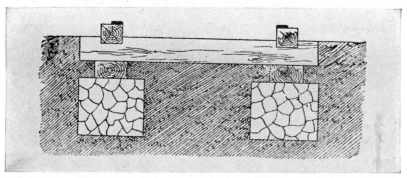

225.—Track of the Albany and Schenectady road, 1837. Foundations of broken stone, topped by timbers; cross-ties of timber; rails of timber, on the inner edges of which were fastened flat strips of iron. From a drawing in the National Museum.

to their credit that few of them permitted themselves to be reduced to the condition which made them incapable of performing their really important work in a safe and proper manner. They were so continually pestered with invitations to drink that they might easily have remained in a state of partial incapacity for months at a time, provided they were permitted to retain their official positions during such an interval.

But it occasionally happened that a driver was false to his duty and forgot the value of the lives entrusted to his care. In cases of that sort disastrous accidents sometimes resulted. One such accident, which occurred in Massachusetts[1] in 1835, received the following newspaper comment:

"The driver, on taking charge of the team at Groton, was observed to be not very well capable of managing his team, which was observed by several persons, one of whom remarked on his incapacity to drive. It is not pretended that he was drunk at the time, but laboring under the stupefying effects of intoxication. After the arrival of the stage at a place called Littleton he took his glass of grog. Mr. Bullard, proprietor of this line of stages, rode on the box with him and had occasion to

[1] The account here quoted is taken from the "Maine Farmer" of April 2, 1835.

arouse him from sleep twice after leaving Groton. Mr. Bullard was still on the box with the driver when they left Littleton. On arriving at the summit of the hill where the accident happened the driver was unable to control his team, four spirited horses, and they ran full speed down the hill, coming in contact with Mr. Powers' six-horse loaded wagon . . . which upset the coach. Mr. Bullard, holding on the railing of the coach as it turned over, swung round and under it upon his side. . . . Previous to expiring Mr. Bullard communicated to those in attendance the facts above stated."

In noting this fatality, which was due to the condition of the driver, the same journal declared: "There is hardly a class of men whose sobriety and habits of carefulness are of as great importance as that of stage drivers. So far as our circumscribed vision extends in regard to this matter, the public around us are happily provided for in this respect; but this is not the case in all places."

One phase of the incident here narrated seems to be worthy of elucidation. The newspaper said, "It is not pretended that he was drunk at the time," but that "he was laboring under the stupefying effects of intoxication." Obviously a distinction is here asserted which the lapse of years has obliterated, and it is, in consequence, necessary to explain that during the period under discussion a man was not pronounced "drunk" unless he was prostrate and unconscious. While he still manifested any glimmering of understanding, or was able to make a distinguishable physical movement, the opprobrium attached to the stronger description could not fairly be applied to him. Until that condition had arrived he was, as explained in connection with the above case, merely "under the stupefying effects of intoxication."

Minor accidents were constantly taking place in the operation of the stages, but it was seldom that a mishap resulted in such unfortunate consequences as those which accompanied the runaway near Groton. Usually a vehicle was overturned and its occupants received a bad shaking up and some bruises; occasionally some one suffered a broken limb. Nor were the elect of the land any more immune from such happenings than the most humble traveller. Even Henry Clay himself, to whose influence more than that of any other man the creation of the Na-

226.—The first rail rolled in the United States. Made in the first American rail mill, at Mount Savage, Maryland, in 1844. A few hundred tons were used on the Baltimore and Ohio road in that year. Weight, 42 pounds to the yard. From the National Museum's illustration of an original specimen. The picture is about three-fourths actual height.

tional Road was due, was involved on one occasion in an upset. He was on his way to Washington at the time, and the driver overturned the coach at Uniontown, in Pennsylvania. The Idol of the West was unhurt, and when he was dragged out of the vehicle he remarked that the Clay of Kentucky had been mixed with the limestone of Pennsylvania. The driver, jolted from his lofty perch by the concussion, alighted on his head and suffered a broken nose.[1]

[1] Searight's "The Old Pike": p. 10.

Another prominent stage-coach passenger who passed through a similar experience was the Indian, Black Hawk. After his capture he was taken to Washington, and journeyed eastward by steamboat on the Ohio River until Wheeling was reached. There he and the entire party of military men and Indians were transferred to coaches and set out over the National Road. While passing through the town of Washington, in Pennsylvania, the driver lost control of the team behind which sat Black Hawk and eight other natives, and after a mad down-hill dash the vehicle left its wheels and rolled over. Black Hawk was the first of the party to emerge, and standing in the street, surrounded by the crowd which speedily gathered, he made a number of remarks in a loud and emphatic tone of voice. Owing to the excitement of the moment no record of the Sac's extemporaneous address was made, but it is safe to say that his opinion of the particular phase of Caucasian civilization with which he had thus suddenly come in contact was not radically different from the opinion that would have been expressed by a white man under similar conditions.

The coming of the railroad and the spread of that new method of movement throughout the East spelled the ultimate doom of stage-coach travel along the National Road and other roads in that part of the country. Various stage lines nevertheless fought hard and well to retain a vestige of their former glory, and some of them succeeded in maintaining a precarious existence until after 1850. But their day as a factor in the upbuilding of the country and in the movement of its population was practically done, and they were destined to survive only amid the sparsely settled regions of the almost limitless West. During the last two or three years in which the old National Road still remained an essential factor in the traffic of the nation the voice of a driver along its way could sometimes be heard as he chanted this ditty in execration of the portentous change that had robbed him of his occupation:

> "Now all you jolly wagoners, who have got good wives,
> Go home to your farms and there spend your lives.
> When your corn is all cribbed and your small grain is good,
> You will have nothing to do but curse the railroad."

But long before the stage-coach and turnpike had ceased to be important factors in the national travel system, a new and radically different method of transportation — the artificial waterway, or canal — had appeared, which was destined for about a generation to play an interesting part in the country's development.

CHAPTER XXXV

AMERICA'S EARLY CANAL PERIOD — THE NATION HAS NOT
DEVELOPED BEYOND THE NEED OF CANALS BUT IS NOW
APPROACHING ITS REAL CANAL EPOCH — CAUSES
OF THE PHENOMENA APPEARING BETWEEN 1817 AND
1845 — FIRST AMERICAN ARTIFICIAL WATERWAYS —
ELKANAH WATSON'S IDEAS AND WORK — NEW YORK
STATE BUILDS THE ERIE CANAL — SCENES AT ITS
OPENING — PENNSYLVANIA'S ACTIVITY — HER EARLY
ERROR — A CHANGE IN POLICY RESULTS IN A RE-
MARKABLE ROUTE TO THE WEST — HOW A TRAVELLER
GOT FROM PHILADELPHIA TO PITTSBURGH

IN considering the subject of canals and canal traffic, in
so far as that method of travel and transportation is
related to the story pursued in these pages, one desirable
point to be kept in mind is that America has not developed
beyond the era of canals but is, on the contrary, apparently
still to enter upon it. The short period of canal construction which appeared in this country between 1817
and 1845 was largely the outgrowth of unusual circumstances, was begun and ended by conditions peculiar to
the country and period, and can best be described as a
sudden, sporadic, forced and exotic phenomenon instead
of the slow and natural outgrowth of broad necessity. It
is improbable that canals would have gained headway at
all had there been even a dim general realization of the
significance contained in the work performed with steam

770

by Fitch, Evans, Stevens, Fulton, and others from 1785 until about 1815. And, once a really valuable though premature canal system was in working order—as was the case by the fourth decade after 1800—it would not have been allowed to disintegrate in large part had there been a general or governmental appreciation of the future needs of the country, coupled with a popular sense of

227.—The earliest American railway passenger trains usually consisted of one car drawn by horses. The car was generally a stage-coach placed on special wheels, or else a two-story affair built on the lines of a stage-coach. That sort of vehicle was the best conveyance yet devised for land travel, and an effort to adapt it to the new transportation method was naturally made. From it the modern railway car slowly developed. Drawn and engraved by the artist Alexander Robb. Date, about 1830. A similar car then in use on the Baltimore and Ohio road was described in the *Baltimore American* of August 5, 1830. See Chapter XLV.

business morality sufficiently strong to resist those blandishments which finally resulted in the crippling or outright abandonment of important, costly and useful public improvements.

Perhaps the first definite idea regarding the building of a canal in America was that of joining the Susquehanna and Schuylkill Rivers in Pennsylvania. The possibility of doing such a thing attracted the attention of the earliest settlers in Philadelphia, and there was some small discussion of the subject even before the year 1700. But it was recognized by the pioneer inhabitants of Pennsylvania that even though the accomplishment of the task might be of benefit, its actual performance was beyond their physical power or financial capacity.

So the first theoretical argument was forgotten, and there was no further serious mention of such a plan for nearly three-quarters of a century. But about the year 1770 it appears that there was a revival of the idea, and two years later Benjamin Franklin—that extraordinary man who had something worth while to say concerning almost every matter of consequence to his country—wrote a letter from England to the mayor of Philadelphia,[1] in which he observed:

"I am glad my Canal Papers were agreeable to you. I fancy work of that kind is set on foot in America. I think it would be saving Money to engage by a handsome Salary an Engineer from here who has been accustomed to such business. . . . With regard to your question, whether it is possible to make the Schuylkill a part of the navigation to the back Country, or whether the Difficulty of that River, subject to inconveniences of floods, ice, etc., will not be greater than the expense of digging, locks, etc., I can only say that here they look on the constant practicability of the navigation, allowing Boats to pass and repass at all Times and Seasons, without hinderance, to be an event of the greatest importance, and therefore they seldom or ever use a River where it can be avoided. . . . Rivers are ungovernable things, especially in hilly countries. Canals are quiet and always manageable. . . . I warmly wish success to every Attempt For Improvement of our dear Country, and am with sincere esteem, yours most affectionately, B. Franklin."

Within a few years after Franklin had written this letter there was authorized the building of the first American canal of any consequence.[2] The action was taken by the Virginia legislature,[3] which formally provided that a canal be built between the towns of Richmond and Westham, a distance of some seven miles, in order that

[1] Mayor Rhoads. The letter was written in August of 1772.
[2] In 1750 there had been dug in Orange county, New York, by Lieutenant-Governor Holder of that province, a short and shallow dyke or ditch, which was used for moving stone loaded on small flatboats, and for other similar construction purposes. This little ditch was technically a canal, and it was probably the first work of such a character in the country.
[3] In 1785.

boats might thus be carried around the falls obstructing the navigation of the James River at that point. The canal was duly dug, and was in part maintained and enlarged through the use of state money. Other similar early American undertakings of the same sort[1] were:

The Dismal Swamp Canal, dug by authorization of Virginia and South Carolina. It was begun in 1787 and finished in 1794.

The Middlesex Canal, which was incorporated in 1789, begun in 1795 and completed in 1808. This canal was about thirty miles long, thirty feet wide at its top, twenty feet wide at the bottom, and three feet deep. It extended from the Merrimac to the Charles River, in Massachusetts. Twenty locks were built throughout its length, and the total cost of the enterprise was more than five hundred thousand dollars.

The small canal constructed around the Patopwick Falls in Massachusetts in 1797. The charter had been granted in 1792.

The Santee Canal, extending for twenty-two miles between the Santee River in South Carolina and the city of Charleston. It was thirty-two feet wide at the top, twenty feet wide at the bottom and four feet deep. This work was completed in 1802.

The Bow Canal in New Hampshire, a small artificial waterway three-quarters of a mile long, which was finished in 1812.

The Schuylkill navigation of Pennsylvania, commenced in 1815 and finished in 1826. Its total length from Fairmount to Mt. Carbon was one hundred and eight miles. The surface width of the canal was thirty-six feet, the bottom width twenty-two feet and the depth three

[1] Compiled from Tanner's "A Description of Canals and Railroads of the United States, Etc., Etc.," New York: 1840.

Exciting Trial of Speed between Mr. Peter Cooper's Locomotive, "Tom Thumb," and one of Stockton & Stokes's Horse-Cars.

The trial took place on the Baltimore and Ohio Railroad, on the 28th August, 1830. The sketch represents the moment the Engine overtook and passed the Horse-Car, the passengers filled with excitement.

(See Mr. Latrobe's description, page 119.)

228.—The Baltimore and Ohio Railway. Test of speed, in 1830, between a horse-drawn car and Peter Cooper's diminutive experimental locomotive known as the "Tom Thumb." Scene as the engine forged ahead. The horse finally won the race. From Brown's *History of the First Locomotives in America.*

and a half feet. The system contained one hundred and twenty-nine locks, and the cost of the project was about two and a half million dollars.

A survey was made in 1762 for a proposed canal between the Schuylkill River at Reading and the Susquehanna at Middleton. No work was performed on the enterprise until 1791 and about four miles were ready for use in 1794, when the undertaking was temporarily abandoned. Work on it was resumed in the year 1821, and in 1827 it was finished and called the Union Canal. Still later it was incorporated into the Pennsylvania Canal.

A canal between the Chesapeake Bay and the Delaware River was proposed in 1764, and the route for it was then surveyed. Actual work on this project was begun in 1804. It was abandoned soon afterward, again revived in 1822 and finished for thirteen miles in 1839.

The various small early canal enterprises here

mentioned were all substantially local in character, and none was planned as a travel and transportation route designed to open extensive new regions of the country or to facilitate movement or commerce between widely separated sections. It is a singular fact that the few artificial waterways created or projected in this country prior to the year 1803 were exciting more interest at that time in the minds of European observers than in the minds of the Americans themselves. In an important work published in London in 1803[1] there appeared the following paragraph:

"We may expect to see the interland parts of that large country so intersected as to bring the produce to market, or for exportation, which will interest Europe, and will make that country in a few years not inferior to the best cultivated and improved states in the old world. The immortal Washington was the original father and promoter of these canals and improvements and well did he deserve the admirable motto 'twice the savior of his country,'—after conducting her to liberty, he opened to her the way to posterity by new roads and canals. Those who wish any further information on these improvements in North-America, I beg leave to refer to the Journal of Mr. Elkanah Watson, a gentleman who has traveled much both in America and Europe."

It is apparent therefore that the two men here mentioned—General Washington and Elkanah Watson—demand attention in connection with the earliest phases of the canal-building period of the country.[2]

Elkanah Watson was a young American who, during the revolution against Great Britain, was sent by Congress to deliver despatches from that body to Benjamin Franklin, then in Paris on public business. Watson remained in Europe for five years—from 1779 until 1784—during which time he examined with attention the canals of Belgium, Holland and England. Soon after his return

---

[1] Philips' "General History of Canals." Fourth edition: p. 581.
[2] Washington's project was for a canal between the Potomac and Ohio Rivers. Its ultimate outgrowth was the Chesapeake and Ohio Canal, later described.

to America, and in the winter of 1785, he visited General Washington at Mount Vernon and at that time discussed with him the subject of river improvements and the project of connecting the waters of the Potomac by a canal with the Ohio or with the waters of the Great Lakes. His European observations and his conversations with Wash-

229.—Popular delight at the introduction of railways was at times manifested by the display of flags on cars and engines. A train of two or more cars was called a "brigade." The locomotive here shown is perhaps intended to represent the *Tom Thumb*. Drawn and engraved by Alexander Robb.

ington made a deep impression on him, and while undertaking extensive trips through many parts of the country during the next three years he found himself giving frequent consideration to the question of canal construction in various localities and to the possible advantages of such undertakings. During these expeditions Watson kept a record of his experiences and ideas, and at a later date the writings, originally brought into being under the conditions thus described, came to be known as the *Journal of Travels* by Elkanah Watson. It so happened that in September of the year 1788 Watson found himself in the interior of New York State, on the Mohawk River, and his thoughts regarding the future economic possibilities of that particular locality were thus set down by him:

"In contemplating the situation of Ft. Stanwix, at the head of Batteaux navigation on the Mohawk River, . . . I am led to think this station will in time become an emporium of commerce to Albany and the vast western world above. . . .

"Should the Little Falls ever be locked,—the obstructions in the Mohawk River removed and the canal between the said river and Wood Creek at this place, formed, so as to unite the waters running east with those running west; and other canals made, and obstructions removed to Fort Oswego,—who can reasonably doubt but that by such operations the state of New York have it within their power by a grand stroke of policy, to divert the full trade of lake Ontario, and the Great Lakes above, from Alexandria and Quebec to Albany and New York. . . .

"In view of escaping by locks from the Hudson into the Mohawk River, it appears to me that the obstacles at this place[1] would be much greater than to cut a canal through the pine plains into a basin back of Albany."[2]

In 1791 Watson began an active campaign of publicity having for its purpose the creation of a sentiment favorable to the making of public improvements and of canals in particular. The New York legislature passed such an act in 1792, and under its provisions Watson was named as one of the commission appointed to explore and lay out a possible route for a canal through the central and western part of the state which should connect the Hudson River with the Great Lakes system. The commission made its report in the autumn of 1792, and improvements in the navigation of the Mohawk River, together with the building of locks for the safe passage of boats at certain points on the stream were soon afterward authorized by the legislature and completed for use by the year 1796. During the next ten years the subject of connecting the Hudson with the Lakes system was brought forward on

[1] Watson here refers to the Cohoes Falls.
[2] The extracts from the Journals as here given are taken from the "History of the Rise, Progress and Existing Conditions of the Western Canals in the State of New York, from September, 1788, to the completion of the Middle Section of the Grand Canal in 1819, Etc., Etc." By Elkanah Watson, Albany, 1820, pp. 15-18,

different occasions by various public men of New York, but with no important or practical result. In the year 1810 the legislature caused a survey to be run which resulted in the recommendation that immediate efforts be put forth to induce the Federal government to adopt the plan as a national undertaking and itself perform the work. This suggestion was made by New York State and rejected by the national administration. New York then applied through her governor and legislature for the aid of Ohio and Indiana and again met with disappointment, although the interior commonwealths recognized and acknowledged the probable value of such a completed undertaking.

Being thus thrown upon her own resources, New York seemed rapidly approaching a decision to undertake the work on her own account, when the outbreak of the second war with Great Britain put an end for the time being to the maturing plans of the state. With the return of peace the subject was at once revived, and public meetings in advocacy of the enterprise were held in New York City and elsewhere. The legislature was memorialized; a new board of commissioners was appointed; and finally, in 1817, a law was passed providing for a system of canals and other internal improvements in New York State. Construction work was begun on the Fourth of July of that year[1] and a small section of the canal—about fifteen miles of waterway between the towns of Utica and Rome —was ready for traffic in October of 1819. The following contemporary letters give descriptions of the scenes attending the first canal boat trip in America:

"On the twenty-second of October, 1819, the first boat sailed on the Erie canal, from Rome to Utica. It was drag'd by a single horse, trot-

[1] In the historical neighborhood of Ft. Stanwix, Oneida county.

230.—The Charleston and Hamburg road. A sailing-car tried in 1829-1830. Before a brisk breeze it carried fifteen passengers at the rate of twelve miles an hour. On one trip the mast and sail, together with several passengers, were carried overboard by the wind. A jury-mast was then rigged and the journey was resumed. From Brown's *History*.

ting on the embankment, in the towpath. It was an elegant boat, constructed to carry passengers, called the Chief Engineer,—a compliment to Benjamin Wright, Esq. The president, and the board of commissioners, attended by many respectable gentlemen and ladies, embarked the ensuing day at Utica, with a band of music, to return to Rome. The Scene was extremely interesting, and highly grateful. The embarkation took place amid the ringing of bells, the roaring of cannon, and the loud acclamations of thousands of exhilarated spectators, male and female, who lined the banks of the new created river. The scene was truly sublime."

"Utica, October 22, 1819.

"The last two days have presented, in this village, a scene of the liveliest interest; and I consider it among the privileges of my life to have been present to witness it. On Friday afternoon I walked to the head of the grand canal, the eastern extremity of which reaches within a very short distance of the village, and from one of the slight and airy bridges which crossed it I had a sight that could not but exhilarate and elevate the mind. The waters were rushing in from the westward, and coming down their untried channel towards the sea. Their course, owing to the absorption of the new banks of the canal, and the distance they had to run from where the stream entered it, was much slower than I had anticipated; they continued gradually to steal along from bridge to bridge, and at first only spreading over the bed of the canal, imperceptibly rose and washed its sides with a gentle wave. It was dark before they reached the eastern extremity; but at sunrise next morning they were on a level, two feet and a half deep throughout the whole distance of thirteen miles. The interest manifested by the whole country, as this new internal river rolled its first waves through the state, can not be described. You might see the people running across the fields, climbing on trees and fences, and crowding the bank of the canal to gaze upon the welcome sight. A boat had been prepared at Rome, and as the waters came down the canal you might mark their progress by that of this new Argo, which floated triumphantly along the Hellespont of the west, accompanied by the shouts of the peasantry, and having on her deck a military band. At nine the next morning the bells began a merry peal, and the commissioners, in carriages, proceeded from Bagg's hotel to the place of embarkation.

"The governor, accompanied by Gen. Van Rensselaer, Rev. Mr. Stansbury of Albany, Rev. Dr. Blatchford of Lansingburgh, Judge Miller of Utica, Mr. Holly, Mr. Seymour, Judge Wright, Col. Lansing, Mr. Childs, Mr. Clark, Mr. Bunner, and a large company of their friends, embarked, at a quarter past nine, and were received with the roll of the drum and the shouts of a large multitude of spectators. The boat, which received them, is built for passengers;—is sixty-one feet in length and seven and a half feet in width;—having two rising cabins, of fourteen feet each, with a flat deck between them. In forty minutes the company reached Whitesborough, a distance of two miles and three-quarters; the boat being drawn by a single horse, which walked on the towing path, attached to a tow rope of about sixty feet long. The horse traveled, apparently, with the utmost ease. The boat, though literally loaded with passengers, drew but fourteen inches of water. A military band played patriotic airs.

"From bridge to bridge, from village to village, the procession was saluted with cannon, and every bell whose sound could reach the canal swung, as with instinctive life, as it passed by. At Whitesborough a number of ladies embarked, and heightened, by their smiles, a scene which wanted but this to make it complete."

The round trip of thirty miles was accomplished in twelve hours and twenty minutes, and the progress of the boat was heralded by the booming of cannon, the ringing of bells, the tooting of innumerable long tin horns, the cheering of the crowds and the music of every fife and drum corps and brass band of that part of the state. "A vast multitude of anxious people," said a local newspaper in its description of the event, "lined the sides of the canal, but everything succeeded according to the most sanguine expectations."

The opening of the successive sections of the Erie Canal formed the subject of description and comment by all the journals of the country. One newspaper[1] published the following correspondence regarding the departure of the first boat from Utica to Rochester on the occasion of the completion of that part of the work in 1823:

"Our village [Utica], on Friday, twenty-fifth inst., presented a scene of bustle and stir never before witnessed here. . . . On Saturday the Packet-Boat for Rochester left here with eighty-four passengers, on her first trip. A boat will leave this place every morning, Sundays excepted, during the season and continue through to the Genesee River. We think this a very judicious arrangement of the Company, as passengers are greatly incommoded by changing from one boat to another. The new boats which have been added to this line are built in the best manner and fitted up in a style of magnificence that could hardly be anticipated in the infancy of canal navigation in this country."[2]

[1] The "Farmers and Mechanics Journal," of Vincennes, Indiana, June 26, 1823. The letter was dated April 20th.
[2] This is a reference to certain early alterations in canal boats that are later discussed.

The same newspaper, on the same date, also printed another letter relating to the event, which read:[1]

"The packet-boat Bouck arrived at the basin on Friday evening last, and left this place yesterday morning crowded with passengers, and we understand that the line of packet-boats have commenced their regular trips. On Wednesday of last week a boat was launched from the yard of H. Goodman & Co., and though we may not announce the event in as lofty language as is used in city prints on like occasions, yet perhaps it was an occurrence equally interesting as the launching of the proudest ship from a seaport. To behold a vessel committed to the water four hundred miles inland, in a place which ten years since was a wilderness, and reflect that it was to navigate a stream erected by the hand of man, two hundred and fifty miles in length, to the naturally navigable waters, excites emotions of no uncommon kind, and must arouse a throb of conscious pride in the breast of everyone who belongs to the state whose enterprise could do and dare so much. Our village at this moment presents something of the bustle and business of a seaport, . . . and even something like ship-building is not wanting here in the forest, as there are several boats of from 20 to 40 tons now nearly ready to be launched which have been built in this place. This is the march of improvement."

Later in the same year of 1823 occurred the passage of the first canal boat from the waters of the canal into the waters of the Hudson River at Albany, and the event was made the occasion of an extraordinary celebration.[2] There was an imposing military display; the firing of innumerable salutes; the delivering of numerous long congratulatory speeches; the discharge of fireworks and the recitation of poems written especially for the occasion; a grand ball; a theatrical performance; and a large public banquet during whose progress those who sat at the tables were requested to drain their glasses to no less than thirteen formal toasts. And after the thirteen toasts had been drunk it appeared to be the consensus of opinion among those present that sufficient honor had not yet been paid to the happy occasion, so twenty-six additional toasts were

[1] This letter was dated at Rochester, New York, April 29, 1823.
[2] On the eighth of October. The festivities took place in Albany.

thereupon proposed and also drunk. The distinguished company finally left the banquet hall wholly convinced that nothing quite so important had ever before happened in the history of the country.

Two years later there was another celebration in honor of the completion of the entire enterprise to Lake Erie, and on that occasion the festivities began in Albany and did not end until a flotilla of western canal boats had finally reached New York City, where they were met by practically the whole population, and where a flask of water from Lake Erie was solemnly poured into the waters of New York Bay in token of their union.[1]

The Erie Canal as originally built was three hundred and sixty-three miles long, forty feet wide at its surface, twenty-eight feet wide at the bottom, and four feet deep. Its cost to the state, including its various branches or feeders, was $12,720,032.25.[2] The revenues of the Erie and Champlain canals of New York began to exceed the expenses of their maintenance in the year 1826, and by the year 1838 the net receipts of the public work in question had paid the interest on the debt created by its construction and had reduced the amount of the debt itself by nearly three and a half million dollars.[3]

In tracing the history of America's primitive canal epoch from the East toward the interior we find that the first important manifestation of Pennsylvania's revived interest in the subject of canals as a practical means of better travel and transportation facilities became visible

[1] A complete account of the celebrations attending the progress of the Erie Canal from 1819 until 1825 is to be found in Volume ii of the "History of Albany, from its Discovery to the Present Time, Etc., Etc." Albany: J. Munsell: 1867. The celebration of 1825 is also described in Colden's book on the subject, printed in 1825.

[2] Figures compiled from Tanner's "A Description of the Canals and Railroads of the United States."

[3] In 1835 work was begun on an enlargement of the prism of the Erie Canal. It is now being still further enlarged, and reconstructed into a ship and barge canal at a further cost of approximately one hundred million dollars.

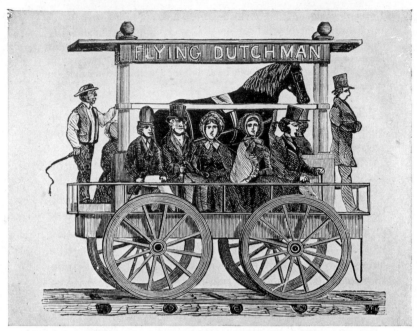

231.—A car propelled by a horse running on an endless platform was also tried by the Charleston and Hamburg road in 1829. Its inventor was awarded $500. This system carried twelve passengers at a speed of twelve miles an hour until the motive power stopped. From Brown's *History*.

in 1789. During that year was organized in Pennsylvania "The Society for Promoting the Improvement of Roads and Inland Navigation," and membership in the society soon increased to more than one hundred, embracing men in numerous sections of the commonwealth. The principal early activity of the association, as stated by a publication which appeared soon afterward,[1] consisted in meeting "on every Monday evening, during the session of the legislature, in order to suggest information, schemes and proposals, for promoting internal trade, manufactures and

[1] "An Historical Account of the Rise, Progress and Present State of the Canal Navigation in Pennsylvania. . . . Containing Abstracts of the Acts of the Legislature since the Year 1790, and Their Grants of Money for Improving Roads and Navigable Waters throughout the State; Etc., Etc." Philadelphia: MDCCXCV.

population, by facilitating every possible communication between the different parts of the state."

In the pursuance of its work the society prepared an elaborate memorial to the legislature in which were discussed the possibility and advantages of creating fourteen different routes of water communication designed to connect various parts of the state and also bring it into closer touch with New York, New Jersey, Maryland, Virginia and the Great Lake system. The memorial further advocated the building of various turnpikes designed for the same general purpose. This address to the representatives of the people was duly signed by its president, Robert Morris, on February 7th of 1791. It was presented to the legislature soon afterward and constituted the first systematic plan for the improvement of internal communications in Pennsylvania. The State Assembly, after some months of deliberation on the subject, decided on the adoption of a course described as follows:[1]

"That the legislators, although animated with the warmest zeal for the improvement of their country by means of roads and, inland navigation, yet could not subject the finances of the state (even if adequate) to the burden of the whole; yet they would make liberal appropriations of public money for the improvement of such roads and navigable waters, as lying too remote from the more populous parts of the country, and the inhabitants, but newly settled, rendered it impracticable for them either to improve their own roads and waters by subscription or the usual county taxes; and the profits of the tolls would yet be too small to induce companies to undertake the work at their own expense; but that in the more settled parts of the country, especially near the metropolis, they would be ready to incorporate companies for the gradual and progressive improvement of roads and waters where the tolls would be sufficient to recompense the subscribers or stockholders, and the charge would fall according to justice upon those who were to be benefited in proportion to the use they might make of such roads and waters."

In accordance with the policy thus announced the state

[1] "An Historical Account, etc., etc.," p. 99

legislature later in the same year passed an act[1] authorizing the incorporation of a company to build a canal between the Schuylkill and Susquehanna Rivers, and during the following year enacted another law[2] authorizing a similar waterway between the Delaware and Schuylkill Rivers. During the two years following the presentation of the memorial the state legislature, in accordance with its newly adopted policy, further appropriated various sums aggregating about $195,000 for use in opening and building roads and for the improvement of natural waterways. Active construction work both on the enterprises undertaken by the state itself and on the incorporated waterways began immediately, and Pennsylvania was thus the first state in point of time to adopt and enter upon a pretentious plan for the improvement of its communication facilities.[3]

But though Pennsylvania was indeed first in chronological order among those states which adopted a broad governmental policy of river and canal improvement, she unfortunately made a somewhat mistaken beginning. Her first effort was largely devoted, not to the exclusive construction of artificial waterways, but to the attempted taming of a number of her rapid, shallow and fluctuating rivers. For about thirty years Pennsylvania clung to the idea that she could create a practical and useful route to the West by utilizing the natural channels of the Susquehanna, Juniata, Conemaugh and the Kiskiminitas. In order successfully to perform such a feat and to build a commercial highway possessing practical value for the purposes of water transportation it would have been

---

[1] The act was approved on September 29, 1791.
[2] Act approved April 10, 1792.
[3] It was soon discovered that the original financial plans of these Pennsylvania canal companies were inadequate for the proposed work, and in 1795 the legislature authorized the two companies to raise $400,000 of additional capital by the selling of lottery tickets.

necessary not only to chain those streams but to surmount by their aid an altitude of almost two thousand and three hundred feet in a westward progress of about three hundred and twenty miles. New York, in joining the Hudson River and Lake Erie, was only confronted by the problem of surmounting an altitude of five hundred feet during a westward progress of about three hundred and sixty miles, and yet the accomplishment of her endeavor cost more than ten millions in money and about eight years of time. It is consequently only necessary to state the physical problem connected with Pennsylvania's first internal navigation scheme to indicate its impracticability as a dependable water transportation route.

It was at last perceived by the commonwealth that nothing practical could be accomplished until—through use of engineering skill—accurate knowledge was obtained regarding those problems of the mountainous district which in a westward route to the Ohio River would have to be encountered and conquered. Accordingly in 1824 the legislature of Pennsylvania authorized the creation of a commission to investigate and report upon the subject, and as one outcome of the explorations conducted by the commission it was discovered that the building of a distinctive lock canal was possible across the entire state from east to west except for a comparatively short distance which embraced the highest ridges of the Alleghany Mountains.[1] Early in 1826, in conse-

---

[1] The commission made its report in February of 1825, and then followed a period of excited public discussion between the advocates of canals and those others who believed that the newly discussed means of transportation called the "railroad" would, if adopted, prove more desirable for the purpose in hand than an artificial waterway. This and the following year were distinguished in Pennsylvania for the vehemence of the debate between the respective advocates of canal and railroad transportation, and one outgrowth of the altercation resulted—as will be seen in a later chapter devoted to railroads—in the action of certain men who sent a civil engineer to England for the purpose of studying railroad development in that country. So clamorous were the Pennsylvania advocates of railroads that on February 7, 1825—three days after the canal commissioners had made their report—the state senate granted their demand for the appointment of an additional commission to investigate the possibility of building a railroad from Philadelphia to Pittsburgh.

quence, the state legislature passed an act[1] definitely committing the commonwealth to the digging of a canal by the use of state funds. It was constructed in two sections, the eastern division of which found its western end at the town of Hollidaysburg at a height of nine hundred and ten feet above the sea level. The western portion of the

Charleston and Hamburg Rail Road, Fig. 69.

232.—Probably drawn before the road had a locomotive. The engine shown is somewhat similar to those used in England previous to the Rocket. A number of sketches of early American railroad trains were thus supplied with engines built by the imagination of the artists.

canal had a terminus at Pittsburgh on the Ohio River, and from there extended eastwardly to Johnstown at a height of eleven hundred and fifty-four feet above sea level. The short intervening distance of thirty-six miles between Hollidaysburg and Johnstown, within which the mountains rose to a height of twenty-two hundred and ninety-one feet, was at first crossed by travellers through the aid of stage-coaches, but was later spanned by a series of

[1] Approved by Governor Shulze on February 25.

mechanical devices which found no parallel in the annals of early American transportation.

There was no delay in commencing the construction work, and the great Pennsylvania Canal was begun at the town of Columbia, on the Susquehanna River, on the Fourth of July, 1826.[1]

The purpose of Pennsylvania in building her principal canal was to obtain for herself a travel and transportation route which should connect her seaport cities with the region west of the mountains, and thereby put herself in a position to compete with New York State for the traffic then largely monopolized by the lately finished Erie Canal. Pennsylvania succeeded in her pretentious effort to create such a highway, but the finished work by whose means the people were enabled to transport themselves and their goods back and forth between Philadelphia and the Ohio valley did not consist exclusively of canal construction. In its final form the line contained two small sections of railway, and since the description of a through trip from East to West over this very important route can only be given—and an understanding of its various physical features can only be obtained—by consideration of the whole work in its final form, it is necessary in this instance to slightly anticipate the occurrence of later historical events and to include at this point a picture of the two railroad links embraced in the Pennsylvania thoroughfare.

The first section of the trip from Philadelphia to Pittsburgh, as undertaken by a traveller after the work was finished, was made by a railroad that extended from Philadelphia to the little town of Columbia on the Susquehanna River. This road, as well as every other part of the route,

[1] The Fourth of July was in those days a pre-eminently popular date for the commencement of an important public work or for the celebration of its completion.

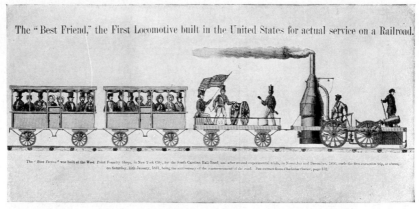

The "Best Friend," the First Locomotive built in the United States for actual service on a Railroad.

The "Best Friend" was built at the West Point Foundry Shops, in New York City, for the South Carolina Rail-Road, and after several experimental trials, in November and December, 1830, made the first excursion trip, as above, on Saturday, 15th January, 1831, being the anniversary of the commencement of the road. See extract from Charleston Courier, page 132.

233.—First American-built locomotive designed for practical service. Made in New York City in 1830 for the Charleston and Hamburg line, and tried during the same year. During a formal trip in January of 1831, United States artillerymen and a cannon were carried on a flatcar to fire salutes in honor of the event. The *Best Friend* was also the first American engine to explode its boiler. A negro fireman was annoyed by the sound of the escaping steam, and stopped it by sitting on the lever which shut the escape valve. From Brown's *History*.

belonged to the state, and was also built by the common-wealth.[1] Twenty miles of the track were ready for use in September of 1832, and in October of 1834 the remaining sixty-one and a half miles of the road were opened for travel.[2]

It should here be explained that although the state built and owned all links of the traffic system to be described, and also installed and operated the motive power on the two railroads included in the system, none of the vehicles used on any part of the route either for the transportation of passengers or freight were owned by Pennsylvania. The railroad cars, stage-coaches and canal boats employed upon it were all owned and operated either by companies or private individuals engaged in transportation as a business enterprise. One of the principal com-

[1] The building of the Philadelphia-Columbia Railroad was authorized by act of legislature on March 24, 1828.
[2] The railroad was 81.6 miles long.

VIEW from the INCLINED PLANE, near Philadelphia.

Lith of J Bowen Phila

A passenger train being pulled up a hill on the Columbia Railroad. Part of the Pioneer Fast Line from Philadelphia to Pittsburgh. Time, four days. F. Lith. Col. Amer.

panies thus organized for the purpose of carrying passengers and goods back and forth between Philadelphia and Pittsburgh was known as the "Pioneer Fast Line," and the experiences of a traveller here to be narrated may be considered such as were encountered after he had committed his person to the custody of that concern in his attempt to reach the western terminus of the route.

The traveller who set out toward Pittsburgh on the completion of the Columbia railroad made the first part of his trip by means of a horse-drawn railroad car.[1] These cars were of divers patterns, varying according to the ideas of their several owners. The earliest of those used somewhat resembled the stage-coaches of the same period. They were, however, mounted on small flanged wheels designed to run on the iron-topped wooden rails which constituted the track. By means of such a primitive railroad car the traveller was conveyed to a distance of about two miles beyond the city, where a considerable hill interrupted his progress in the vehicle in which he set forth. This acclivity was surmounted by an inclined plane two thousand eight hundred and five feet long, by which a height of one hundred and eighty-seven feet was overcome. Brigades of cars[2] were pulled up this inclined plane by an immense hawser nine inches in circumference, the cost of which was two thousand eight hundred dollars.[3]

The cars were pulled up the inclined plane by station-

---

[1] A contemporary picture of such a car, as it stood in the streets of Philadelphia before starting westward, is reproduced elsewhere.

[2] Trains of cars were at first called "brigades" of cars.

[3] The first hawser so installed was only six and three-quarter inches in circumference and proved inadequate to the work demanded of it. It lasted but a year, after which it was supplanted by the larger ropes mentioned. These hawsers considerably exceeded a mile in length. The total cost of the ropes used on the inclined planes on the Philadelphia-Pittsburgh route up to 1840 exceeded eleven thousand dollars.

ary engines of sixty horse-power. A contemporary colored lithograph, giving a view of this curious feature of an early American railway, is reproduced in its original colors elsewhere. After having reached the top of the hill near Philadelphia the traveller continued on his journey, and in the course of some eight or ten hours—if conditions were favorable—he finally reached the end of the railroad.[1]

The Columbia terminus was at first also distinguished by another inclined plane eighteen hundred feet long, built to surmount a height of ninety feet, but this plane was soon eliminated by the rebuilding of a section of the road for a distance of six miles. Some few miles of the track were laid with granite ties and wooden rails topped with flat bars of iron, but for most of the distance the track construction consisted of wooden ties and similar rails.[2]

The state derived its income from the road[3] through a system of charges here named:

Tolls for passengers, one cent a mile;

Tolls for passenger cars, one cent a mile for each pair of wheels;

Tolls for baggage cars, two cents a mile.

The three charges thus stated were exacted for the use

[1] From the autumn of 1832, when the first twenty miles of the road were opened for travel, until it was finished for its entire length in 1834, this part of the trip was made in horse-drawn cars. Steam locomotives then supplanted animals as a means of propulsion.

[2] About 1840 the primitive rails were discarded and replaced by rails of rolled iron, fifteen feet long and weighing about forty-one pounds to the yard. The total cost of the Philadelphia-Columbia road to 1840 was four million, two hundred and ninety-six thousand, seven hundred and ninety-six dollars.

The operating expenses of the road for the year ending October 31, 1838,
 were $177,854.13
Its receipts for the same time (composed of tolls paid by the companies and
 individuals using the road) were...................................$397,641.49
Its profits to the state for the same fiscal year were.....................$219,787.36
The passengers using the road during the same fiscal year numbered..... 103,336
These figures are taken from Tanner's "A Description of the Canals and Railroads of the United States," p. 121.

[3] Exclusive of that obtained from the transit of merchandise.

The "West Point," the Second Locomotive built in the United States for actual service on a Railroad.

234.—The *West Point* was also created for the Charleston and Hamburg road in 1830-1831, and put in commission on March 5, 1831. A car loaded with cotton bales was hitched immediately behind the locomotive as a protection to the passengers in case the engine blew up. A further degree of safety was assured to the public by placing a negro brass band behind the cotton. No accident marred the occasion. From Brown's *History*.

of the tracks. After the introduction of state-owned locomotives on the road the state also collected additional fees for the use of its motive power, as follows:

One cent a mile for each passenger;

One cent a mile for each four-wheeled passenger car;

Two cents a mile for each eight-wheeled passenger car.

The owners of the cars paid all the above listed tolls to the state and collected three dollars and twenty-five cents from each passenger for conveying him from Philadelphia to Columbia. This was at a rate of four cents a mile.[1]

On arriving at Columbia the traveller at once embarked on a packet-boat and set forth for his voyage over the central division of the Pennsylvania Canal. That part of his journey was one hundred and seventy-two miles long and terminated at the little town of Hollidays-

[1] In Tanner's "A Description of the Canals and Railroads of the United States" (at pages 122-125) are presented tables designed to show that had the rolling stock of this road been owned and operated by the state it would have been a more profitable enterprise than any railroad operated elsewhere by a corporation at that time.

burg. The canal was forty feet wide at its top, twenty-eight feet wide at the bottom, four feet in depth, and the voyager passed through no less than one hundred and eight locks in advancing one hundred and seventy-two miles westward.

At Hollidaysburg he confronted the most unusual part of his journey, namely the thirty-six and a half miles intervening between that town on the east and Johnstown on the west. Between those two settlements the crest of the Alleghany Mountains attained a height of almost two thousand three hundred feet, and it had long been recognized that the lifting of canal-boats over such an obstacle by means of locks was commercially impracticable even if possible from an engineering standpoint. It had, therefore, been decided by the state legislature early in 1831 that the route should be carried over the mountains at this point by means of a railroad consisting of a series of inclined planes which should rise no less than one thousand three hundred and ninety-eight and seven-tenths feet in the first ten miles west of Hollidaysburg, and which should then drop one thousand one hundred and seventy-one and fifty-eight hundredths feet in the twenty-six and a half miles intervening between the highest point of the hills and Johnstown on the west. There was thus a total rise and fall of more than two thousand five hundred and seventy feet to be compassed by whatsoever vehicles moved over the thirty-six and a half miles constituting this part of the line. The difficulty was surmounted by building the inclined planes, as stated, and railroad cars were pulled from Hollidaysburg up the planes to the summit of the range by ropes and stationary engines similar to those employed near Philadelphia, and were then lowered down the slope to Johnstown.

This method of overcoming mountains was unique in the history of the early railroads of the country. Before actual track laying was begun it was necessary to cut a path through a dense forest for more than thirty miles, at a cost of thirty thousand dollars. An iron railroad was then laid in the shape of rails weighing about forty pounds to the yard[1] and resting on wooden cross-ties. Two stationary engines of thirty-five horse-power each[2] were installed at the top of every inclined plane, and the cars were pulled up by endless ropes.[3]

When the west-bound traveller reached Hollidaysburg—during the early days following the completion of the entire route—he left his canal boat, took a seat in one of the little cars designed to carry him over the mountains and in it was transported some thirty-six and a half miles farther along his westward way. These cars—like the canal boat he had just quitted—were private or corporation vehicles which paid Pennsylvania for the work of hauling them up and down hill.

The English story-writer, Charles Dickens, passed over the Pennsylvania route between Philadelphia and Pittsburgh during his first trip to this country, and in the book he afterward wrote describing his experiences while here[4] he gave this description of his journey over the Alleghany Mountains:

"On Sunday morning we arrived at the foot of the mountain which is crossed by railroad. There are ten inclined planes, five ascending and

---

[1] The rails used in building these inclined planes were eighteen feet long, and were imported from England. The total cost of building the thirty-six and a half miles of railroad across the mountains was $1,634,357. Locomotives were customarily used for pulling the cars along the comparatively few level places. Of the total rise and fall of more than two thousand, five hundred and seventy feet between Hollidaysburg and Johnstown two thousand and seven feet were encompassed by pulling and lowering the cars at the end of ropes.

[2] Only one was used at a time, the other being held in reserve in case of a breakdown or other emergency.

[3] Previous to March, 1834, when the railroad here described was completed, passengers were conveyed between Hollidaysburg and Johnstown in stage-coaches.

[4] "American Notes."

five descending; the carriages are dragged up the former, and let slowly down the latter by means of stationary engines; the comparatively level spaces between being traversed sometimes by horse and sometimes by engine power, as the case demands. Occasionally the rails are laid upon the extreme verge of a giddy precipice; and looking from the carriage window the traveler gazed sheer down without a stone or scrap of fence between, into the mountain depths below. The journey is very carefully made, however, only two carriages traveling together; and while proper precautions are taken is not to be dreaded for its dangers."

CHAPTER XXXVI

STILL ON THE ROAD TO PITTSBURGH — CANAL BOATS CAR-
RIED BODILY OVER THE MOUNTAINS ON THE SERIES OF
INCLINED PLANES — ORIGIN OF THE DEVICE — PAS-
SENGERS BY THE PIONEER LINE PROMISED A QUICK
TRIP OF FOUR DAYS — COST OF REACHING THE
INTERIOR CITIES BY THE PENNSYLVANIA ROUTE —
THE CHESAPEAKE AND OHIO CANAL — ITS EVOLUTION
FROM WASHINGTON'S "POTOMAC COMPANY" —
JEALOUSIES OF STATES INTERESTED IN THE PROJ-
ECT — THE FEDERAL GOVERNMENT BECOMES A
PARTNER IN THE WORK — MONROE APPROVES —
JOHN QUINCY ADAMS' SHOVEL STRIKES A ROOT —
FINAL COMPLETION OF THE CANAL AFTER MANY
DELAYS

B UT a still more remarkable scheme was soon put into
operation on this rugged part of the road. In order
that the traveller might not be subjected to the inconvenience entailed by so many shiftings from one vehicle to
another while making his trip, some of the transportation
companies built passenger canal boats that could be taken
apart into sections, placed on railroad cars constructed for
the purpose, and thus carried bodily over the mountains
while the people in each section of the dismembered
canal boat remained on board the water craft undisturbed.
After this plan was put in operation the traveller on his

arrival at Hollidaysburg did not disembark from the canal packet, but felt himself placed on wheels and lifted up over the hills.[1] Thus he came at last to Johnstown, and there he again slid into the water on the reassembled vessel and continued on his way along the artificial river toward Pittsburgh.

The custom of conveying canal boats over the mountains from Hollidaysburg on the east to Johnstown on the west by loading them on railroad cars had its origin in an incident happening in 1834. During that year a Pennsylvanian who lived on the Lackawanna River decided to remove with his family to the West and undertook to make the first part of his journey by boat. He accordingly built a suitable craft—somewhat on the plan of a western flatboat but considerably smaller in size—and embarked on it together with his family and household goods. He floated down the Lackawanna and Susquehanna and thence continued by canal to Hollidaysburg, where according to his original idea he had planned to sell his boat. But when he got to Hollidaysburg it was suggested to him that it might be possible to take the boat itself over the mountains by means of the inclined planes, in which case he could reëmbark in the canal at Johnstown, proceed to Pittsburgh on the canal and then enter the Ohio River for the remainder of his journey to Missouri.

The emigrant agreed that the attempt might be made, and so his floating house was taken out of the water, put on a specially prepared car and successfully transported over the series of inclined planes to Johnstown. There the boat entered once more into its proper element

[1] Despite all the ingenious methods used on this part of the Philadelphia-Pittsburgh route the physical difficulties encountered made its commercial success impossible after engineering science had become able to operate an all-rail route between the two cities.

and the migrating family set sail again for another
thousand miles of the voyage to St. Louis.[1]

The length of the remaining canal from Johnstown
to Pittsburgh was one hundred and four miles, within
which distance sixty-six locks were encountered. The
entire distance spanned by the traveller in advancing over
the state-owned route from Philadelphia to Pittsburgh
was three hundred and ninety-four miles, and, as earlier
mentioned, the advertised time required for the journey
was four days. But it can readily be understood that the
complicated processes and many changes of vehicle and
motive power involved in the trip made it impossible to
maintain any regular schedule. In fact any such thing as
a time schedule in the present-day sense of the word was
not possible, since the railroad tracks and rolling stock
were not under the same management, and the state was
only called upon to furnish power and lockage facilities
upon the arrival of some railroad car or canal boat.

A traveller's guide book published in 1836[2] had this
to say concerning transportation over the highway here
described, and its use in reaching the cities of the interior:

"The Pioneer Line on this route is exclusively for passengers, and
professes to reach Pittsburg in four days—but is sometimes behind

[1] The American use of inclined planes for the purpose of conveying canal boats
from one level to another, although more spectacularly shown on the Portage railroad in
Pennsylvania, was not confined exclusively to that thoroughfare. A somewhat similar
device was also employed on the Morris Canal across New Jersey between the Hudson
River and the Delaware. The inclined planes of the Morris Canal were described soon
after their installation by the Scotch engineer, Stevenson, who came to this country in
1837. He said:
"The boats are moved from different levels by means of inclined planes instead of
locks. The whole rise and fall on the Morris Canal is 1557 feet, of which 223 feet are
overcome by locks, and the remaining 1334 by means of 23 inclined planes. . . . The
car . . . consists of strongly-made wooden crib or cradle, . . . on which the
body rests, supported on two iron wagons running on four wheels. . . . The cars
run on plate rails laid on the inclined planes, and are raised and lowered by means of
machinery. . . . The railway on which the car runs extends along the bottom of
the canal for a short distance from the lower extremity of the plane; when a boat is to
be raised, the car is lowered into the water and the boat being floated over it, is made
fast to the part of the framework which projects above the gunwale . . . the
machinery is then put in motion; and the car bearing the boat drawn by a chain to the
top of the inclined plane, at which there is a lock for its reception."
The above description is from David Stevenson's "Sketch of the Civil Engineering of North America." London: MDCCCXXXVIII, pp. 128-9.
[2] "A New Guide for Emigrants to the West." By J. M. Peck. Boston: 1836, pp.
369, 373-374.

several hours. Fare through, $10.00. Passengers pay for meals.

"Leach's line, called the 'Western Transportation Line,' takes both freight and passengers. The packet-boats advertise to go through to Pittsburg in five days for $7.00.

"Mid-ship and steerage passengers in the transportation line [meaning on a line-boat] in six and a half days; merchandise delivered in eight days. Generally, however, there is some delay. . . . The price of meals on the boat is about thirty-seven and a half cents.

"The whole expense of a single person from New York to St. Louis, via Philadelphia and Pittsburg, with cabin passage on the river, will range about $40 to $45. The time from 12 to 15 days.

"Taking the transportation lines on the Pennsylvania Canal, a deck passage will range between $20 and $25, supposing the person buys his meals at 25 cents and eats twice a day. If he carry his own provisions, the passage, etc., will be from $15 to $18.

"The following is from an advertisement of the Western Transportation, or Leach's Line, from Philadelphia:

	Miles	Days	
"Fare to Pittsburg	400	6½	$6.00
" " Cincinnati	900	8½	8.50
" " Louisville	1050	9½	9.00
" " Nashville	1650	13½	13.00
" " St. Louis	1750	14	13.00

"The above does not include meals.

"Packet-boats for cabin passengers same line:

	Miles	Days	
"Fare to Pittsburg	400	5	$7.00
" " Cincinnati	900	8	17.00
" " Louisville	1050	9	19.00
" " Nashville	1650	13	27.00
" " St. Louis	1750	13	27.00

"Emigrants and travelers will find it to their interest always to be a little sceptical relative to the statements of stage, steam and canal-boat agents, to make some allowance in their own calculations for delays, difficulties and expenses, and, above all, to feel perfectly patient and in good humor with themselves, the officers, company, and the world, even if they do not move quite as rapid, and fare quite as well as they desire."

The first canal packet to reach the Ohio River from the East was the *Pittsburgh*. She was seventy-two feet long, eleven feet wide and eight feet high. The underbody of the boat was painted red and black, and the cabin

The First Steam Railroad Passenger Train in America.

235.—The Mohawk and Hudson Railroad train of 1831. First steam railway in New York State. Sketched just before the trip of August 9 by William Brown, a travelling silhouette artist of the time. The original silhouette made by Brown, from his drawing, is now in the collections of the Connecticut Historical Society. The picture here reproduced is accurate, but several of the printed statements on the lithograph are incorrect. It was not the first steam railroad passenger train in America; David Matthew of New York and not John Hampson of England was the engineer, and the locomotive was the American built *DeWitt Clinton* and not the English engine *John Bull*. The engine and cars of this train, on its first trip, were connected by short and heavy chains of three links each.

structure was a dazzling white. Along each side of the superstructure extended a row of twenty small windows with green shutters. She carried a crew of nine persons, and had accommodations for one hundred and fifty passengers.[1]

Although the early plans for joining the Schuylkill and Susquehanna Rivers were suffered to lapse they were revived in 1811 by an act of legislature providing for the incorporation of an enterprise known as "The Union Canal Company of Pennsylvania." This project was in substance a consolidation of the two old plans for joining the Delaware and Schuylkill Rivers to the Susquehanna,

[1] "Accommodations for passengers" on a canal packet did not have the same meaning possessed by that phrase to-day as applied to ocean steamships. It did not mean that the number of passengers "accommodated" could all be supplied with sleeping quarters. A canal packet frequently carried more than twice as many travellers as could be provided with berths. The surplus number slept on the floor or supper tables.

the early companies which had been organized for that purpose having failed and dissolved. Again did the War of 1812 interfere and cause a temporary abandonment of a transportation enterprise, but the Union Canal was aided by additional legislation in 1819 and 1821, when lotteries were authorized as a means of getting money whereby arrears of interest might be obtained for the holders of the stock authorized in 1811. Construction work was resumed in 1821 and the enterprise was completed in 1828, thirty-seven years after the first work on it was begun. The Union Canal was about eighty-two miles long and extended from Middletown on the Susquehanna to Reading on the Schuylkill. At Middletown it joined the Pennsylvania Canal, thus giving it a westward outlet to Pittsburgh, and at Reading it joined the Schuylkill Navigation project, by which it gained access to Philadelphia. The waterway never acquired unusual importance as a transportation route, and one of the principal causes of its failure in that respect was the inadequacy of the locking facilities throughout its length. Its locks were but seventeen feet wide.

By the year 1840 the state of Pennsylvania owned and operated six hundred and eight miles of canals and one hundred and eighteen miles of railways, the total length of the transportation system built by the state thus being seven hundred and twenty-six miles. The Union Canal was constructed and owned by a corporation, as was the Schuylkill Navigation scheme with one hundred and eight miles of navigable water; the Lehigh Navigation, whose length was eighty-four and a half miles; the Conestoga Canal, the Susquehanna Canal and various other minor waterways.

One other important canal begun in the East remains

to be noticed in a review of the early efforts that were made to join the East and the interior by means of artificial water communications. This was the Chesapeake and Ohio Canal, a work that had its inspiration in a plan promulgated by General Washington as early as the year 1784. Washington was an ardent advocate of better transportation facilities to the Ohio valley and the West, and as one means of acquiring a suitable route to the westward he favored the improvement of the Potomac River, together with the building of short canals around various obstructions to the navigation of that stream. The organization of a corporation known as "The Potomac Company" was largely due to his endeavors, and the company was incorporated by Virginia and Maryland in 1784-1785 with Washington himself as its president.

Although there had been as yet no really extensive movement of population toward the West—except for the local though highly important enterprises which followed Boone's exploits—it was dimly seen that the future of the new nation would be profoundly swayed by the relations later to exist between the original colonies and the vast region lying on the far side of the Alleghany Mountains. At that time the Spaniards still held the Mississippi River and it was feared—possibly with some reason—that if the future English speaking population of the interior was permitted to maintain close social and economic relations with them, without such opportunity to enjoy like associations with the East as would be afforded by better facilities for intercommunication, the result of that state of affairs might gradually produce a political effect injurious to the nation. Doubtless some such considerations as these were involved in all the early efforts to bring about a closer union of the seaboard and the interior by means of projects for better communications between the two regions, including the Potomac Company idea, although that enterprise was ostensibly a commercial one only.

After Washington's death the importance of the Potomac Company decreased rapidly, and at last became

RAIL ROAD SCENE.

236.—An engraving intended to depict a scene on the Mohawk and Hudson Railroad, in New York State. Published in Cincinnati about 1838. The locomotive shown is fictitious. It slightly resembles a primitive English type of which none was used in America. When the picture was printed there was but one locomotive in Ohio, and it was in the northern part of the state. Perhaps the western artist had never seen one, or even a good representation of such a machine.

virtually negligible. Yet the idea of creating a traffic route between the Potomac and the Ohio Rivers still maintained a spark of life, and the year 1816 witnessed its emphatic revival. In that year the Virginia Board of Public Works made the first new suggestion that a canal be built to join the waters of the Potomac and the

Ohio, and four years later, in 1820, Virginia began a survey to search into the practicability of such a plan. As an outcome of that survey the states of Virginia and Maryland engaged in a joint inquiry which resulted in the decision that the still existing Potomac Company was no longer useful and that its route ought to be supplanted by an artificial canal constructed by the two states in question. It was at once proposed to build such a canal westward along the Maryland shore of the Potomac from George-town on the east to the base of the Alleghany Mountains on the west,[1] and that the canal should be thirty feet in width and three feet in depth. The expense of such a work was originally estimated at about a million and a half dollars, but the final cost of the canal to Maryland was more than eleven million dollars, and other sums contributed to its construction by the Federal government and various cities brought the total to about fifteen million dollars.[2]

The first practical step which led to the building of what afterward became known as the Chesapeake and Ohio Canal was an act passed by Virginia in 1823 authorizing the incorporation of "The Potomac Canal Company." Maryland, influenced by the interstate jealousies of the period, at first refused to give her legislative endorsement to the project, and her non-action inspired the numerous advocates of the plan to begin an aggressive fight in its behalf. Public meetings were held throughout Maryland, Virginia and Pennsylvania in 1823, and delegates were appointed by those assemblies to meet in a convention in the city of Washington in November of that year to consider the whole subject and take measures for its material advancement. When the convention duly

[1] With Cumberland as the western terminus.
[2] See "Report to the Stockholders on Completion of the Canal to Cumberland," 1850.

assembled its membership was composed of thirty-one delegates from Maryland, thirty-eight from Virginia, twenty-four from the District of Columbia, one from Pennsylvania and several self-appointed gentlemen from Ohio on whom were bestowed honorary memberships in recognition of their active interest in the undertaking. The reason for Pennsylvania's scanty representation in the convention is to be found in the fact that the state was already beginning to consider its own plans for a route to the West, for which reason its people were disinclined to participate actively in an enterprise that would no doubt compete with whatever plan they themselves might adopt. The convention[1] proceeded enthusiastically to the consideration of the subject it had assembled to discuss, and its opinion was ultimately embodied in a declaration which read:

"Whereas, The connection of the Atlantic and Western waters by a canal leading from the city of the National Government to the River Ohio, regarded as a local object, is one of the highest importance to the states immediately interested therein, and considered in a national view is of inestimable consequence to the future union, security and happiness of the United States,

"*Resolved,* That it is expedient to substitute for the present defective navigation of the Potomac River, above tide water, a navigable canal from Cumberland to the . . . eastern base of the Alleghany, and to extend such canal as soon thereafter as practicable to the highest constant steamboat navigation of the Monongahela or Ohio River."[2]

In the minds of many of the men who took part in the convention of 1823 the ultimate terminus of the proposed canal was Lake Erie, but they proposed to confine their first energies to the building of a section about two hundred miles long from tide water to the mountains. The existing Federal policy and public opinion in favor of using government funds in the construction of new trans-

[1] It sat in the Federal capitol.
[2] "Proceedings of the Chesapeake and Ohio Canal Convention." Washington, 1823.

237.—Another picture probably containing as much imagination as actuality. The passenger car may have been a truthful delineation, but the engine is the English *Novelty*. The last car, which is a horse-equipage standing on a platform, is the first published intimation of the private car of the future.

RAIL-ROAD, ENGINE, AND CARRIAGES.

Private Carriage.   Carriage for Passengers.   Car with Freight.   Locomotive Engine.

portation routes—which policy was again destined to dominate Congress and to sweep the country as a political issue within the next two years—was also visible in the action of the convention, which proposed a scheme of ownership for the waterway that would distribute its capital shares according to the following plan:

The United States to own one million dollars' worth of stock; Virginia to own seven hundred and fifty thousand dollars' worth of stock; Maryland to own five hundred thousand dollars' worth of stock; the District of Columbia to own five hundred thousand dollars' worth of stock.[1]

It was also resolved that the United States should control and be responsible for all stock, and have a dominant voice in the management of the project. It was further decided to call the enterprise "The Chesapeake and Ohio Canal."

According to the ideas of the convention, therefore, the Federal government and certain of the states were to be partners in the undertaking, and the consent of all was necessary before it could be completed. The acquiescence of the national administration and of Virginia, Maryland and Pennsylvania was requisite before it could be begun. This condition of affairs resulted in a delay of not less than five years between the date of the convention and the day on which actual construction work was commenced. For a long time previous—and even during the period under immediate consideration—the individual states of the union had been and still were at odds on the subject of their interstate communications,[2] and jealousies born of

---

[1] At this time it was calculated that the cost of the enterprise from Georgetown to the mountains would be about $2,600,000.
[2] The action of the New York court in declaring that steamboats from another state could be prevented from entering New York, just as if they were infected goods dangerous to public health, will be recalled.

RAILROAD DEPOT AT PHILADELPHIA.

238.—Early Pennsylvania roads. Terminus and passenger car of the Philadelphia, Germantown and Norristown Railway in 1831 or 1832. First railroad in Philadelphia. The line did not then have a locomotive, and the artist supplied the deficiency by a good drawing of Stevenson's *Rocket*. The passenger car is the best contemporary portrayal of such an early American vehicle thus far found.

those relations had much to do with the postponement of the plan.

Virginia granted a charter to the company early in 1824, adding to her endorsement of it a declaration of her opinion on the constitutional question involved by the proposed use of government money in the enterprise. This she was compelled to do in order to maintain her established position respecting state's rights as opposed to broad Federal authority. Maryland refused for a time to pass a law permitting the organization of the proposed company, and Pennsylvania likewise declined to take any action. The attitude of both those commonwealths was in large part due to state jealousies and to a fear that the contemplated undertaking would bring more benefit to other communities than to themselves. Indeed, this apprehension was openly avowed during the next session of the Maryland legislature, and it was then believed by members of that body that the proposed canal would bring Washington and Georgetown into close touch with the West and thereby benefit those cities rather than Baltimore. Maryland finally did grant the desired charter, but only on condition that she might have the right to extend the canal in such manner as to bring the eastern end of it to her own metropolis.[1]

At this time, as has been shown by the history of the National Road, the Federal Congress believed that the country might constitutionally use its money in the building of travel and transportation routes, and a few weeks later that body passed a law confirming the action of Virginia and Maryland. President Monroe signed the act on his last day in office,[2] thus giving his endorsement to a

[1] See "Laws of Maryland: December Session 1824." Maryland's confirmation of the charter was under date of January 31, 1825.
[2] March 3, 1825. His approval of the extension of the Cumberland Road through Ohio, Indiana and Illinois was also recorded on the same day.

governmental policy which he himself had previously believed to be unconstitutional. So in 1825, practically two years after corporations began to apply for railroad charters, the nation was engaged in interstate turnpike and canal building in an effort to create a more efficient transportation system by public funds. The Pennsylvania legislature sanctioned the canal plan in 1826,[1] and for a short time everything seemed favorable for the commencement of actual work. But all the states involved discovered in the plan, as it then existed, certain conditions which they believed would operate against them individually, and numerous amendments to the canal charter were therefore passed by them. Some of these amendments required adoption by all parties to the enterprise, and not until 1830 were legal obstacles removed from the path of the desired highway.

Still another cause that entailed delay in beginning the canal lay in a hitherto unmentioned feature of the Federal policy toward the subject of constructing public improvements. Congress had passed a bill in 1824 appropriating funds to obtain "the necessary surveys and estimates on the subject of roads and canals," and President Monroe had given his executive signature to the act, which created a Federal "Board of Internal Improvements." This board had been directed to "make immediate reconnaissance of the country between the waters of the Potomac and the head of navigation on the Ohio, and between the Ohio and Lake Erie for the purpose of ascertaining the practicability of communications between these points, of discussing the most suitable route for the same and of forming plans and estimates in total of the

[1] February 9.

expense of erection."[1]   In the spring of 1826 the Board of Public Improvements had reported that the eastern section of the proposed canal—that part lying between Georgetown and Cumberland—would cost over eight millions of dollars.

The announcement of this estimate was a serious blow to the advocates of the plan and gave corresponding encouragement to all those throughout the country who were turning toward railroads as the most desirable solution of the problem presented by the need for better physical communications between the East and the interior.

But sturdy believers in the Chesapeake and Ohio Canal refused to be overwhelmed.   Another convention of its supporters assembled in Washington in December of 1826 and characterized the unfavorable financial estimate as excessive.   A new survey of the proposed route between Georgetown and Cumberland was therefore made and a revised report was sent to Congress in March of 1828, in which it was stated that the work could be done for four and a half million dollars.   The public began to subscribe for stock in the proposed company in the autumn of 1827, and within six weeks more than one million and a half dollars had been pledged.   On May 24, 1828, Congress authorized the United States treasurer to subscribe to one million dollars' worth of stock and also guaranteed similar subscriptions made by the towns of Washington, Georgetown and Alexandria to the amount of one and a half million dollars.   The United States therefore became a partner in the undertaking to the extent of two and a half million dollars.[2]

[1] Senate Document No. 32; 18th Congress, 2nd Session.
[2] The amounts subscribed by the three municipalities here named were paid by the Treasury to foreign stockholders who had bought the securities under the Congressional guarantee.

239.—A carefully drawn but crude print of *Old Ironsides,* first locomotive of the Philadelphia, Germantown and Norristown railroad, and the first engine made by Baldwin. Built and put in commission in 1832. The car, also sketched with obvious care, is seemingly the same vehicle shown in the preceding print.

The Chesapeake and Ohio Canal Company was finally organized in June, 1828, and ground was broken during the same summer—the date of course being July 4th. The usual procession, speeches and other ingredients of a public celebration characterized the occasion, and when all was ready for the climax of the day President John Quincy Adams stepped forward and dramatically thrust his shovel into the ground. It struck a root, and his effort to bring up a clod of earth was a failure. So he laid down his shovel, took off his coat and hat, picked up the shovel again and made a second and more vigorous effort in his temporary occupation of day laborer. This time he was successful, and the work was at last begun.[1]

[1] A description of the day's ceremonies was printed in Vol. 34 of "Niles' Register," p. 325.

The building details proceeded slowly amid many physical obstacles whose seriousness had not been properly appreciated, and the cost of going ahead assumed formidable proportions. There were times during the next two years when the question of continuing the project or abandoning it seemed to hang almost by a hair as a consequence of the extent to which the cost of progress exceeded the original estimates. One of these occasions developed in 1830, and is portrayed in a letter then written to President Mercer of the company by Richard Rush, one of its legal advisers. The letter ran:

"Private.

"Washington, April 17, 1830.

"My dear Sir: I have just returned from a short visit to Annapolis. I there learned that great pains have been taken to impress the Governor and Council with the belief that to complete the canal as far as Cumberland on the plan on which the work is now going on will require twelve or fifteen hundred thousand dollars more than the company now have, of all funds, including the Dutch loan; for it was so that I understood my informant. I was amazed, and stated my entire disbelief in the above representation, but had no facts in detail to repell it authoritatively.

"The Governor and Council have been vested with authority to vote the proxy of Maryland, and will endeavor by their votes to undo everything, I imagine, unless they get better information before the time arrives. I write you this letter confidentially. You, my dear sir, in conjunction with any of the Board to whom you may show it, will best know what to do on the occasion. It strikes me, however, that not one day should be lost in sending a proper person to Annapolis charged with materials for making known the facts as they truly are representing the cost, and in the most authentic way that the case will admit of.

"I remain as ever, my dear sir, sincerely yours,

"MR. MERCER."   "RICHARD RUSH."

This and other similar crises were successfully passed in one way or another, and by the summer of 1831 twenty miles of the canal at its eastern end had been finished. The company then found itself involved in a legal controversy with the Baltimore and Ohio Railroad over questions growing out of the physical location of the two enterprises.

By the year 1832 the canal company had disentangled itself from obstacles temporarily interposed against its extension, but in the meantime it had used up all its money and could make no further progress until it had found another source of financial help. The Federal government had decided that it would withdraw from active participation in the undertaking. Maryland had already expended more than half a million dollars, and could expect no returns on her investment unless she followed it with a much larger sum. Two years of debate ensued over the best policy to be pursued in these circumstances, and in 1834 the Maryland general assembly authorized the state to loan the company two million dollars. Pennsylvania and Ohio were already deeply engrossed in the construction of their own canal systems, and Virginia declined to do anything further unless those more western states could be relied on for a share of the support necessary to carry the enterprise ahead. So the whole burden fell upon Maryland, several million dollars more were supplied, and by the middle of 1837 the canal had been finished to a point a little more than one hundred miles west of Georgetown. The financial panic which swept over the country in 1837 brought still further trouble to the company, and in the following year the state was compelled to subscribe to its stock in the additional amount of one million, three hundred and seventy-five thousand dollars. Three years later, in 1841, the work was again brought to a halt through lack of funds and Maryland itself was involved in financial difficulty. About one hundred and fifty miles of canal were then in operation and bringing in some revenues, though its receipts were less than the outlay necessary for its maintenance. A final exertion by Maryland in 1844 resulted in bringing more help to the canal, and it was at last finished to Cumberland in the year 1850.[1]

At a considerably later day[2] the Federal government again displayed an interest in the original proposition of 1823, which was to complete the canal from Cumberland to Pittsburgh and the Ohio River. Surveys were then made in accordance with the plan, but it was never carried out.

It will thus be seen that no less than three important and extensive schemes for connecting the East and the West by artificial waterways characterized the early canal-building epoch of the country. Those of New York and Pennsylvania were pushed on to their intended destinations, and the southernmost of the three projected routes was carried almost two hundred miles into the interior. By the first of these three canals the waters of the Hudson were connected with Lake Erie and eventually also with the interior of the state of Ohio, with the Muskingum, Scioto and Miami Rivers, with the Ohio River, with the interior of Indiana, and with the Wabash River. By the Pennsylvania Canal and the two state-owned railroads operated in connection with it, the waters of the Delaware and Schuylkill Rivers were connected with the Ohio valley. The scheme out of which the Chesapeake and Ohio Canal grew was not carried to its intended conclusion, and so that important work did not become a thoroughfare comparable with those two which

---

[1] An elaborate history of the Chesapeake and Ohio Canal is contained in "The Early Development of the Chesapeake and Ohio Canal Project," by George Washington Ward. Baltimore: 1899, the same be:ng Nos. 9, 10, 11 of Series XVII of the "Johns Hopkins University Studies in Historical and Political Science."
[2] 1870.

lay to the northward of it. But the two that finally did reach the Great Lakes and the head waters of the Ohio linked the eastern seaboard with the populous interior valley and formed practicable routes of transportation over which flowed for many years a constant stream of human and commercial traffic.

It is now desirable to trace the further development of the first American canal period, by which the public works just discussed were extended westward through the states of Ohio and Indiana, where extensive canal building by Federal and state aid finally came to an end, and was soon afterward overtaken and superseded by the use of steam and railed tracks.

CHAPTER XXXVII

THE history of the canal system of the Middle West can best be outlined by dividing it into two sections. Ohio first began the work of construction, and Indiana carried it on. The later efforts of the two states to create an artificial water route which should join them with the East were so closely interwoven as to demand a simultaneous consideration, but the first attempt of the interior to improve and expand a national transportation system by the making of canals was centered in and confined to Ohio. Ohio's pretentious undertaking during the early days of actual canal building was closely connected with the ambitious project of New York State that has already been described, but a well-defined agitation for the creation of canals existed in Ohio even before New York built her waterway from the Hudson to Lake Erie. As early as the year 1807 a Federal senator from Ohio had urged in Congress that the national administration interest itself in the subject of canals and turnpikes.[1]

It has already been said that the Erie Canal Commission of New York made an attempt, soon after its organization in 1810, to secure Federal support for the proposed Hudson and Erie Canal. When that endeavor failed the New York Commission turned to Ohio for help, and the western state made a prompt and favorable reply to New York's appeal. The Ohio legislature passed a resolution[2] declaring its opinion that the digging of a waterway which should unite the Hudson River with the lake system was a matter of interstate and national importance, and that in its judgment the general government should itself undertake the work. The outbreak of the second war with Great Britain temporarily obscured the consequence of this and all similar internal concerns, however, and no action was taken by Congress. At the close of the war, after New York had finally abandoned her desire to secure Federal aid in building the Erie Canal, she again appealed to Ohio for assistance in carrying out her contemplated effort. Ohio's executive[3] laid before the legislature of his state in December of 1816 a letter written by De Witt Clinton in which that eminent advocate of canals asked Ohio to join in the creation of the New York waterway, and pointed out the advantages which would accrue to Ohio by such procedure.[4] But by

[1] A resolution to that effect was then introduced by Senator Worthington.
[2] On January fifteenth, 1812.
[3] Worthington, who as Senator had introduced the resolution of 1807.
[4] See "Ohio Senate Journal" for 1816, p. 68.

that time Ohio was beginning to discuss the building of canals within her own limits, and her legislature in consequence did not favor New York's appeal for financial help. During the next five years the question of canal construction in Ohio received the constantly increasing attention of the people of that state, and various plans for

240.—Another print of *Old Ironsides*. Showing the two types of passenger vehicles then most widely used. Drawn and engraved by Alexander Robb, who lived in Philadelphia at the time. Richard Imlay, the car-builder, who made for the Baltimore and Ohio road, in 1830, a car almost identical with the first one here portrayed, also had his shop in Philadelphia. Robb was therefore in position to see both locomotive and passenger coach. He duplicated the first of these cars in his engraving shown by illustration No. 227.

the suggested work were at all times before the assembly. Finally, in 1822, the legislature passed a bill providing that surveys and estimates be made for one or more canals which should extend across the state from north to south and join the waters of Lake Erie and the Ohio River. Again the mutual interests of Ohio and New York were disclosed, and the eastern state loaned to her western sister one of the few competent Americans[1] of that day who possessed sufficient engineering knowledge to perform the task which Ohio desired to begin.

Ohio's survey and further consideration of the contemplated ditch extended over the following three years, and early in 1825 her lawmakers entered on the

[1] James Geddes, who had been prominent in the construction of the Erie Canal up to that time. He made the Ohio survey.

policy of canal building.[1]   By the terms of the act then passed the canals were to be undertaken wholly as a state enterprise and by means of borrowed funds, and a state tax system was devised by which it was expected that a sinking fund would be formed to meet the interest on the proposed loans and gradually retire the principal thereof until such period as the profits of the canals should be sufficient to meet those duties.   At the time Ohio formulated her plan of canal digging it was estimated that the cost would be about $6,600,000.   This estimate, as was usually the case in such matters, was much too low, and some $16,000,000 were ultimately expended before the state's system of artificial waterways was completed.[2]

Two canals were authorized by the Ohio act of 1825. One of these was to extend from Portsmouth on the Ohio River, following the course of the Scioto River in a generally northward direction to a point in Franklin county near the center of the state, from which it was to swing northeastward to Tuscarawas county, and thence proceed almost directly north until it terminated at the village of Cleveland on the shore of Lake Erie.   The other route was to begin at Cincinnati and extend northward until it reached the valley of the Great Miami River, whence it was later to extend still farther northward until it entered the valley of the Maumee, and was thence to proceed along the Maumee until it joined the waters of Lake Erie at Toledo.   Actual commencement of the work was set for July Fourth of 1825, and was attended by elaborate ceremonies and popular rejoicing.   Governor Clinton of New

[1] By a law passed on February 4th entitled "An Act to Provide for the Internal Improvement of the State of Ohio by Navigable Canals."

[2] The profit produced by the operation of the canals did not suffice to pay the interest charges on the canal loans by the year 1837, as expected.   The panic of 1837 and the financial and economic conditions produced by the introduction of railroads also exercised a powerful influence on Ohio canals and the monetary scheme originally devised for their creation.   As a consequence the state debt incurred was not wiped out until a recent period.

York journeyed from Albany to be present on the occasion, and he lifted the first spadeful of earth that marked the beginning of the undertaking. Governor Morrow of Ohio dug the second shovelful, and as he and his colleague of the Empire State thus inaugurated the physical effort on which the commonwealth was embarked a mighty cheer arose from the thousands who had gathered to witness the scene.[1] Governor Clinton also took part in the festivities at Middletown, later in the same month, where the Miami and Erie Canal was begun.

After Governors Morrow and Clinton had laid aside their spades the further process of excavation was continued by thousands of laborers who were paid thirty cents a day and their subsistence for working from sunrise to sunset. For a few months those more capable though less celebrated diggers were also furnished with a daily allowance of whisky amounting to a quantity then termed a "jiggerful."[2]

Work on both canals went on without serious interruption, and the first completed section of the waterway between Portsmouth and Cleveland was opened to traffic exactly two years after the enterprise was begun. This part of the canal extended northward from Akron[3] to Cleveland, and was about thirty-seven miles long. The first packet passed along the waters of these thirty-seven miles on the Fourth of July, 1827, and an account of its triumphal progress was contained in the next annual message of the governor[4] in which he said of the boat: "She was cheered in her passage by thousands of our delighted

[1] This first digging took place at Licking Summit, in Licking county.
[2] Howe's "Historical Collections of Ohio," 1847. The precise amount of liquor contained in a "jiggerful" can not now be stated, and even at that time there may have been jiggers of varying capacities. But it is likely that even a small jigger held a substantial drink.
[3] The present city of Akron, in Ohio, had its beginning in a temporary encampment of laborers who were engaged in canal work between 1825 and 1827.
[4] Governor Trimble's message of December 4, 1827.

241.—Scene in Philadelphia showing a railway car of the "Pioneer Fast Line" to Pittsburgh. Passengers were transported between the two cities over a system of canals and railroads built and owned by Pennsylvania. The boats and cars were owned and operated by private companies, of which the Pioneer Line was one. Advertised time of passage, four days. Date, 1833-1834.

citizens who had assembled from the adjacent country at different points on the canal to witness the novel and interesting sight." A small division of the Miami Canal was also opened during the same year, to the accompaniment of similar popular enthusiasm. In an official account of the occasion it was said: "Three fine boats, crowded with citizens delighted with the event and interest of the occasion, left the basin six miles north of Cincinnati and proceeded to Middletown with the most perfect success. The progress of the boats was about three miles an hour, including locks and other detentions. The return trip was made with equal success."[1]

Additional parts of the Ohio system as originally planned were in succession opened for traffic, and the Miami Canal was practically finished before 1829. The channel between Portsmouth and Cleveland[2] was completed in 1833, and Ohio then owned more than four hundred miles of navigable canals. These additions to the transportation system of the state were never less than twenty-six feet wide at the bottom, forty feet wide at the surface and four feet deep. In many places the dimensions named were exceeded, for the state commissioners always caused the excavation of a larger channel than was called for by the law in regions where such a policy might be followed without materially increasing the estimated cost of the work. In consequence of this wise plan some portions of both canals were from fifty to one hundred and fifty feet wide, and from five to ten feet deep. So it came about that by the close of the year 1833, and through use of the Hudson River, the Erie Canal, Lake Erie, the Ohio and Erie Canal and the Ohio River, all cities and settle-

[1] "Sixth Annual Report of the Ohio Canal Commission," January 5, 1828. The trip described took place on November 28, 1827.
[2] Together with a number of short lateral canals connected with it.

824

ments along the Ohio River and many of the towns throughout the whole extent of the state of Ohio were connected by direct water communication with New York and the Atlantic coast.

At this point in the history of the canals of the interior it is desirable to introduce Indiana as a factor in the further extension of the system of artificial waterways built in the middle states.[1]

One of the considerations—in addition to those heretofore mentioned—which convinced both East and West that increased facilities of communication were necessary between the two sections, was the experience derived by the country from the War of 1812. It was recognized during and after the war that the existing wilderness roads extending out through Virginia and North Carolina to Tennessee and Kentucky, and the Ohio River, not only failed to furnish a sufficient means of transit for travel and commerce in time of peace, but that the lack of better

[1] The most important historical study of the Ohio Canal system is a monograph published by the Ohio State Archeological and Historical Society in 1905, under the title "History of the Ohio Canals: Their Construction, Cost, Use and Partial Abandonment." This is a careful work of one hundred and eighty-one pages, and was prepared by C. C. Huntington and C. P. McClelland, under the direction of Professor Haggerty of Ohio University. It not only deals with the history and construction of the canals of the state, but with their finances and economic value.

There have been two recent monographs dealing with the history of the Indiana canals. The earliest of these in point of date is Number Twelve of Cottman's historical pamphlets, entitled "Canals of Indiana." This is a twenty-four page pamphlet containing material previously published in Volume Three, Number Three of the "Indiana Magazine of History." The other recent item discussing the Indiana Canal System is Volume Five, Number Two of the publications of the Indiana Historical Society, its title being, "Internal Improvements in Early Indiana," by Logan Esarey, Indianapolis, 1912. Esarey's monograph is a book of one hundred and fifty-eight pages and constitutes the most elaborate historical review of Indiana's early road and canal system that has as yet appeared. Its narrative and facts were drawn from substantially the same sources as those used by the author of these volumes, namely the early official state records, and files of early newspapers in the collections of the Indiana State Library. It is proper to say in this connection that Mr. Esarey's investigation of the subject was made prior to that of the writer, although his monograph was not published until some months after material intended for use in these present volumes had been collected and put in form. When considered in relation to Indiana's early population and resources, that state's activity in an attempt to construct a system of public improvements was the most pretentious, as well as the most disastrous and significant in its lessons, of all similar pioneer efforts. The subject of such former state enterprises is receiving a constantly increasing attention, and the publication of Esarey's contribution to the social and economic history of the canal period, prior to the appearance of these volumes, has fortunately enabled the author of this history to abbreviate the space which he would otherwise have felt compelled to devote to Indiana's undertaking and the significance of its collapse. Esarey's work should be read in connection with Benton's "The Wabash Trade Route in the Development of the Old Northwest": Baltimore, The Johns Hopkins Press, 1903.

transportation facilities also left the interior almost defenseless against England in time of war. The conflict emphasized the need of continuing at once along the general lines of the national policy previously outlined by the road building provision in the Ohio Act of 1802 and the Cumberland Road Act of 1806.

Congress in 1816 passed a bill appropriating about one million and a half dollars, together with an annual sum of about four hundred thousand dollars thereafter, to be used for the construction of interstate roads and canals. The success of the bill in Congress was mainly due to the support it received from the interior commonwealths. They advocated the measure as an economic and social necessity rather than as a military expedient, but were not especially concerned over the reasons leading to its approval by the East so long as the object designed by the bill was attained.

President Madison vetoed the act, despite his previous approval of six laws in favor of the Cumberland Road. His decision on that occasion was perhaps the final determining influence that impelled the four states of New York, Pennsylvania, Ohio and Indiana to enter upon the creation of extensive canal systems as state undertakings. It was in 1817 that New York committed herself to the building of the Erie Canal. Pennsylvania, in the same year, passed a legislative resolution inviting Virginia, Kentucky, Ohio and Indiana to join with herself in a conference having for its purpose the improvement of communication facilities in the middle and western states. Clinton, of New York, also wrote to Governor Jennings of Indiana in 1817 in reference to the need of canals which should join the lake system of waters with the Ohio and Mississippi Rivers, and Indiana's governor discussed

Clinton's letter and its subject matter in his message to the state legislature later in the same year.[1] At this time the small population and limited wealth of Indiana[2] made it impossible for the young state to embark upon any such pretentious scheme of public works as was under way in the East, but public discussion of the subject continued to increase during the next three years.

The opening of the Erie Canal in New York, the commencement of work on the Ohio canal system in 1825, the rumors which came from England about a new method of transportation called the "railroad," Strickland's book on railroads published in 1826,[3] and numerous other similar events served still further to concentrate Indiana's attention upon the subject, and the active history of her early scheme of public improvements soon began.

During the preceding two or three years the state legislature had been petitioning Congress for a donation of public lands through whose sale she might secure funds for canal building. While one of these requests was before the national House of Representatives, in 1823, objection was made to the proposal on the ground that the land in question had been given to the Federal government by the state of Virginia with a proviso that it should not be used except for purposes of common benefit to all the states. The opponents of the suggested measure argued that the projected Indiana canal was a local work and of state importance only. Those legislators who opposed governmental aid to proposed internal improvements in the Ohio valley also pointed to Pennsylvania, where similar work was being done at that state's own expense.

[1] See "Journal of the Indiana House of Representatives" for 1817, p. 8.
[2] Even at as late a date as 1824 the yearly income of the state was only about forty thousand dollars.
[3] Strickland's work is discussed in a later chapter.

242.—A train of the Pioneer Fast Line passing through a Pennsylvania town at a
considerably later period, when locomotives were common. Date, probably
about 1842. The canals which constituted part of the system built by the
state were sold to private companies between 1845 and 1858, and the main
line of railway was sold in 1857.

But to this the western states retorted that Pennsylvania
owned her own public lands, whereas in the West the
public domain belonged to the general government and
so could not be made the basis of state credit. It was
finally decided that the proposed western artificial waterway was of national importance, and in 1827 the Federal
government gave to the state a considerable amount of
land in the neighborhood of the Fort Wayne portage on
condition that Indiana create a canal connecting the
navigable waters of the Maumee and Wabash Rivers.
This donation was accepted in 1828, and the state thus
stood committed to the building of the designated artificial
traffic thoroughfare.

At this time the whole country, both East and West,
was in a veritable frenzy of excitement over the subject of
improving its travel and transportation routes. The
National Road was being pushed westward through

Ohio; the Erie Canal was in successful operation throughout its entire length; Pennsylvania was spending large sums on her canals, some sections of which were in operation; parts of both the Ohio canals had already been opened to traffic; railroad cars pulled by horses were regularly travelling back and forth over a few miles of the new Baltimore and Ohio Railroad; South Carolina was preparing to build a long railroad from Charleston to Hamburg; the country was rapidly increasing in prosperity; thousands of its citizens in all the states were hastening to invest their savings in the stocks of projected railroads or canals; the subject of better travel and traffic facilities was the principal question occupying the attention of the newspaper press; and political parties achieved ascendency or encountered defeat in accordance with their attitude on the topic of universal public interest.

As soon as Indiana began her survey for the projected canal between the waters of the Wabash and the Maumee it was discovered that a part of the canal would necessarily have to lie in Ohio. This complication resulted in a conference at Cincinnati in 1829 between representatives of the two states, and it was agreed that Ohio should undertake that portion of the waterway within her own borders and accept some of the Federal land as recompense for her work. It was further agreed that each state should enjoy identical rights throughout the entire length of the canal. Indiana ratified the Cincinnati agreement, but Ohio refused to indorse it, and maintained her attitude of opposition for a number of years. Her position constituted another of those numerous instances of state jealousy or sectional narrow-mindedness which from time to time characterized the early history of the national transportation system. Ohio's attitude was due to the fact that she was already digging two canals designed to unite Lake Erie and the towns along her southern border, and one of these[1] was to extend north and south throughout the length of the state and but a short distance to the eastward of the Indiana boundary. If the canal planned by Indiana and aided by the Federal government was created, and Lake Erie and the Maumee were by it joined to the Wabash and lower Ohio, it was obvious that a considerable amount of water travel and commercial business would thereby be diverted through Indiana as interstate traffic, instead of flowing southward to Cincinnati on a waterway controlled exclusively by Ohio. Nevertheless Ohio did finally consent, in 1836, to the physical union of her system with that of her western neighbor. Work on the Indiana part of the canal had already been begun near Fort Wayne early in the year 1832.

This was a critical era in the history of the transportation utilities of the Middle West. Scarcely a month went by that did not bring to the interior fresh news concerning the rapid advance of the railroad idea in the eastern states. To many minds it was already apparent that the railway was destined to spread over the land and ultimately revolutionize the conditions of its social and economic life. Those who entertained this belief were profoundly convinced that the adoption, in the comparatively sparsely settled interior, of a public policy committing the states to the immediate building of extensive canal systems would constitute a serious error. Though no less anxious than all other of their fellow citizens that facilities for movement and commerce should be increased, they felt it would be the part of caution, and better in the end, if they should wait yet a little while

[1] That between Cincinnati and Toledo.

longer in order to be sure of the wisdom of their course. And meanwhile an equal—or perhaps still larger—portion of the people of the West pointed to the established success of the Erie Canal and to the benefits it had brought to the commonwealth which had constructed it. And they

243.—A train on the West Chester railroad in Pennsylvania. The road was built in 1835 and was nine miles long. Horse-drawn cars were also employed on the West Chester line. Engraved in mezzotint by John Sartain from a drawing by the artist Thomas Ashton.

also advanced the argument that action of some sort was necessary if the West was to attain the place its undeveloped opportunities and potential strength entitled it to occupy. They failed to see that the Erie Canal—under the peculiar national economic conditions then existing held a position which was not only unique in the communication system of the nation but one which could not elsewhere be duplicated until the interior itself possessed in substantially equal degree those circumstances of social development and industrial progress which then characterized the East. Amid conditions then prevailing the Erie Canal was not, and could not be, an artery through which might flow equal and reciprocal advantages for both sections. It was rather a broad estuary of trade movement into which rolled many smaller streams of traffic, and it became mighty in its effect in the region where it existed only because it resembled, in a sense, a natural river fed by innumerable tributaries.[1]

It was this error in estimating the economic relationship of a canal to a population that led the West to its early embarkation on the policy of canal construction. The people of the interior were carried away by their own desperate need, and failed to see that an extensive canal system is not a transportation device suited to a vast region of scanty population and undeveloped resources, but is preëminently a device suitable for such conditions as are gradually appearing throughout the whole region east of the Mississippi River, wherein the benefits of such a system might now be distributed with something like an approximate equality through all the districts connected and served by it.

So Indiana finally committed herself to the policy of canal building, but even after the legislature had formally acted on the question there still ensued a delay of several years, due in part to a continuation of the debate over the relative merits of canals and railroads. Nevertheless

---

[1] By the year 1847 the canal business concentrating at Albany was greater than that derived by New Orleans, in the same year, from the Mississippi River and its tributaries. In 1872 but one-twelfth of the tonnage reaching Albany by means of the Erie and Oswego Canals originated in New York State. The other eleven-twelfths came from outside states. The relative proportions here mentioned did not exhibit quite such a striking contrast in the early days of the Erie Canal, but the economic principle governing them existed from the first, and its effects were visible, though they were not taken into account by those of the interior who believed that Mississippi valley canals would at that time have corresponding value to the Middle West.

L. Crepon del.   Amb* of H.P Osborn Bethlehem.   P.S.Duval & Sons lith Phil.

M⁺ PISGAH PLANE AT MAUCH CHUNK.

Length 2322 feet. Elevation 662 feet.

244.—Several of the early railways of Pennsylvania, the Mohawk and Hudson
line in New York, one in Indiana, and one or two roads in New England, at
first surmounted steep grades by means of inclined planes. The cars were
lifted and lowered by means of stationary engines and huge cables. But the
delay and cost of such practise, and accidents, resulted in the substitution of
détours and more gradual ascents.

the state eventually adhered to its decision, and one of the considerations impelling it to that course was the argument that all materials and labor for the making of a canal could be found in Indiana, and all the money expended in its construction would therefore remain in the state, whereas if a railroad was decided on, all the iron and many other materials for it would necessarily come from the East and the money representing their cost would leave the commonwealth.

When the day arrived whereon it had been agreed by the legislature to take a vote on the proposed measure the issue seemed to hang in the balance. The chamber of the House of Representatives was crowded with spectators and a powerful speech had just been made against the bill, when up rose Colonel John McNairy, a famous backwoods orator of the upper Wabash valley. Raising himself almost on tiptoe he secured recognition from the Chair, and then at the very highest pitch of his voice he shouted "Mr. Speaker, our population on the Wabash am great, but our resources for salt am slim. Salt! They cannot emigrate up the Wabash!" This speech settled the matter. No one asked for the floor to reply. The question was put from the Chair and the bill passed by a decisive majority. "The cannon were fired, the city was illuminated, and all was joy and hilarity at the capital for weeks thereafter."[1]

The Federal lands donated to the state had been put on sale in 1830, and Indiana permitted their purchase on a payment of one-seventh of the cost price in cash, the remainder to be paid in six equal annual installments.[2]

[1] This account of the incident and McNairy's address are taken from Smith's "Early Indiana Trials: And Sketches." Indiana's act was passed in January of 1832, and therein it was directed that work begin by March of the same year.
[2] Insufficient cash for the commencement of operations was obtained through this method, and the state was compelled to borrow $600,000 in addition to the sums thus received.—"Sessions Laws of Indiana" for 1831-2-4.

At the time work on the canal was begun at Fort Wayne, some of the country near that town was still owned and occupied by the Miami Indians, and the canal was built through their territory for part of its length. The natives had granted permission for the necessary work by treaty with the United States in language which read: "It is agreed that the State of Indiana may lay out a canal or road through any of these reservations."[1]

During the construction of the canal through the Indian village of White Raccoon[2] it was observed that a cabin belonging to Cha-pine, orator of the tribe, was situated precisely on the line chosen by the surveyors for the location of the waterway. Cha-pine's home was therefore taken down, moved and rebuilt at the expense of the canal fund of Indiana. The artificial river was dug literally through and among Indian villages and native farms.

The moving of the Miami orator's lodge by the consent of himself and his people carried a significance more important than the act itself. It typified the process by which America's modern transportation system came into being. In like manner were the Indians, group by group, set to one side in order that their habitations as a race might not interfere with the intercommunications of the white Americans.

The first section of the Wabash Canal, some thirty miles long and extending from Fort Wayne to the town of Huntington, was opened for business on the Fourth of July in 1835. During the same year the proposal was made that the state embark on the construction of an extensive system of canals, railroads and turnpikes whose

[1] Treaty of 1826 between the United States and the Miamis.
[2] White Raccoon was a chief of the tribe.

total cost was to be about six million dollars. The plan at once became the principal political issue before the people, and the elections held later in the same year were fought and decided upon it. When the legislature assembled for its next session public opinion was known to be in favor of the proposed law and it was overwhelmingly passed.[1] With the enactment of this legislation, which was without question based on the desire of the people and that contained some features of merit Indiana entered on a course of action destined to lead her for more than thirty years through a series of unhappy experiences and embarrassments. The main feature of the proposed system of internal improvements was to be the Wabash and Erie Canal, extending in a generally southwestward direction from the Ohio state line to the town of Terre Haute, near the Illinois boundary. About a dozen other canals, railroads and turnpikes were also provided for by the bill, all of which were to connect either with the main canal, the Ohio River or Lake Erie.

The principal weakness embodied in the elaborate scheme thus undertaken was the geographical distribution of the proposed new thoroughfares. Local and sectional jealousies played a dominant part in the final shaping of the plan, and various projects of undoubted value embraced in it were only enabled to obtain legislative support by the inclusion of other features introduced for the purpose of giving all parts of the state a share in the desired public work. As finally adopted the law was so drawn that only seven counties of the state were not included among those touched by the proposed improvements. The process of framing the legislation and adopting the policy to which it committed the state was sub-

[1] In January of 1836.

stantially identical with that which has long prevailed in the Federal congress in connection with the periodic passage of national laws providing for the improvement of rivers and harbors and for the erection of public buildings.[1] Under the operation of such a method important enterprises of undoubted general value can only secure support in legislative bodies by indefensible concessions permitting the expenditure of public money in needless and wasteful undertakings.

Another feature of the Indiana law was its establishment of a Board of Internal Improvements consisting of nine members, to each of whom was assigned supervision of certain portions of the construction work. The several members of this board made immediate haste to push the separate parts of the plan allotted to their individual jurisdictions, without giving attention to the big question of physical coöperation and connection between all the scattered units of the system or to public revenues that could only be derived from finished work.

During the years from 1836 to 1839 inclusive, Indiana borrowed $6,673,000 for the purpose of expanding her traffic routes, of which sum all but $400,000 was obtained for use on the new enterprises authorized by the law of 1836. The heavy loans thus negotiated in behalf of the general system seriously disturbed those financial arrangements planned for the obtaining of money to complete the previously authorized Wabash Canal, on which trunk line of the system the success of all its other parts to a large extent depended.[2] No plan for connecting adjoining sections of the whole scheme was followed. These oversights,

[1] In the national Congress the process came to be known as "You scratch my back and I'll scratch yours." The representatives of various states would combine to obstruct or defeat such a bill unless their commonwealths were included among those in which money was to be expended.

[2] The state also sold bonds on credit to eastern speculators and lost over three million dollars by those transactions.

together with the panic of 1837, the increased cost of labor and material, and heavy monetary losses due to lax methods employed in disposing of state bonds finally wrecked the whole pretentious enterprise. The almost complete collapse of Indiana's internal improvement policy was pictured by a newspaper of the state[1] in these words:

"The policy of constructing the work and parts of works simultaneously was so well pursued that no considerable portion of any work was completed or fit for use. . . . There lies the system still, its unfinished excavations, embankments, locks, culverts, aqueducts and bridges hastening to ruin."

The State Board of Public Improvements was unable to pay its bills by 1839 and ended its attempt to build the turnpikes, canals and railroads so auspiciously begun but three years before with the enthusiastic approval of the whole population. In 1841 the state offered to transfer nearly all the system to such private companies as might be willing to take its units, on condition that they be completed. Only the Wabash and Erie Canal was omitted from this offer and it remained the property of the state. Indiana's debt due to the work done on her improvements project then amounted to $9,500,000. To balance this expenditure she possessed only two hundred miles of canal in operation, from which she obtained about five thousand dollars a year in tolls; two little railroads whose similar receipts were $26,500; and various incomplete sections of smaller canals and turnpikes. A few of the unfinished transportation links were taken over by private companies and others were abandoned outright. Among those abandoned was a half-made turnpike between Jeffersonville and Crawfordsville on which $350,000 had been expended. The state-owned railroad between the towns of

[1] "The Tippecanoe Journal," Lafayette, Indiana, Dec. 1, 1841.

245.—The New York and Harlem Railroad. Original passenger car on the line, or one substantially identical with it. The road was formally opened by the use of two such horse-drawn vehicles, and the day was marked by the first American railway collision. Drawn and engraved by Alexander Robb, who pictured a similar car in his drawing shown by illustration No. 240. Date, about 1832.

Madison and Indianapolis was bought by a corporation after it had cost the commonwealth $1,600,000 and had yielded $63,000. Indiana continued the operation of that part of the Wabash and Erie Canal already opened, and undertook to complete it to Terre Haute.

Meantime the canal had reached the town of Peru in 1837, Logansport in 1838, and the Tippecanoe River in 1841. Ohio at last complied with her pledge to connect her own Miami Canal with Indiana's Wabash Canal, and that part of the work lying within the limits of Ohio was ready for use in 1843. Its opening gave Indiana a water outlet to the eastward. She was then enabled to reach Lake Erie at Maumee Bay over the northern part of Ohio's Miami Canal, and to reach the city of Cincinnati by using the southern section of the Miami Canal from the point where that waterway was tapped by the Wabash Canal. The length of the Wabash and Erie Canal at the time was two hundred and fifteen miles, of which the first seventy-one miles westward from Lake Erie lay in Ohio and the remainder, one hundred and forty-four miles, in Indiana. Internal communication by water was then possible by means of the Hudson River, Lake Erie, and the Wabash and Erie Canal to the town of Lafayette on the Wabash River in Indiana.[1] Through traffic began in both directions in 1843 and the tolls received by the Wabash and Erie Canal increased no less than six hundred per cent. Yet even then its income amounted to less than the costs of maintenance and operation.

During this period a number of states had found themselves involved in serious financial difficulties due in most instances to errors of judgment connected with their plans for internal improvements. Indiana's condition has been indicated. Pennsylvania postponed payments on a part of her debt. Ohio was compelled to establish a tax rate of seventy-five cents on each hundred dollars in order to pay the interest on her public debt. Michigan's plan for internal improvements had encountered grave difficulties similar in some respects to those experienced by Indiana, and for a time she could not pay the interest on her obligations.[2] The states of Illinois, Maryland and Mississippi were also unable to meet their interest charges.[3]

Illinois by her own foresight fortunately escaped a fate similar to that which befell Indiana. She, as well as her sister commonwealths to the eastward, had decided to embark on the enterprise of pretentious canal construction, but altered her plan and used most of the money derived from her grant of public lands for the building of railroads. Her principal railway[4] prospered, and Indiana's canal project failed.

The first interstate packet-boats began to ply on the

[1] Indiana's canal reached Lafayette in 1843.
[2] Michigan negotiated a loan for the purpose of making internal improvements. She also sold her securities to financial houses that failed before she had received but a fraction of the amount due to her.
[3] For a detailed statement regarding the situation in the several states as here outlined, see Scott's "Repudiation of State Debts."
[4] The Illinois Central. Another of the early Illinois railways, however—a state enterprise—was not successful and was sold.

Wabash and Erie Canal in 1843. At first they did not run according to any fixed schedule but started on their trips after a profitable number of passengers was assured. Neither was there any attempt during the earliest months of the service to make regular time along the way or to reach destinations on any given day. Sometimes the passengers got their meals at farmhouses along the line of the canal. The first schedule service was announced in 1844, when two enterprising men[1] of Dayton, Ohio, established a packet line connecting Cincinnati on the south with Toledo on the north, and another joining Toledo on the east with Lafayette in the west. These lines of packets continued in operation until the opening of the Toledo and Wabash Railroad in 1854. One of the boats was the packet *Indiana,* which is mentioned in the following pages in connection with some experiences encountered by a family travelling on it.[2] The *Indiana* was an especially popular vessel, and her arrival at Fort Wayne was always the signal for a public concert given at the wharf by two enthusiastic citizens of the town named Ed Parker and Bill Patchen. When the well-known sound of the captain's horn rang through the streets of the village, announcing the coming of the craft, each member of the orchestra abandoned whatever work might be occupying him at the moment. Ed seized his clarinet, Bill grabbed his fiddle, and together they raced to the landing place, there to entertain the disembarking passengers as a token of the town's hospitality.

The distance traversed by a packet-boat from Toledo

---

[1] Samuel Doyle and William Dickey.
[2] Other boats employed by the same lines on the Miami and the Wabash and Erie Canals were named for different states and were called the "Ohio," the "Illinois," the "Missouri" and the "Kentucky"; still others were known as the "Atlantic," the "Banner," the "Erie," the "Fashion," the "Tempest," the "Cataract" and the "Niagara." The "Niagara" was a steam-propelled canal boat costing ten thousand dollars. She was a financial failure.

to Lafayette was two hundred and forty-two miles, and after a regular schedule had been established the trip between the two towns was regularly made in two days and eight hours. The rates of passage and distances between the four principal cities joined by the Miami Canal of Ohio and the Wabash and Erie Canal of Indiana were as follows:[1]

Trip	Distance	Cost of Ticket
Cincinnati to Fort Wayne	221 miles	$6.75
Lafayette to Fort Wayne	138 "	3.75
Fort Wayne to Toledo	104 "	3.25

The Federal government was to some extent involved in the disaster attending Indiana's plan for public improvements, since it had donated a part of the public domain on condition that the state build a canal by means of money received through a disposal of the lands thus given. Hence the Congress was compelled to give its consent to those plans of the state which followed the collapse, and under which the work of pushing the canal southward from Terre Haute toward the Ohio River was begun. The town of Evansville was at last reached in the year 1853. The length of the Wabash and Erie Canal was then four hundred and fifty-eight miles, and it was the longest artificial waterway in the country. From 1847 to 1856 its business steadily grew, but the action of Indiana in granting charters permitting railroads to parallel the course of the canal[2] later resulted in a pronounced decrease in its traffic, and it fell into disuse. Indiana could not refuse to adopt a new means of transportation in order that she might cling to the slower method

[1] These figures are taken from an advertisement published in the "Fort Wayne Times and People's Press," of October 21, 1847.
[2] The Wabash Valley Railroad, extending westward from Toledo, was finished to Lafayette in 1856. Another railroad extending northward from Evansville through the region occupied by the canal was also authorized by the state.

already established. Yet it is true that the state's action, in availing herself of progress and a new traffic system, did work harm to those of her creditors who held securities based on the older means of communication whose utility and value were thus impaired.

The first packet reached the Indiana town of Terre Haute from Toledo over the Wabash and Erie Canal in 1849, and some idea of the passenger traffic carried on it during that year can be obtained from the following figures:

Total mileage of boats clearing from Fort Wayne in 1849.... 209,982
Total mileage travelled by passengers departing from or arriving at Fort Wayne in 1849...... 519,336
Total mileage of boats clearing from Lafayette in 1849...... 162,297
Total mileage travelled by passengers departing from or arriving at Lafayette in 1849...... 505,397

The number of miles travelled by the canal boats departing from or arriving at the four Indiana towns of Fort Wayne, Lafayette, Logansport and Covington during the year 1849 was 485,736. The number of miles travelled by passengers departing from or arriving at the same towns during the year 1849 was 1,294,701.[1]

The number of canal passengers arriving at Fort Wayne during 1850 was 3,419. In 1851 the number of people who reached the same town by canal was 3,083, and those departing numbered 3,108. During the year 1852 no less than 76,962 pounds of passengers' baggage and furniture reached Terre Haute in canal boats, and 291,489 pounds of similar baggage and furniture belonging to west-bound travellers arrived at Lafayette during the same year. The similar figures for Fort Wayne were

[1] The above statistics are compiled from the "Annual Report of the Trustees of the Wabash and Erie Canal": December, 1849. Although passengers could then proceed as far as Terre Haute, the similar figures for that town had not yet been prepared by the company.

still larger, being 455,236 pounds. In those later days of its active history the waterway was exerting an important influence in the settlement of the region through which it extended.

The concluding years of the Wabash and Erie Canal were characterized by active public hostility toward the

246.—A later variety of car on the New York and Harlem. The captain stood on a very small platform at the rear. Horses were employed on the road for several years.

enterprise in some parts of Indiana, and its usefulness was several times destroyed as a result of mob violence. In May of 1854 a mob cut the embankment of a reservoir whose waters were necessary for feeding the canal, thereby disabling that part of the work extending from Terre Haute southward toward Evansville. In May of the following year the water necessary for the operation of the canal was again drained from a reservoir by similar means. The damage was committed by armed men, who worked with blackened faces at mid-day. After this outbreak the governor sent state troops to the spot while repairs were being made, but as soon as the reservoir walls were built up they were once more demolished. Numerous inhabitants of the disaffected region were arrested and charged with complicity in the destruction but were discharged by the local courts. During the same year of 1855 one of the aqueducts of the canal was set on fire by a mob and partially destroyed. The system was by this time falling into disrepair, and the toll receipts became insufficient for its maintenance. A long dispute then ensued between the state and holders of canal bonds, and gradually the whole pretentious work fell to pieces, ceased to exist as a practical transportation route, and was at last abandoned.

The ultimate extent of Ohio's artificial waterway system as it appeared in 1850, after the era of active construction had ended and before the period of partial abandonment began in that state, will be disclosed in the following table:

Length of the Miami and Erie Canal............... 301.49 miles
Length of the Ohio Canal .... 512.26 "
Length of the Pennsylvania and Ohio Canal......... 76 "
Length of the Sandy and Beaver Canal............. 79 "
Length of the Whitewater Canal .... 32 "

Total ....1000.75 miles

In building these canals Ohio had expended about fifteen millions of dollars.

The material result of the canal-building era throughout the whole country has thus been summed up and discussed by the government:[1]

"Adding together the totals of operating and abandoned canals, we have a grand total of 4,468 miles of canals, costing approximately $214,-

[1] In its review of "Agencies of Transportation," in the United States Census Report for 1880.

041,802. Of these, 1,953 miles are now abandoned, and a large portion of the remaining 2,515 is not paying expenses. This is largely due to railroad competition. All the canals of the New England States are abandoned for commercial purposes. . . . In New York State, 356 miles of lateral canals, costing $10,235,314, have been abandoned; in Pennsylvania 477 miles are abandoned, costing $12,745,780; in Ohio, 205 miles, costing $3,000,000, have been abandoned. Indiana, with the aid of her creditors, constructed 379 miles of canals, costing $6,-325,262, all of which were abandoned upon the construction of railroads along the lines of the canals."

Just as the National Road—as a macadamized turnpike—paused in its westward course when it had reached the western limits of Indiana, so also did extensive canal building under the direct control or indirect patronage of governmental enterprise finally halt after it had reached the same region. The extension of the Wabash and Erie Canal southward from Terre Haute to Evansville, and its operation to the last-named town for a comparatively brief interval, virtually marked the end of the early canal-building epoch.[1] By the use of the artificial water routes which had up to that time been made through the states of New York, New Jersey, Pennsylvania, Ohio and Indiana, and the further use in conjunction with them of the Great Lakes and the waters of the Ohio and Mississippi Rivers, an immense system of combined natural and artificial interior waterways had been created. Several hundred thousand square miles of territory between the Atlantic Ocean and the Mississippi River had been roughly linked together, and the resultant canal travel undertaken by large numbers of people was for some time a prominent feature of national life.

[1] Although one waterway of the sort—the Illinois and Michigan Canal—was built in Illinois. It extended from Chicago to Peru, and was one hundred miles long.

CHAPTER XXXVIII

TRAVEL ON THE CANALS — THE EARLY BOATS PATTERNED AFTER KEEL-BOATS AND BARGES — CHANGES IN THEIR FORM AND ARRANGEMENT—LINE-BOATS AND PACKET-BOATS — GOING TO BED ON A CANAL PACKET — THE SLEEPING BUNKS — WHY A TRAVELLER SOME-TIMES HESITATED TO CHOOSE A LOWER BERTH — CONDITIONS ON A CROWDED CRAFT — SLEEPING ON THE FLOOR AND TABLES — THE CLOTHES-LINE — EX-PERIENCES OF AN UPPER-BERTH PASSENGER IN AN EFFORT TO GET OUT ON THE ROOF — DELIGHTS OF CANAL TRAVEL — THE "FIVE CENTS A MILE" SCHEME — ADVENTURES OF AN ENGLISHMAN AND OF HORACE GREELEY

THE subject of American travel by means of artificial waterways is one that has received small attention in discussions of the canal-building epoch and its effect on human movement and the settlement of the country. Doubtless this has been because our canals—to an extent greater than was involved in the history of any other early means of transportation—were built more for the avowed purpose of freight traffic than for any other reason. The arguments in favor of a canal-building policy contained little or nothing regarding their possible development as important factors in public travel. Yet no sooner were man-made water courses constructed toward the West than they were seized upon by the people as a means of

847

moving themselves from place to place, and preëxisting plans for their operation underwent material alteration in consequence of the popular attitude.

The first canal line affording any extensive opportunity for human travel was the one by which New York State connected the waters of the Hudson River with those of Lake Erie. And, even before that immense undertaking was completed in its entirety, the finishing of intermediate sections of the work at once proved that the people looked upon canals not only as routes for commodities but also as useful means for their own journeyings.

While the canals themselves were the enterprises of the states within whose limits they lay, the boats that navigated their waters were the property either of individuals or of companies organized for the purpose of operating them. The conflicting methods of those who built the first boats for canal traffic disclosed a considerable diversity of opinion regarding the most desirable form for such a craft. In fact, though the career of the vehicle was more brief, its history conformed in a general way to the life-story which we have already observed in following the development of the stage-coach. It underwent various changes and alterations in size, appearance and arrangement, and by a process of evolution at last emerged into a standard type which thereafter prevailed throughout the country.

The first canal boats varied in their construction and plan in accordance with the ideas of their builders, but all of them were more or less patterned after the keel-boat and barge of venerable and worthy memory. Indeed, numerous keel-boats and barges were still in use on various rivers, and were employed thereon for the same purposes for which canal boats were likewise being constructed. It was therefore only natural that the first builders of canal boats should turn to the older craft when seeking models for the new means of conveyance. This they did, and so the earliest canal boats were usually from fifty to sixty-five feet long, rather sharp at both bow and stern, and with rounded bottoms. Not even in their width did they ma-

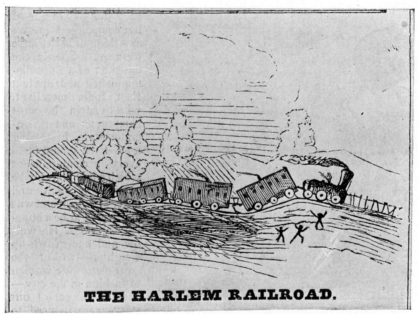

THE HARLEM RAILROAD.

247.—Cartoon suggesting that the roadbed of the Harlem Railway. which extended through the New York City streets, was too rough and undulatory for popular approval. The cars are apparently of the type shown in the preceding, and a locomotive has been substituted for animal power. Date, about 1840-1842.

terially differ from their narrow aquatic ancestors.[1] They also adopted from the barge those small superstructures, or cabins, which had been formerly added to the keel-boat as living places for the crew and passengers. They even

[1] A model of the first passenger canal boat which appeared on the Erie Canal in 1819 has been preserved by the Buffalo Historical Society, and it shows the similarity between the keel-boat and barge and their canal descendants. The canal packet of 1819 was but seven and a half feet wide and was sixty-five feet long.

took the sleeping bunks of the barge, and the berths were arranged in tiers along the sides of the canal-boat cabins in the immemorial fashion. A very scanty allowance of space was originally made for the important activities of the cook.

The first material alterations that were soon to result in a standard type of vessel were an increase in width and a change in the shape of both bow and stern, which were made much more blunt and rounded in form. Most of the primitive vehicles were designed either for the exclusive carriage of freight, or for the accommodation of perhaps half a dozen passengers in connection with a cargo of bulky goods. But the immediate adoption of the canal as a means of human travel—considerably to the surprise of the official and mercantile mind—speedily made it apparent that the original notions of the companies and builders were not altogether in harmony with popular ideas and the needs of the occasion. The people demanded transportation facilities for themselves to such an extent—especially as long stretches of water were opened—that arrangements obviously had to be made for meeting the unexpected emergency. The "step lively" principle, as far as it was applicable to progress by canal, also appeared, and the cry for speed was intensified whenever a route in process of construction opened for traffic a new extension which permitted farther penetration of the country by that means. As a consequence of these manifestations of public desire it soon developed that the shipment of both passengers and freight on the same vessel was poor policy, and so the building of boats designed exclusively for the use of travellers began.

At this point still another phase of the same general subject appeared. That part of the travelling public which desired to use the canals was evidently divided into two classes. One of these classes was composed of individuals or families who were removing permanently from their former homes to new locations in the West, and to whom time—measured in hours or days—was not of great importance. The other portion of the canal-patronizing public was made up of travellers who really had need to arrive at their destinations within the shortest possible period, and they demanded the swiftest progress that could be made. Persons such as these were willing to pay an increased price for quick transportation if necessary, while the first-named class wanted to move ahead at the cheapest possible cost. The same canal boat obviously was not an appropriate vehicle for carrying both these sorts of people, and so was brought about a division of passenger boats into two types, one of which came to be known as the line-boat and the other as the packet-boat. A line-boat somewhat resembled in its functions the modern second-class railroad car or railroad train. That is to say, it moved more slowly and was not equipped with such attention to the comfort of its occupants as were those boats designed for the other sort of patronage. Usually, though not invariably, a line-boat supplied its passengers with neither bedding nor food, and it advanced at about two or two and a half miles an hour. A canal packet[1] on the contrary was considerably more luxurious in its interior fittings and arrangements, was pulled by a better breed of live stock, charged one or two cents a mile more for its tickets, and progressed at the rate of three or three and a half miles an hour. If a line-boat and a packet-boat left a given point simultaneously, at the end

---

[1] The term "packet-boat," as given to canal craft so distinguished, was adopted from the term "packet" that had long been applied to the swifter sort of ocean sailing craft.

of twenty-four hours the lucky passengers on the packet-boat would find themselves about twenty-four miles ahead of their less fortunate fellow-travellers. After a week of steady travel they would probably be more than a hundred and fifty miles ahead.

Another feature wherein early canal boats at once began to deviate in external appearance from keel-boats and barges lay in the matter of their outward decoration. Scanty indeed had been the attention given to the esthetic inclinations of the floating public during the scores of years in which keel-boats, flatboats and barges had been the only means of water conveyance. During those times no fastidious sense of the voyager impelled him to refuse passage on a water craft because it was dingy or uninviting. All he then considered was the fact that it was going in the direction he desired to follow, and that with good luck it would convey him on his way. But the unknown man who first painted the sides of his Conestoga wagon in bright colors established a decorative principle in American travel conveyances which was speedily adopted thereafter by the owners of all other vehicles both on land and water. If a dozen line-boats or packet-boats were gathered together in one spot the chances were that most of them would be floating symphonies in either green, yellow, brown, red, white or blue, each being further embellished with panels and window frames done in other colors harmonizing with the general scheme.

In its internal arrangements the passenger canal boat also speedily assumed a standard pattern. In the bow was a small covered cabin containing five or six bunks for the crew, and this part of the vessel was separated from the rest of it by a partition. Nearly all the space aft of the crew's cabin was devoted to the accommodation of the

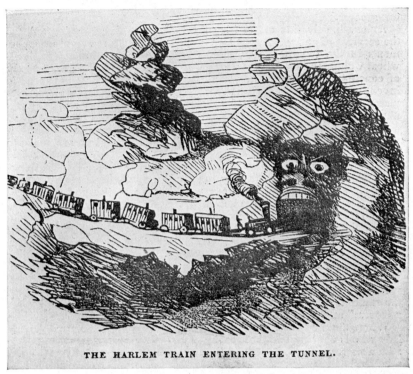

THE HARLEM TRAIN ENTERING THE TUNNEL.

248.—Another cartoon, published about the same time as the foregoing, and depicting a Harlem Railway train entering the tunnel through which it ran from 34th Street to 42nd Street, New York City. The tunnel still exists and is used by a street railway line.

public, and was divided into a number of compartments. The first of these was usually a wash-room and dressing-room for women, and following it was the women's cabin. The largest compartment of all immediately adjoined the women's quarters, and it was devoted to a variety of uses. This large room, usually about forty-five feet in length, served by day as a place of general assembly, and on stormy passages was the spot in which men travellers gathered for protection from the elements. Here they might write their letters, and here also they could as-

853

semble to participate in those exciting games of checkers or backgammon that served to dissipate the tedium of the voyage. Here they would gather for their discussions regarding the political condition of the country or to sing their rollicking choruses. If the boat by chance possessed an organ—as a few of the most pretentious did—that musical instrument was located in the compartment here described. Nearly all the hand-baggage of the travellers likewise found its resting place in this big room.

Thrice each day, at morning, noon and evening, the captain and two other members of the crew[1] appeared and speedily converted the apartment into a dining-room. The process was effected by setting up a long table composed of wide boards placed on a system of trestle-work.[2] These necessary appurtenances of lumber, when not in use, were stowed away somewhere in a small storeroom. As soon as the meal was finished the tables were taken down and the main cabin again assumed its function of general gathering place. In short, this principal section of the boat combined within itself all those features of utility and comfort which are now to be found in the various lounging-rooms, restaurants, libraries, reading-rooms and smoking-rooms of a modern ocean steamship.

At night there came still another change and the big compartment[3]—through a metamorphosis likewise accomplished by the captain and two of his assistants—was converted into a floating dormitory. Small shelves of wood, about six feet long and three-and-a-half feet wide, were attached to the walls. These were held up at their

[1] The captain's two assistants on these occasions usually being the steersman and mule driver who were not at that time pursuing their regular duties.
[2] Many of the boats were equipped with tables of more solid contruction that remained permanently in the room.
[3] The entire superstructure of a canal passenger boat extended upward for some six feet or more above the sides of the hull proper, and the whole was covered by a nearly flat roof which served as a promenade and lounging place by day. The inner height of the main cabin was usually about nine feet.

outer edges by slender supports of wood or wrought iron,[1] and became the beds on which the men passengers were privileged to repose. Each shelf was equipped with a thin clump of clotted straw contained in a flat rectangular bag of blue canvas, the whole being commonly known as a mattress. A similar contrivance very much smaller in size, but closely allied to the mattress in species and called a pillow, was also placed on each shelf, and one blanket was likewise supplied. The beds were ranged in tiers, the lowest being within a few inches of the floor and the one immediately above being at a distance of about three feet from the bottommost bunk. A like interval of space separated the middle shelf from the upper one. The space between the top bunk and the cabin roof was usually not so great as that between the lower beds. There were thus three identical compartments in each tier, and a large packet generally had seven tiers of bunks along each side of the cabin. This arrangement permitted forty-two passengers to complete those preparations which are ordinarily followed by sleep. But as the cabin was practically devoid of ventilation, and as sundry other conditions that are about to be described entered into conflict with the ostensible purpose of sleeping berths on a canal boat, a comfortable night's rest under such circumstances was hardly to be expected. It should here be said that the night arrangements in the women's cabin were substantially identical with those just mentioned.

The usual method of allotting berths on a canal boat was to permit the passengers to choose their sleeping quarters in the order in which they embarked. Travellers customarily chose lower shelves as long as any still remained vacant, though a lower bunk had one undesirable

[1] Or sometimes by ropes.

feature in that there always existed the possibility of a collapse of those immediately above it. In such cases— especially when the catastrophe began by the giving way of the top shelf—the occupant of the bottom pigeon-hole generally found himself in the most awkward position of all the passengers involved. But accidents of that sort were rather uncommon on canal packets and could not be depended upon to occur with any degree of certainty. During periods of especially heavy travel it constantly happened that the number of people embarking on a canal boat far exceeded the number of sleeping berths with which it was equipped. At those times it was the necessary practise to permit late arrivals to sleep on the floor, and extra mattresses, blankets and pillows were carried for use in such emergencies. When the floor was full there still remained the dinner tables, which also were converted into beds when occasion required. Sometimes seventy-five or eighty or even a hundred men were thus closely packed into a room designed for the accommodation of forty-two. Few indeed were the canal-boat voyagers who dared to venture upon such preparations for a night's repose as were usual under home conditions. A man would take off his hat, collar, cravat, and his coat and waistcoat, and then climb into his allotted bunk. If unusually fastidious he would also divest himself of his trousers and shoes before retiring, but such passengers as went to the extreme here indicated were not uncommonly regarded as "fops" or "swells."

There remains still another condition which arose during the process of going to bed on a crowded canal boat. When the floor and tables were all occupied, as well as the shelves, it became necessary to erect a zigzag series of clothes-lines back and forth across the cabin on which the discarded garments of the passengers might be hung, and the scenic effect produced in the sleeping room when this process had been completed somewhat resembled that displayed by the back-yard of a modern tenement house on wash-day. Finally, after all the travellers were spread out upon their berths and on the tables and floor, and the light had been put out, the unhappy assemblage subsided into a restless but unseen throng in which the stillness was only broken by faint moanings, the creaking of the boat and an occasional stentorian snore. After suffering for several hours amid the conditions here outlined it was a common occurrence that some passenger abandoned his endeavor to obtain rest in an upper berth and decided to quit it for the better air and greater comfort to be found on the roof. He therefore cautiously lowered his feet in the direction of some table whose position as it stood when he went to bed was remembered by him. He would try to perform this operation of getting a foothold with utmost quietude, in order that he might not disturb his fellow-travellers. Hanging from his shelf by his elbows, and feeling in the darkness with his foot for the table he was seeking he might at last find it, only to step on the prostrate form of some belated passenger to whom it had been allotted. When that mischance occurred—and being anxious to comply with the sudden protest which it evoked —he would hastily try to shift the position of his feet, only to discover that he was astraddle of one of the clothes-lines. He then abandoned further hope of a peaceful solution of his difficulties and let go, without caring where he alighted, or how.

With the first indication of dawn the passengers emerged from their night's surroundings and sought the open air. The men's wash-room was so small as to be en-

249.—A still later picture of a train on the Harlem road. No enclosed cab or shelter had as yet been provided for locomotive engineers. The car shows a tendency toward improvement. All railways had abandoned the old stage-coach curves for passenger coaches, and had adopted the rectangular car bodies introduced by the South Carolina enterprise.

tirely inadequate for the use of any considerable number of persons, and members of the crew or some of the travellers themselves would in consequence lower buckets over the side of the boat and draw up water for their ablutions. Such of the group as were particular about their personal appearance afterward formed in line to secure use of the massive comb and brush that were always chained to the wall of the wash-room. While the passengers were thus resuming their daytime appearance the allotted members of the crew were busily dismantling the sleeping berths and converting the cabin into an eating room. The cook in his little cabin at the extreme after end of the boat had been busy since four o'clock at his work of preparing breakfast, and that meal was generally announced at six. Everything was put on the table at once, after the custom prevailing in the taverns of the day, and the man who ate most swiftly was most certain to secure a substantial meal, be its after effects what they might. From the very nature of things it was not possible to serve on a canal boat a meal of such variety or excellence as could be obtained on dry land. The food was limited in variety and, sad to say, often limited in quantity also. The breakfast in the women's cabin[1] was served at the same time to all the women and children on board, and after the meal was finished it again became the privilege of the two sexes to meet and spend the coming day together. Families were once more united.

Despite the slowness and apparent monotony of canal travel there was much to commend it to those who were starting upon extended journeys, especially if they had not previously visited the regions to be traversed. In the first place the method of movement was a safe one. It was true that a canal boat was occasionally halted by a sunken stump or rock, or reposed for an hour or two on a mud bank, but no accidents could occur on one similar to the almost countless collisions and explosions that daily wrought such appalling havoc on the river steamboats. Most of the big canals extended through interesting sections of the country, and parts of them penetrated districts wherein the scenery was attractive and often beautiful. Some canals skirted precipitous cliffs or ran between rugged and forest-covered hills. Certain of the routes contained deep cuttings that were almost tunnel-like, and in a situation of that sort the horses or mules were compelled to pick their way carefully along a narrow ledge built on the side of a wall far above the canal boat itself.

[1] The women's cabin was always called "Ladies' Cabin."

Such an unusual bit of canal scenery was displayed on the Erie Canal through New York State near the village of Lockport.[1] The process of passing a boat through a lock or series of locks was a never-ceasing matter of interest to the passengers, and whenever this operation was performed all but the most habitual canal travellers assembled on the roof to observe the work necessary for a transfer to a higher or lower level, and to comment critically on the manner and time in which it was accomplished. Numerous rivers and smaller streams were crossed by the voyagers on lofty aqueducts of wood or stone, and some few of the canals even had inclined planes on which the boats were placed and then pulled bodily up or lowered down to a different level of water.

No more delightful experience of travel could be obtained in all the country than that encountered by a canal-boat passenger while moving through a region of wooded hills during the hours of a moonlit summer night. Ahead he could see the plodding horses and their driver. The lights from the open windows gleamed on the towpath and the rugged hillsides, and each new turn of the waterway brought into vision some new scene of shadowy loveliness. From the cabins beneath came the sound of laughter and children's voices, and if by chance he was embarked upon a boat which boasted of an organ he heard the strains produced by its manipulation, accompanied by rollicking choruses from a score of voices in which he himself no doubt also joined. And even if there was no organ aboard it was a rare ship's company that did not possess among its membership some individuals accompanied by flutes, fiddles and accordions. Those universally en-

---

[1] The excavation of this deep cut, and a view of it after its completion, are elsewhere shown by reproduction of contemporary pictures.

countered instruments of melody were brought forth on every possible occasion and formed an orchestra whose harmonies, however vigorously produced, were often drowned by the terrific vocal outbursts they inspired.

The cost of passage on a line-boat which provided neither sleeping accommodations nor food for its patrons

On the Norwich & Worcester Rail Road

250.—The road between Norwich and Worcester was built in 1840, and was 66 miles long. The wheels on the cars are shown to be outside of the car bodies, as was sometimes the practise in early construction.

was small; often but fifty cents a day. The cost of a ticket on a packet-boat, which also included the price of meals and sleeping bunk, usually amounted to about five cents for a mile of distance traversed. This price of five cents a mile for packet canal travel was early established and for a time formed the basis of an ingenious scheme that was frequently used by pedestrian travellers who were following the route of a canal. Such a man based his plan on the knowledge that a packet moved at the rate of about a mile in twenty minutes, and that the meals aboard the boats were served at certain regular times. As the hour for the canal-boat meal drew near he made himself prominent at a convenient spot on the bank of the waterway, and when the boat selected as the scene of his imposition approached he indicated by signal his desire to embark. The steersman would thereupon so divert the course of the craft as to enable the man to spring aboard, and as the repast was at that moment announced, he hastened to the table and consumed as much of the food before him as could be done in fifteen or twenty minutes. He then conscientiously paid the captain five cents and signified his desire to be put ashore. So generally was this petty trick practised for a number of years that at last it became necessary to issue rules which made it impossible, and thereafter a minimum sum of from fifteen to twenty-five cents was demanded from a passenger, no matter how short his trip might be.

The crew of a canal boat usually consisted of the captain, two steersmen, two drivers and the cook. The captain was on duty from dawn until after the passengers were in bed. The steersmen worked alternately throughout the twenty-four hours, and each guided the craft for a period of six hours before relinquishing the helm to his alternate; the two drivers worked in like manner with the steersmen. The cook worked all the time. The drivers were the most humble members of the crew, and if one of them displayed unusual care in performing his work he was eventually promoted to the position of helmsman: a helmsman in similar way sometimes became a captain, provided the boat was owned and operated by a company. In a case wherein the boat was the property of an individual the owner himself often acted as its captain. A captain ordinarily received fifty or sixty dollars a

251.—First train on the Erie Railroad, 1837. The eastern terminus of the road was on the west shore of the Hudson River, about 30 miles above New York City and just north of the New Jersey state line. New York would not then let the enterprise cross her boundary. But little work was done on the railway in 1837, and it is possible the first train was assembled for its legal value in relation to the franchise. Modern copy of an engraving printed in 1837 from a sketch made by the early American artist, A. C. Morton.

month, a steersman from thirty-five to fifty dollars a month, and a driver about twenty dollars a month. All members of the crew were also supplied with their food and with such lodging as the boat provided.[1]

In addition to the freight boats and the two sorts of passenger boats already mentioned there was also another variety of canal boat whose uses formed a not inconsiderable feature of life along the early artificial water routes of the country. This fourth species of craft was composed of what may with some propriety be called family boats, since they were both the homes and travelling conveyances of entire families, and were used for no other purpose. In fact they were closely analogous in their use and slightly resembled in appearance the flatboats of the interior rivers. They were considerably shorter and often a little wider than the public canal boats and with relation to their interior arrangements were fitted up in each instance in accordance with the desires or interests of the families who lived or travelled in them. They were domestic establishments in the literal sense of the word, and their various apartments contained such furniture as might be found in any ordinary unpretentious dwelling on the land. The owner of such a boat even kept his own horses on board when those animals were not engaged in pulling it along the surface of the water. A few of these boats were built for use in conveying families or other groups of people to the West, and some of them made very extensive journeys. They occasionally traversed the Erie Canal to Lake Erie, thence proceeded slowly by means of towing to one of the Ohio canals, and in that manner either reached southern Ohio or continued on westward through

---

[1] James A. Garfield, later President of the United States, was for a short time, while a youth, a driver on the Portsmouth and Erie Canal in Ohio.

Indiana by means of the Wabash and Erie Canal. Others of the same type did not migrate to such extreme distances from the place of their origin, but were employed as the homes of people whose lives were spent in canal work, or whose money was invested in canal enterprises.

On another page is reproduced a cartoon of the canal period, wherein an artist of the time has suggested that even such a staid and prosaic method of travel as that under discussion might have its accidents. This was perhaps true, though not to the extent that pilgrims on a canal packet might ever expect actual danger through the agency of tempest, wreck or collision. When a collision occurred—which was quite often—its only result was an unpleasant bump as the two heavy boats came together; and in the unimaginable emergency of a wreck the only resultant unpleasantness to the passenger would have been the necessity of wading ashore through three or four feet of mud and water. If a traveller happened to be standing at the edge of a boat when it came in collision with another and was overbalanced and thrown into the water by the shock, all he had to do was to clamber aboard again, change his clothes, and spend the rest of the day in expressing his opinion about the mules, the driver, the steersman, the captain and everybody else who had any part in the calamity.

But on numerous canals of the country, and especially on those parts of them which were in reality rivers used for canal purposes, there were many embarrassing obstacles to quick and comfortable travel.[1] This condition of affairs was so well recognized that two or three of the early canals of the country had guide books written about

---

[1] That is, to quick travel in the canal meaning of the term; namely, three or three and a half miles an hour.

252.—Pioneer American locomotives and locomotive building. The Rogers Machine Works, at Paterson, New Jersey, as they appeared in 1832. Outgrowth of a little machinery-making shop founded by Thomas Rogers in 1819. The initial railway work undertaken by the firm was the making of a hundred sets of wheels and axles for the Charleston and Hamburg road. Rogers, Ketchum and Grosvenor was the first name of the company.

them, in which the passengers and captains of the boats were warned of certain well-recognized obstacles to their safe navigation. In one such guide book[1] it was said in the preface:

"The Schuylkill Canal is considered very difficult without an experienced navigator, or proper directions; especially the lower section from Reading to Philadelphia, occasioned by points, rocks, and bars."

Certain of the directions contained in this guide book indicate some of the troubles which beset the Schuylkill voyager. A captain ascending the canal was cautioned in this manner:[2] "Tow the whole way to Manyunk—let the horse go at a slow walk—attend to the line—keep a look

[1] "The Schuylkill Canal Navigator," by S. Alspach. Philadelphia, 1827.
[2] Ibid., pp. 3-4.

out for stumps and rocks—keep out about 10 or 15 feet, according to the situation of the place, till you pass through the Little Canal, then keep out about 30 feet till you come to Young's Landing—then keep the tow-path channel at the Falls about 10 or 12 feet from shore, and so continue till you have passed the rocks; then you may keep farther from shore till you come to Manyunk Landing— tow the boat above the landing and take on the horse— make for the Locks by using the poles."[1]

Another urgent caution was directed by the same publication to canal-boat captains who were passing a point known as "Little Catfish Dam." Here, the publication read, "Keep out about 30 feet from shore, avoid stumps and rocks." At "Little Dam" the boatman was warned "to keep out about 30 feet; by going in much nearer to shore there is danger of sticking on the rocks," and of another section of the canal, twenty-two miles long, it was declared that "caution must be used to prevent running the boat aground in the short turns and narrow places; also in passing other boats, by running against them." Of that part of the canal between Reading and Mt. Carbon the navigating directions proudly stated:

"It is in such complete order that it may be passed without danger, only observing to keep out from the tow-path about 10 or 12 feet from the dams—by going farther out there is danger of sticking on rocks or stumps in the canal—keep in the middle."

But no records of canal disasters have come down to us, nor do the printed annals of those days—recent as they were—contain more than a few striking accounts of canal travel in any of its features. Most of the contemporary descriptions of packet trips are condensed into a para-

---

[1] Long iron-tipped poles were also carried by many canal boats for use in turning the craft, releasing it from rocks or sand-bars, or navigating it into a harbor or basin. These necessary poles were a survival of the earlier keel-boats, from which canal boats themselves had descended.

graph or two, as though the travellers preferred to forget their experiences as soon as possible rather than revive their memories through the process of telling them. One of the best relations of a canal voyage preserved in the words of former times is that written and published by an Englishman who, with his family, journeyed eastward from Terre Haute across Indiana and Ohio over the Wabash and Erie route. He travelled in the packet *Indiana,* previously mentioned, and the internal arrangements of the boat, according to the description set forth in his book,[1] were as follows: At the stern were the kitchen, steward's room and offices. In the center of the boat was the large salon—the sitting-room of all by day and the sleeping room of male passengers by night. Adjoining it toward the bow was the ladies' apartment, beyond which again was a small cabin. In this small cabin were a looking-glass, a hand basin, two towels, and a comb and a brush for the use of the ladies. It was a rule on all canal boats, said Beste, that no gentleman might go into the ladies' salon without express invitation from the ladies there present, even though one of them was his own wife.

When dusk began to descend the numerous young children of the Englishman's family, who had been exploring the mysteries of the boat with great interest, returned and asked their parents where they were to sleep. "The steward, however," Beste went on to say, "soon solved their doubts by hanging up some shelves to the wall, and laying mattresses and sheets[2] upon them. After tea[3] we all began a most murderous attack upon the mosquitoes that swarmed on the windows and inside our berths in expecta-

[1] "The Wabash, or Adventure of an English Gentleman's Family in the Interior of Indiana." By J. Richard Beste, London, 1855.
[2] The sheets were unusual, though the journey in question was made after 1850, and by that period such bedclothes may have become more common than formerly.
[3] Meaning the repast then known in America as "supper," which was served on canal boats about six o'clock in the evening.

tion of feasting upon us as soon as we should go to bed; but those on whom we made war were soon replaced by others, and the more we killed the more they seemed to come to be killed. . . . At last we gave up the task as hope-

253.—The Baldwin Locomotive Works in Philadelphia and types of engines they made. Baldwin's first locomotive was *Old Ironsides*. Engraved in mezzotint by John Sartain after a drawing by the artist William Mason.

less and resigned ourselves as well as we could to passing a sleepless night."

A description of the efforts of the travellers to enjoy repose in the berths hung on the wall was written at the time by Lucy Beste, a grown daughter of the family, and her statement of the conditions she encountered was incorporated by the author in the published story of his family's journey. Lucy Beste's remarks read:

"The berths were in tiers three rows high. I was put in the top one. . . . I lay awake, but still, for a long time. At last I heard every one turning and sighing with the heat, so I gave way to my own feelings and did so, too. But the shelves or tiers on which we lay were so short that I found my pillow constantly slipping down below my head; and if I put it lower down my feet hung out at the other end; so that, although I was not very tall I was obliged, at last, to curl myself up and be quite still, while the mosquitoes devoured and the heat melted me."

At last the night ended, and with the first gleam of sunlight the travellers left their beds and prepared for another day. In order to wash their hands and faces they were compelled to lower a pail overboard at the end of a rope, by which means they secured from the canal itself the water necessary for that purpose. Lucy Beste continued in her diary:

"Then came the breakfast. The bread was hot and very heavy, and the beefsteaks were dry, small, and much underdone. I do not know how papa managed. Captain Davis looked very black if any one asked to be helped a second time."

The Englishman after thus permitting his daughter to interject certain of her observations into his narrative, went on to describe the scenery through which the canal boat moved as it crawled toward the East. He said:

"We passed through scores and scores of miles of woodland that had never heard the axe; passed thousands of acres where trees were rotting in the steaming pools collected about them. . . . I never saw more magnificent timber than shaded the valleys. . . . Great sticks of black oak shot up straight from the bottoms without a knot or branch, until their heads spread out some scores of feet above, like the tufted summits of the Italian pine. At times partial clearings or little prairies offered vistas in the land beyond, and still the same noble timber everywhere arose. On the banks of the canal, as on mounds of higher earth, the spaces between the trees were filled with wild and untrodden copses. Shrubs with large, gorgeous leaves shot up amid creepers of various hues, and glistened in the sun."

At length the boat bearing the English family reached the eastern terminus of the Wabash Canal at a little place called Junction, and there its members trans-shipped to another packet, destined to carry them southward on the Miami Canal toward Cincinnati. In changing boats at Junction the passengers stepped directly from one to the other, as both lay side by side in the canal basin. The south-bound boat happened to be exceedingly crowded, and Beste described the conditions upon it in these words:

"I never saw people packed so close as they were that night in the men's saloon. I and my remaining son had our accustomed berths in a corner: every other one of the three tiers around the walls was occupied. Mattresses completely covered the floor, on which people lay as close as possible. The dinner table was covered with sleeping humanity more thickly than Captain Davis ever strewed it with beefsteaks; and those who lay under the table thought themselves favored, inasmuch as they could not be trodden upon."

A description of a trip between Albany and Buffalo, made on an Erie Canal line-boat by an American more famous than the Englishman Beste, well serves as an example of those narratives that suggest a desire to forget the conditions described. It reads:[1]

"I made the journey by way of the Erie Canal, on those line-boats whose 'cent and a half a mile, mile and a half an hour' so many yet remember.[2] Railroads, as yet, were not. The days passed slowly yet smoothly on those arks, being enlivened by various sedentary games. But the nights were tedious beyond any sleeping-car experience. At daybreak you were routed out of the shabby shelf-like berth, and driven on deck to swallow fog, while the cabin was cleared of its beds and made ready for breakfast. I say nothing about 'the good old times'; but if anyone would recall the good old line-boats, I object."

When Greeley made his western trip to Buffalo there were not, as he says, any such things as railroads. But when Beste moved slowly eastward on the *Indiana,* in 1854, the early American canal period had virtually reached its end. Already the locomotive had penetrated to the same region in its westward progress, and three years afterward the Mississippi River could be attained over iron rails extending continuously to the Atlantic Ocean. The railway age had come, bringing with it in a few years changes infinitely more important than had taken place during the two preceding centuries.

[1] From "Recollections of a Busy Life," by Horace Greeley: p. 64.
[2] These figures indicate a speed of 36 miles a day at a cost of 54 cents a day.

CHAPTER XXXIX

THE FOSSIL RAILWAYS OF AMERICA—GENERAL FEATURES
CONNECTED WITH THE FIRST APPEARANCE AND USE
OF THE RAIL HIGHWAY PRINCIPLE IN THIS COUNTRY
—OLIVER EVANS' PROPOSITION OF 1812—DESCRIPTION
OF THE RAILWAYS BUILT BEFORE 1827—JOHN
STEVENS, IN 1812, URGES ON CONGRESS THE IMPOR-
TANCE OF BUILDING RAILROADS AS A NATIONAL UN-
DERTAKING—CONGRESS CONSIDERS THE MATTER
UNIMPORTANT—OBJECT LESSON OF THE STEAMBOAT
IGNORED—THE NEW TRANSPORTATION METHOD IS
DESTINED TO DEVELOP UNDER THE GUIDANCE OF
PRIVATE ENTERPRISE

THE acceptance of railways by the United States as an improvement over other methods of movement already in use was a process that somewhat resembled, both in slowness and its relationship to national conditions, the previous introduction of steamboats.

In tracing the circumstances connected with America's pioneer railroads and the endorsement finally given to them, four general features of the period between 1807 and 1829 appeal for notice. First of all, the earliest and exceedingly crude rail highways of this country were designed by their builders simply as mechanical improvements of existing turnpikes, and were intended to facilitate the movement of wheeled vehicles usually drawn by horses. Second, there were a few men with understanding of the

872

254.—The engine *York*. Named from the Pennsylvania town where it was made. Built by Phineas Davis, a watchmaker, in 1831-1832, to obtain a prize of $4,000 offered by the Baltimore and Ohio management. After some alterations it was accepted and used on that road for several years. It had a vertical boiler, ran on four wheels, weighted 3½ tons, and could pull a load of 15 tons at a speed of 15 miles an hour on a level track.

possibilities contained in the new idea, who put their be-liefs on record and persistently—with ultimate success—strove to interest the public in the subject. Third, there was at first no widespread opinion that the principle of a rigid and permanent track, thus applied to land trans-portation, would soon be associated with steam as a motive power and alter almost every phase of man's affairs. Finally—though in no degree impeaching the value and primacy of George Stephenson's practical locomotive building in England and the world's obligation to him—it is more than probable that steam railways would soon have been developed on this side of the Atlantic even had Stephenson not built his *Rocket*[1] locomotive in 1829, or even if he had never lived at all.

The conditions prevailing in this country with respect to the projection and building of railroads prior to the era opened by the memorable trial of the *Rocket* go far toward justifying such a conclusion, and a brief account of the primitive railway ideas and actual enterprises of America is therefore desirable.

We find, then, that in 1786 a petition was presented to the legislature of Pennsylvania by Oliver Evans[2] of Philadelphia in which he asked for the sole right to use wagons propelled by steam on the highways of that state. In the same memorial he also requested a similar right in connection with a steam flour mill. The legislators listened with tolerance and some interest while the inventor explained the principles of his mill, but when he began to discuss a vehicle designed to move along roads by its own power and mechanism their patience came to an end, and a belief arose that Evans' mental capacity was becoming seriously impaired. His similar application, made shortly afterward to the lawmakers of Maryland, was more successful. They bestowed the privilege he asked on the ground that such action on their part could harm nobody.

[1] The "Rocket" was built in response to a proposal by the Liverpool and Manchester Railway, then under construction, and which offered a prize of £500 for a locomotive that would do certain specified work. Not one other civil or mechanical engineer in England believed moving engines would furnish high speed or satisfactory motive power for railroads. Most of them, except Stephenson, advocated the use of stationary engines. The "Rocket," in October of 1829, pulled a train weighing 13 tons at an average speed of 15 miles an hour and attained a maximum speed, when running alone, of 35 miles an hour. The engine itself weighed 4½ tons. It was the first machine of the sort to demonstrate the practicability of moving locomotives for railways. The performance of the "Rocket" was largely due to the use of the multitubular boiler, originally devised by John Fitch, improved by Voight, and patented by John Stevens in 1791 and 1803 (in America) and in 1805 (in England). Stevens used multitubular boilers in his screw propellers of 1804 and 1805.

[2] About a year after Fitch, his acquaintance, had invented boats propelled by steam.

Armed with Maryland's monopolistic grant Evans labored diligently among the moneyed men of the day in an effort to arouse interest in steam-propelled land vehicles, and to secure capital by which he might give the plan a practical test. Failure attended his efforts to enlist aid for the enterprise. Finally, when he built his little five-

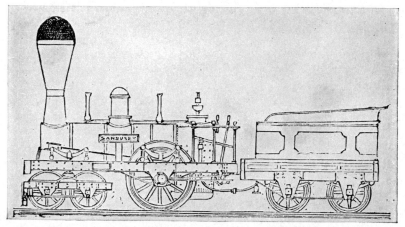

255.—The *Sandusky,* first engine made by Rogers, Ketchum and Grosvenor. It was finished in 1837, and was originally designed for a New Jersey line. Bought by the Mad River road of Ohio, where it arrived in November of 1837, before any track had been laid to receive it. The road was built to fit the engine, and its gauge of 4 feet 10 inches dictated the width of the pioneer rail highways of Ohio.

horse-power steamboat in 1804 he put wheels under it and ran it through the streets of Philadelphia as proof that his idea for operating land wagons by mechanical power was a sound one. Still he met nothing but skepticism. Those who did give attention to the demonstration argued that the speed attained by the clumsy boat during its trip across the city was too slow to be useful. "I silenced them," said Evans, "by answering that I would make a carriage, to be propelled by steam, for a bet of $3,000, to run upon a level road against the swiftest horse they would produce. I was then as confident as I am now that such velocity could be given to carriages . . . I am still willing to make a steam carriage that will run fifteen miles an hour, on good, level railways, on condition that I have double price if it shall run with that velocity, and nothing for it if it shall not come up to that velocity."

By thus declaring, in 1812, the necessary and intimate relationship between steam locomotive and railed track in order to procure valuable results and high speed for overland vehicles, Evans anticipated the more famous comparison made by Stephenson of England.

Actual railways, though short and unimportant, had already appeared in several localities of the eastern states when Evans wrote the words above quoted. It is possible that the first application of the principle in America was the construction of an inclined plane in Boston, about the year 1795. A brick kiln in that city stood on a certain high spot known as Beacon Hill, and an inclined plane, some two feet wide and equipped with wooden rails, is believed to have been used in lowering the finished product of the kiln to a street below. The loaded cars ran down the track and were hauled up by a cable when emptied. Twelve years later, in 1807, a short railway was built in Boston by Silas Whitney near the location of the previous inclined plane. It was without such an abrupt grade, and was intended to facilitate the movement of horse-drawn wagons.[1]

Still another early American application of the railed-track principle was that of Thomas Leiper in 1809. Leiper owned a stone quarry in Delaware county, Pennsylvania, and he conceived the notion that parallel wooden rails such as had long been used for wagons in the coal

[1] Concerning these two Boston railroads but little is known.

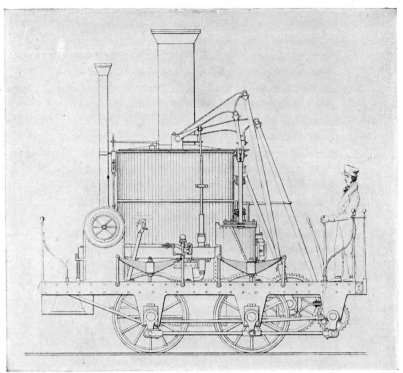

256.—A locomotive used on the Baltimore and Washington railway in 1837. Closely resembling the *York,* but weighing eight tons. Built by Gillingham and Winans, at Baltimore. From a drawing made by the Scotch engineer David Stevenson, in 1837.

mining regions of England and Wales could be intro- duced with advantage in his quarry. He accordingly hired a Scotchman familiar with such devices to lay an experimental track, and one was put down near the Bull's Head tavern, Philadelphia, in September of 1809. The little railroad near the tavern was about sixty yards long, and so satisfactory does it seem to have been[1] that Leiper at once began to make a similar track on his quarry prop- erty. The Delaware county railway was built under the

[1] As an experiment. It of course had no other value.

direction of a man named John Thompson, whose son, J. Edgar Thompson, became in his turn a distinguished civil engineer and president of the Pennsylvania Railroad. The original map and plan of the Leiper road, as drawn by John Thompson, afterward came into possession of the Delaware County Institute of Science. Leiper's railway was about three-quarters of a mile long and cost approximately $1,500[1].

Virginia probably witnessed the building of the next railroad on this side of the ocean, since in the year 1811 a similar but longer and more elaborate construction was undertaken at Falling's Creek, about ten miles from Richmond, for the purpose of more easily moving the product of a powder mill. This road was planned and erected by George Magers, and the most authentic record of it is contained in a statement written by Thomas McKibben of Baltimore. The account says:[2]

"It was about a mile long, and run between the magazine and the mill. . . . Cross ties or floor joists were laid, and the rails, of hard wood, were laid about an ordinary wagon gauge. One rail was grooved and the other tongued. The rails were cut out of the solid timber, and between them a flooring, securely fastened to the cross ties, was laid the entire length of the road. The country was very hilly, and at one point on its length it passed over a valley about a quarter of a mile wide. Across this valley the inventor erected an immense trestle some 75 feet high. . . . The wagon that ran upon it was very large, 18 or 20 feet long in the body, running upon low wooden wheels about two feet in diameter, composed of double plank of hard wood, cross-grained to each other, and securely fastened. The wheels one side were tongued, and the others grooved, to suit their respective rails, and there was a lever or brake to control the speed down to the magazine. When the car was unloaded it was hauled up again by a stout rope winding on a huge vertical drum, operated by the water wheels at the mill. . . . My uncle returned to Baltimore in 1823, and at that time the railway was still in use, but only as a curiosity, as the mill blew up in 1819.

[1] See "Minutes of the Proceedings of the Delaware County Institute of Science" for Feb. 1, 1873, for an account of Leiper's enterprise.
[2] Prepared from descriptions given to McKibben by a relative, and published in the "American Engineer" for 1886.

257.—The engine *Hackensack,* of the Hackensack and New York Railroad. Date, about 1846. Locomotives of the time were usually painted in bright red, blue, green and other colors and fitted with much ornamental brasswork. Cabs for the engineers were coming into general use. Built by Rogers.

The railway was not affected by the 'blow up,' and the people around the country used to visit it, the hands living in the neighborhood operating it for their own amusement, making excursions on the road."

The details of this Virginia railway show that in its general features it was not far removed from similar constructions then being used in England, and that in a few things it excelled them.[1]

No doubt there were numerous railed roads laid down in various places in America during the first years of the century, but their use was either unnoticed in the printed

[1] But not in the use of motive power or iron rails. Cast iron rails—three or four feet long—were made in England in 1767 and used on a road in Loughborough in that year, and Trevithick's first locomotive ran in 1804.

annals of the time or else told so obscurely that a list of all of them cannot now be made. Of several others, however, there are contemporary accounts, and they, like those already mentioned, were efforts to create a track which should be an improvement over existing highways and designed for the easier use of existing vehicles. There was a little railway built at Kiskiminetas Creek, Pennsylvania, in 1816, and one at Bear Creek, in the same state, in 1818. The last-named road was devised to move the iron made at a furnace. Its rails were also of wood. Another short railway was laid at Nashua, New Hampshire, in 1825.

One of the earliest American roads on which iron rails were used, if not the first, was constructed in Massachusetts in 1826. The Bunker Hill monument was then being put up, and Gridley Bryant, owner of the quarries from which stone for the monument was taken, built the railway in order to transport blocks of granite from his quarry to tide water at Neponset. Its foundation consisted of stone sills, or sleepers, placed eight feet apart. On top of the cross-ties ponderous wooden rails were laid. These were beams a foot high and six inches thick. Flat strips of iron three inches wide and one-fourth of an inch thick were then fastened by spikes to the top of the wooden rails and the construction was complete. The road was about three miles long, and the wagons which ran on it were drawn by horses.

During these first years of American railway building the plans and visions of a few men had sped far ahead of actual creation. Another early native engineer who realized the practical value of the new transportation idea was John Stevens of Hoboken, whose previous work in steamboat enterprises—from 1804 to 1809—has already been observed. In 1811 Stevens applied to the New Jersey legislature for a charter empowering him to construct a railroad,[1] but he almost immediately shifted to the opinion that all such extensions of the internal communications system should be created by, and belong to, either the national government or the several states. So when

258.—The *Victory,* a type of railway engine used about 1848. Built by Rogers. For twenty-five years nearly every American-built locomotive was given a name.

New York's plan for digging the Erie Canal began to take shape a year later, he advocated the making of a railway instead of the contemplated water highway, as the most practical and best connecting link between the Hudson River and the Great Lakes. Stevens even went to the extent of writing a pamphlet[2] in advocacy of railroad building. In his arguments upholding the advantages of a rail-

[1] First application of the sort in America.
[2] "Documents Tending to Prove the Superior Advantages of Railways and Steam Carriages over Canal Navigation." New York. Published by T. and J. Swords, 1812. Doubtless the first American printed work on the subject.

road over the proposed canal then under discussion he said, among other things:

"Let a railway of timber be formed, by the nearest practicable route, between Lake Erie and Albany. The angle of elevation in no part to exceed one degree, or such an elevation, whatever it may be, as will admit of wheel carriages to remain stationary when no power is exerted to impel them forward. This railway, throughout its course, to be supported on pillars raised from three to five or six feet above the surface of the ground. The carriage wheels of cast-iron, the rims flat with projecting flanges, to fit the surface of the railways. The moving power to be a steam engine, nearly similar to the one on board the Juliana, a ferry boat plying between this city and Hoboken."

Stevens also foresaw much of the economic relationship of railroads to the country as a whole, and urged the desirability of Federal activity in their construction and control. In that regard his action, appeal, and unselfish motive were similar to the previous attitude of Fitch in connection with the steamboat. Stevens said:[1]

"I consider it [the building of railroads] in every point of view, so exclusively an object of national concern that I shall give no encouragement to private speculations until it is ascertained that Congress will not be disposed to pay any attention to it. Should it, however, be destined to remain unnoticed by the General Government, I must confess I shall feel much regret, not so much from personal as from public considerations. I am anxious and ambitious that my native country should have the honor of being the first to introduce an improvement of such immense importance to society at large, and should feel the utmost reluctance at being compelled to resort to foreigners in the first instance. As no doubt exists in my mind but that the value of the improvement would be duly appreciated and carried into immediate effect by transatlantic governments, I have been the more urgent in pressing the subject on the attention of Congress. Whatever then may be its fate, should this appeal be considered obtrusive and unimportant, or, from whatever other cause or motive, should it be suffered to remain unheeded, I still have the consolation of having performed what I conceive to be a public duty."

This was in 1812.

Congress considered the subject unimportant. Its

[1] Ibid.

members had before them the recent history of the steamboat from 1785 onward, and beheld the results that had flowed from a failure to accept, on behalf of the people, Fitch's offer in an identical case. The steamboat, instead of being a national possession free for employment by every man in every locality, had fallen into private hands and its use had become subject to the whims of separate states, to political influence, and to monopolistic grants that forbade its general utilization on pain of fine and imprisonment. Here was another and even broader opportunity to seize and apply the same principle of steam transportation for the benefit of the country at large, and yet, even with the parallel example and existing conditions before them, the sifted leaders of public thought and action once again failed to grasp an opportunity. They even refused to make a proposed test of the new method of locomotion whereby vehicles propelled by steam were to be run on land tracks instead of on water.

No governmental action was taken, and the introduction and building of railways—most powerful of all instruments affecting the development of the nation—thereafter proceeded under private auspices, without systematic experimentation, control, uniformity of construction, or harmonious relationship as parts of one continental system designed and operated as the chief mechanical servant of the public. Instead—and for two generations or more—the railways of the country were usually brought into being without sufficient regard for their need, coöperation or location; were built with more thought of cheapness than of efficiency and safety; sometimes became political machines that ruled cities or dominated whole commonwealths; occasionally came into the hands of unscrupulous men who systematically used them to filch money from others; and at last the entire fabric—drunk with a fallacious belief in its own power—fell into such a state of moral collapse that its members conspired both with outsiders and among themselves, to injure communities, to destroy private enterprises, and to favor one man at the expense of another.

Within recent years these conditions, methods and acts have gradually been disappearing. The people have indicated a desire that they cease. A better, wiser, more far-seeing and competent species of guiding minds has slowly been coming into control of the vast system on which the progress, prosperity and happiness of the country so largely depend. This is not a proper occasion for analytical discussion regarding the desirability or undesirability of governmental ownership or regulation of transportation routes, nor is the discussion of that complex and important question here undertaken. It is, however, necessary to state the government's attitude at the beginning of the railroad era as a historical incident relevant to the matter in hand; to suggest the alternatives in development methods which then offered; and briefly to summarize certain other historical conditions that later prevailed. The relation between private ownership of transportation facilities and the physical and administrative excellencies and demerits of those existing facilities in America, together with comparisons between American conditions and similar systems governmentally controlled elsewhere, are already the subject of a large and accessible literature in which popular interest is increasingly manifested.

CHAPTER XL

THE MODERN RAILROAD ACCURATELY FORESEEN AND DE-
SCRIBED BY AMERICAN ENGINEERS BETWEEN 1813 AND
1819—STEVENS ABANDONS HOPE OF NATIONAL AC-
TION—DEARBORN MAKES ANOTHER APPEAL TO CON-
GRESS IN 1819—STEVENS BUILDS A LOCOMOTIVE AND
EXPERIMENTAL ROAD AT HOBOKEN—HIS TEST OF
1820 THE FIRST INCIDENT IN A SERIES OF EVENTS
THAT LED TO AMERICAN ADOPTION OF THE IDEA—
THE PENNSYLVANIA CHARTER OF 1823—PUBLIC
DISCUSSION—ATTITUDE OF THE MONEYED MEN—
ORGANIZATION OF THE PENNSYLVANIA INTERNAL
IMPROVEMENTS SOCIETY

IT was suggested in the first chapter of this narrative
that the development of our national transportation
system had on several occasions been affected—usually
to its disadvantage—by the occurrence, at critical periods,
of important or spectacular events that attracted the attention of the people and made it impossible for the public
mind to see opportunities which, had they been improved,
would have saved many years. Stevens' proposal of 1812,
urging Congress to consider railroad building as an object
of national concern and to take appropriate action in ac-
cord with such a policy, epitomized another critical period
of the sort referred to. But it so happened that an emergency in the political life of the country had to be faced at
the same time, and the needs of the future were, as always, hid by the imperative demands of the present. A

second war with England naturally absorbed all the government's energy and claimed public interest as well, and the new subject of railroads could command no thought.

Whether Congress' failure to embark on a systematic course of railroad investigation and development at that time operated to advantage or to disadvantage in the expansion and later history of our transportation facilities is a fair subject of debate. Whichever conclusion is reached by the individual man will largely depend on his prejudice against, or in favor of, governmental ownership and control of railways. It is not too much to assume, however, that if a tranquil condition of public affairs and sufficient publicity had induced the people and their representatives then to give serious consideration to the subject in some proportion to its importance, the existing and very striking object lesson of the steamboat would have had an effect, and the after-history of our railroad system would in some degree have differed from the form it was destined to take. And in the same connection it is desirable to bear in mind that during the ten years just preceding the Federal government had also adopted and maintained a policy which had for its purpose a further expansion of existing traffic routes by means of an interstate land highway built by treasury funds. Governmental adoption and use of the railroad idea at that time would have entailed no change in national policy.

Oliver Evans, in the same narrative of his early endeavors previously quoted,[1] also discussed the railway plan proposed by Stevens to the New York Canal Commission and then went on to say:

"When we reflect upon the obstinate opposition that has been made by a great majority to every step toward improvement; from bad roads

[1] The account published in "Niles' Register" in 1812.

"LOCOMOTIVE COMING ALONG THE SUSQUEHANNAH STATION."

259.—An Erie engine of about 1850. The smokestacks on some locomotives of the period were enormous.

to turnpikes, from turnpikes to canal, from canal to railways for horse carriages, it is too much to expect the monstrous leap from bad roads to railways for steam carriages, at once. One step in a generation is all we can hope for. If the present shall adopt canals, the next may try the railways with horses, and the third generation use the steam carriage. . . . I do verily believe that the time will come when carriages propelled by steam will be in general use, as well for the transportation of passengers as goods, traveling at the rate of fifteen miles an hour, or 300 miles per day."[1]

Within a year Evans' conviction of the speed to be obtained by the use of steam railroads had still further strengthened, and he declared:

"The time will come when people will travel in stages moved by steam engines, from one city to another, almost as fast as birds fly, fifteen

[1] This was two years before George Stephenson built his first locomotive, in 1814. It made four miles an hour.

or twenty miles an hour. A carriage will set out from Washington in the morning, the passengers will breakfast at Baltimore, dine at Philadelphia, and sup at New York, the same day. To accomplish this two sets of rails[1] will be laid, so nearly level as not in any place to deviate more than two degrees from the horizontal line, made of wood or iron on smooth paths of broken stone or gravel, with a rail to guide the carriages, so that they may pass each other in different directions, and travel by night as well as by day; and the passengers will sleep in these stages as comfortably as they now do in steam boats."

The neglect shown to the subject by the national government and New York State caused Stevens to revive his plan for the securing of a charter from New Jersey, and his request received favorable consideration three years later, in 1815, when he was authorized to build a railway between Trenton and New Brunswick. He could not get the financial help necessary to construct the road. In 1819 he urged the Pennsylvania legislature to build a railroad from Philadelphia to Pittsburgh, and that effort likewise received no encouragement. A similar fate befell the proposal addressed to Congress in the same year by Benjamin Dearborn, of Boston, whose ideas and plans were expressed in part as follows:[2]

"The memorial of Benjamin Dearborn, of Boston, respectfully represents that he has devised in theory a mode of propelling wheel-carriages in a manner probably unknown in any country; and has perfectly satisfied his own mind of the practicability of conveying mails and passengers with such celerity as has never before been accomplished, and with complete security from robberies on the highway.

"For obtaining these results, he relies on carriages propelled by steam, on level railroads, and contemplates that they be furnished with accommodations for passengers to take their meals and their rest during the passage, as in packets; that they be sufficiently high for persons to walk in without stooping, and so capacious as to accommodate twenty, thirty, or more passengers, with their baggage . . . and he feels confident that whenever such an establishment shall be advanced to its most improved state, the carriages will move with a rapidity at least equal to a mile in three minutes.

[1] Meaning that a double track road would be laid.
[2] Brown's "History of the First Locomotives in America," pp. 72-73.

"Protection from the attacks of assailants will be insured;[1] not only by the celerity of the movement, but by weapons of defense belonging to the carriage, and always kept ready in it to be wielded by the number of passengers constantly travelling in this spacious vehicle, where they would have liberty to stand erect, and to exercise their arms in their own defense.

"The practicability of running steam-carriages on the common road was long since advocated in a publication by that ingenious and useful citizen, Oliver Evans; your memorialist, therefore, does not assume the merit of originating the idea of steam carriages, but only of modifying the system in such a manner as to produce the results here stated, which could not be effected on a common road.

"Relying upon the candor of the National Council, this memorial is laid before them with the desire that ingenious and scientific artists in the different sections of the country may be consulted, by direction of Congress, on the probability of accomplishing the purposes here anticipated; and that an experiment be made, if sanctioned by their favorable opinions; for if the design can be put into successful operation by the government, a great revenue would eventually be derived from the establishment, besides the advantages before enumerated."

Dearborn's proposal was referred to the Committee on Commerce and Manufactures, and nobody ever heard of it again.

By the year 1820 Stevens had become exasperated because other people did not see the value of railroads as quickly and clearly as he did, and he resolved to prove, out of his own pocket, that the travel method urged by him was not a nonsensical scheme. He had been laughed at, disputed and called a maniac long enough. During the year named, therefore, and on his own estate in Hoboken, New Jersey, Stevens built a little railway of narrow gauge and a small steam locomotive. The engine was his own handiwork. He put the locomotive on the track with cars behind it, and so ran it repeatedly with himself as a passenger, to the amazement of those before whom the demonstration was made. As far as is now known that was the first steam

[1] Reminiscent of the precautions taken on the Cincinnati packets of the Ohio River in the flatboat age, about 1790. In 1819 there was much robbing of stage-coaches by highwaymen.

railway locomotive to be built or to be run on a track in America.[1]

The practical test of 1820, though made on a small scale, had far-reaching results. From it can be traced a series of subsequent events that by degrees, and with an

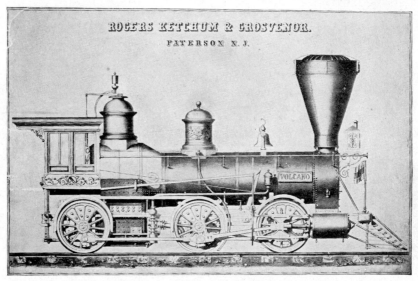

260.—The *Volcano*. Also a product of the Paterson builders. Date, about 1854. It, in conjunction with the three foregoing machines, shows a steady development toward the modern type of locomotive.

ever-increasing pressure, forced the public to give closer heed to the subject and, through popular discussion, at last brought money from its hiding place to take up the work demanded.

The various primitive railroad enterprises then in operation; the published discussions in newspapers and pamphlets; the arguments and predictions; the experiments; the appeals to legislatures and the petitions to

---

[1] Unless Fitch's last model—that of 1798—was designed as a railroad engine and run on rails by him before his death.

Congress heretofore recounted, were open to the knowledge of public men and far-seeing minds for about three years before President Monroe vetoed a National Road bill and stated that the work then being carried on by the government implied its power to create a complete interstate system of public improvements.

Stevens had abandoned hope that the Federal government would assume charge of national railroad construction, and no other path was left open to him but private enterprise authorized by separate states. He continued his campaign for support,[1] and by 1823 had enlisted some aid and secured a charter from Pennsylvania empowering him and his associates to build a railway from Philadelphia to Columbia. No work of the same nature had previously been undertaken on such a scale in this country, and the projectors could not, with sufficient accuracy, inform the lawmakers how much money they would expend or what amount of capital stock would be needed. As a consequence the financial provisions of the charter of 1823 were so framed as to make them of peculiar interest at this present time. Pennsylvania fixed the capital stock of the road at six hundred thousand dollars, but since it could not be foretold whether the actual cost of the work would be greater or less than the amount of money subscribed by the public, the following proviso was made by the legislature:

"That on the completion of said railroad the president and directors are hereby required to ascertain precisely the amount of the sum total of expenses incurred in the construction of the same, and said sum total shall constitute the existing capital of said railroad company."

Thus did an American commonwealth, in 1823, foresee that stock in such an enterprise might be issued without

[1] Though himself a well-to-do man for those days he could not, alone, bear the heavy burden necessary in building a railway.

equivalent value behind it, and thus did the state safeguard intending investors by providing against the possibility of such an action. Whether or not the sordid minds of the period also glimpsed the possibilities of gaining easy wealth by such unscrupulous financial methods, and whether or not the outcry which arose about that time in opposition to Federal building of traffic routes was due, in some measure, to their realization that governmental building of new national transportation facilities would destroy a large opportunity for acquiring ill-gained wealth, are questions perhaps impossible of answer at the present day.

Two other features of this early railroad charter deserve mention because of the archaic transportation viewpoints they reveal. One of them gave to Stevens—by inference at least—certain rights similar to those of a patentee, for it provided that all profits of the road, above twelve per cent., were to go to Stevens or his legal assignee. The other interesting feature of the charter dealt with remuneration which the road might exact for service rendered. It empowered the company to charge three and a half cents a mile on every ton of freight moving eastward, and seven cents a mile for a ton going west.[1]

No sooner had the legislature given permission to build and operate the road than a public discussion began over the mechanical possibility of doing such a thing. It was admitted that railways were practical for small distances, because a number of short highways of that description really did exist in various states, and vehicles were moved over them. But the proposed new road, of the stupendous length of seventy-three miles, was altogether

[1] Because westward movement was on an up grade.

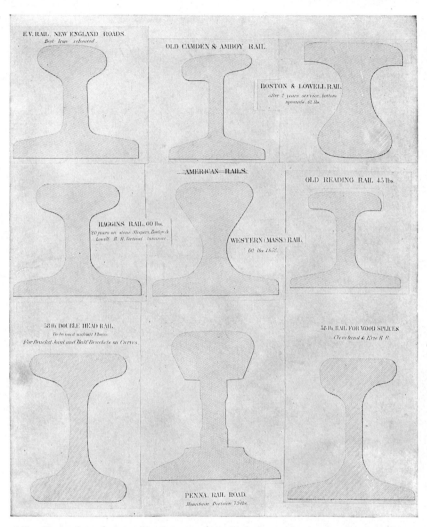

E.V. RAIL. NEW ENGLAND ROADS.
Best Iron rcheated.

OLD CAMDEN & AMBOY RAIL.

BOSTON & LOWELL RAIL.
*after 2 years service, bottom
upwards. 62 lbs.*

AMERICAN RAILS.

OLD READING RAIL. 45 lbs.

HAGGINS RAIL. 60 lbs.
*10 years on stone Sleepers, Boston &
Lowell R. R. Vertical lamina.*

WESTERN (MASS.) RAIL.
60 lbs. 1852.

58 lb. DOUBLE HEAD RAIL.
*To be used without Chairs.
For Bracket Joint and Half Brackets on Curves.*

58 lb. RAIL FOR WOOD SPLICES.
Cleveland & Erie R. R.

PENNA. RAIL ROAD.
Mountain Division 75 lbs.

261.—Examples of the rails that supplanted timbers edged with flat iron bars.
Many experiments were still tried, but a steady drift toward the T rail
and a standard pattern was apparent. Some of the Boston and Lowell rails
were laid upside down, and were used that way. Dates, from 1832 to 1852.

another matter. When this vocal obstacle to the project arose, Stevens promptly set about to overcome it. With outward calmness—and it may be imagined with what inward raging—he tried to make the skeptics see that if a short railway was practical then a long one, of identical construction and grade, was also practical; that the traversing of each new mile was but a repetition of what the vehicle had already successfully performed. He wrote and distributed a long circular letter, addressed to the public, in which he elaborately explained the disputed point. In part it ran:

"Philadelphia, 1823.

"Sir:—It is now generally admitted that a railroad is not a mere visionary project but is actually practicable. An erroneous idea has, however, prevailed among its opponents, that it is only practicable to short distances, and that the contemplated extension of a railroad to a distance of 73 miles is ridiculous.

"As the railroad will, throughout its course, be, in its construction, exactly similar, it is only in its deviations from a horizontal line that any difference in the progressive motion of carriages thereon can take place. The charter contains a provision that the railroad in its progress shall in no part rise above an angle of two degrees with the plane of the horizon.

"Now let us suppose that a section of the intended railroad be constructed in the immediate vicinity of the city, of one mile in extent, in the progress of which elevations of two degrees do actually occur. Should it, however, be practicable, on such section of the intended railroad, to cause loaded carriages to move forward and backward, without encountering any impediment or difficulty, would it not be presumable that the effect would be precisely the same were a similar road to be extended ever so far?

". . . And when this great improvement in transportation shall have been extended to Pittsburgh, and thence into the heart of the extensive and fertile state of Ohio, and also to the great western lakes, Philadelphia may then become the great emporium of the western country."

Stevens' argument certainly sounded plausible, even if it did not produce the desired effect. The men who were both rich and honest could not refute his conclusions, nor did they try to. They simply held aloof and refused to embark their fortunes in enterprises such as he was urging.

One reason for their attitude was this: they could not at once bring themselves to believe that the old order was changing, and that the immemorial, undisputed sway of pack-horse, stage-coach, wagon train and water craft was seriously threatened. For two centuries the country had got along with those methods of travel and transportation. They themselves had come to manhood and won places of leadership without knowledge or thought of any other means of movement. Every act and circumstance of their affairs—the whole fabric of their lives—was bound up with, and based upon, the old ways. Now they were suddenly bedeviled by a lot of fanatics who bombarded them with strange and unanswerable questions; who proposed impossible, unheard-of, quixotic things; who waved countless diagrams, plans, surveys and calculations; and who demanded money for the immediate construction of fantastical rails and engines by means whereof the people might buzz about the country like bees in a clover patch.

It was too much. Never had it been necessary to perform a problem in trigonometry previous to the beginning of a stage-coach trip, nor even while waiting for the steamboat to slide off a sand-bar. What had science to do with going somewhere? If a man wanted to go to Pittsburgh or Ohio then let him begone, and have it over.

Yet there were a few things the big men were willing to admit. They conceded that these railroads concerning which they heard so much would very probably answer as improved portages between two natural or artificial waterways, and that short constructions of the kind might under certain conditions be otherwise useful. But the rivers were more reliable, the stage-coaches averaged six

PORTAGE BRIDGE.

OVER GENESEE RIVER AT PORTAGEVILLE.

262.—A common method of timber bridge construction. Some bridges were of massive masonry. Iron was rarely used.

or eight miles an hour on good turnpikes, numerous canals were already in operation and many others were either in process of building or under consideration. Canals promised to be profitable, and millions of money had been expended on them already. On the whole it was better to attend strictly to business and let well enough alone.

As an outcome of this attitude Stevens and his comrades failed to get the cash they needed.[1] But though his reasoning then failed to sway the men who could have aided him, the uproar, wrangle and debate produced by his seventy-three-mile railway proposition did arouse such

[1] And their charter was repealed in 1826.

a deep interest in the public mind that other and lasting effects soon appeared. The country—as far as the adoption of a new system of locomotion was concerned—stood literally at the parting of the ways. Canals and railroads both had their partisans, and the clash of opinion regarding the relative value of the two methods of communication speedily brought about a general hubbub and intensity of feeling such as had never before been aroused in this country by the discussion of any question unrelated to national politics or warfare.

This state of affairs was especially noticeable in Pennsylvania, and out of it grew the organization, late in 1824, of the Pennsylvania Society for the Promotion of Internal Improvements in the Commonwealth. Its members were business men, chiefly of Philadelphia, who had determined to take an active part in definitely settling the question then uppermost in the thoughts of the people.

CHAPTER XLI

STRICKLAND IS SENT TO ENGLAND—THE INSTRUCTIONS
GIVEN TO HIM—EXCITEMENT IN THIS COUNTRY
OVER THE SUBJECT OF RAILWAYS—STRICKLAND'S
DRAWINGS AND THEIR EFFECT—A BASIS FOR ACTION
AT LAST—COMPARISON OF THE TWO METHODS BY
WHICH ENGLAND AND AMERICA APPROACHED A CON-
CRETE REALIZATION OF THE RAILROAD—UNDERLYING
CAUSES OF THE ADVANTAGE POSSESSED BY THE AMER-
ICANS—THEY COULD SEE THE FINISHED CANOE
IN THE TRUNK OF THE UNTOUCHED TREE—THE
VINDICATION OF THE DREAMERS

ENGLAND, at that time, had enjoyed a more extensive experience both with canals and railroads
than had the United States, and the Pennsylvania association believed there was benefit to be derived from a study
of English methods used in the building and equipment
of the two systems of internal communication. It hoped
to utilize those foreign methods—as far as desirable—in
conjunction with some of the ambitious hopes already
discussed on this side of the water.

Swift action by the Pennsylvanians followed their conclusions. They at once employed an American civil engineer,[1] and sent him to England under secret instructions,[2]

[1] William Strickland.
[2] The injunction requiring Strickland to pursue his work as quietly as possible was
no doubt prompted by a natural desire on the part of the society to obtain the first
knowledge of his investigations, in order that its members might use the information
collected by him in business enterprises if they wished to do so.

898

263.—A "lookout pole." For about twenty years there was no way by which a railroad might discover the location or adventures of its trains after they had disappeared from sight. Nor could waiting travellers along the line be informed when the trains would reach them. So it became the custom of station agents, or of the roads themselves, to set up stout masts at stopping places, and shortly before a train was due the agent climbed his pole, sat himself in a little seat at its top, and watched the horizon for smoke. If successful, as was often the case, he shouted bulletins to those below. Otherwise there was nothing to do but wait.

enjoining him to prepare a report on the subject for which they were organized. The date of the society's confidential letter to its representative was March 25, 1825, and various essential parts of it read as follows:

"It is not a knowledge of abstract principles, nor an indefinite and general account of their application to the great works of Europe we desire to possess through your labors. . . . What we earnestly wish to obtain, is the means of executing all those works in the best manner, and with the greatest economy and certainty. . . .

"Of the utility of railways, and their importance as a means of transporting large burdens, we have full knowledge. Of the mode of constructing them, and of their cost, nothing is known with certainty. . . . You will bear in mind in your investigations of this subject that we have, as yet, no complete railway in Pennsylvania; and you will, therefore, so exhibit your facts, as that they may be understood by reference to the drawings which you may make. . . . Locomotive machinery will command your attention and inquiry. This is entirely unknown in the United States, and we authorize you to procure a model of the most improved locomotive machine, at the expense of the society."

It will be seen from the spirit and literal wording of these instructions[1] that the men responsible for them were in no uncertain state of mind regarding their own beliefs. They were not sending a man to England to find out whether railroads were of value or not. That point they already considered as settled. They wanted to find out how railroads were built, and how locomotives were built. No sooner had Strickland begun his work than clamor over the subject of internal improvements in America became louder than ever before, and increased popular interest in the question was reflected in a further instruction which was sent by the society to its representative on September 19th. The committee's letter to Strickland under that date said, in part:

"Canals and railways present the most important of all subjects for your attention. Upon every matter connected with both you will be expected to be well informed. . . . Much excitement prevails in this state upon the question whether railways are superior to canals, and the inquiries that are in progress in relation to them are in the hands of men of ingenuity and well disposed to the cause of internal improvement. It is, however, feared by many that the question between canals and railways will have an injurious influence in Pennsylvania, as it will divide the friends of the cause of improvement, and thus postpone, if not prevent, the commencement of the work. The importance of correct information in relation to them is thus greatly increased."

The society's representative brought back with him in 1826 a model of an English railroad locomotive of the inefficient type then in use[2] and during August of the same year his report was published by the society, together with many large reproductions of the drawings he had made

[1] The full text was put in type by the society at the time, in a confidential pamphlet of four printed pages.
[2] Which later came into possession of the Franklin Institute, of Philadelphia.

while abroad.[1] Strickland's elaborate and important volume produced an overwhelming impression; not so much through the comparatively short text giving its author's observations as by means of the engravings it contained. An intelligent pictorial appeal to the understanding is always effective, and when the matter illustrated happens

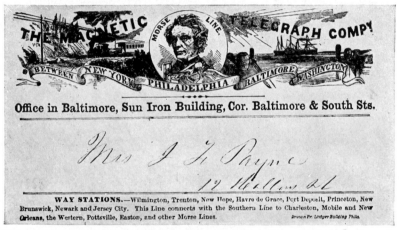

Office in Baltimore, Sun Iron Building, Cor. Baltimore & South Sts.

WAY STATIONS.—Wilmington, Trenton, New Hope, Havre de Grace, Port Deposit, Princeton, New Brunswick, Newark and Jersey City. This Line connects with the Southern Line to Charleston, Mobile and New Orleans, the Western, Pottsville, Easton, and other Morse Lines.   *Brown Pr. Ledger Building Phila.*

264.—A telegraphic message sent by the first Morse line. Design used on the delivery envelope. The telegraph was first used in connection with railway operation by the Erie road in 1851, and all other railroads immediately followed its example. The lookout pole then became extinct.

to be one concerning which the public is vitally interested —as was true in the case mentioned—and regarding which it has no other reliable information in similar form, then such presentation of a subject has a power difficult to exaggerate.

It should not be understood that the famous book in question was a familiar object in every household, for nothing could be further from the fact. Only a few

[1] Contained in a large folio atlas entitled, "Reports on Canals, Railways, Roads, and Other Subjects, made to the Pennsylvania Society for the Promotion of Internal Improvement. By William Strickland, Architect and Engineer, while Engaged in the Service of the Society." Strickland's drawings are reproduced in 72 very fine folio plates engraved on copper, and include every detail of railway, canal and other public works construction as then practised in England.

hundred copies of it were printed,[1] and its high cost[2] effectually removed it from the class to which popular novels belong. But it did show for the first time—not only in America, but in the world[3]—and in a manner easily comprehended, the whole process then employed in building and equipping a railroad. It furnished a basis for action. It was practical. The mass of the people never saw the book for which their clamor was directly responsible, yet the public felt its result at once, for it passed into the hands of, and influenced, those who had money, those who could do the work it described, and those in high station.[4] Again had the nameless thousands, represented this time by a group of citizens whose identity is discoverable only by the antiquarian, furnished the impulse destined to sweep others into tardy action and bring about a revolution.

There is a proverb which says every human act exerts a never-ending influence; that its consequences will in some way radiate to remotest time. Maybe the saying is true. Sometimes it surely is, and the deeds of men are strangely interwoven. The madman of Conjurer's Point dreamed a steamboat, and made one. From his work John Stevens of Hoboken gained inspiration for similar endeavor, and Stevens, in course of time, put wheels under his engine instead of a keel. A group of Pennsylvanians joined with Stevens in a plan to introduce those wheeled engines here, and out of the discussion attending that effort grew an organization which sent a man to England.

[1] The "List of Subscribers" indicates but 334 copies, and probably the whole issue did not exceed 500.

[2] The engravings it contains represent an expenditure of perhaps three thousand dollars, and it was sold for $10.00 a copy.

[3] For not even in England had any work been published which remotely approached Strickland's atlas in importance or value.

[4] Among the subscribers were the United States Post Office Department, the Navy Department, the War Department, the West Point Military School, and the national House of Representatives, which took 25 copies! The government was waking up.

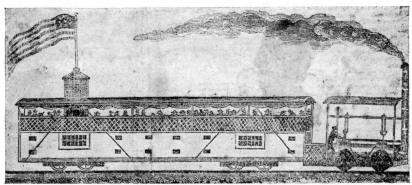

265.—Beginning a series of eleven illustrations showing the evolution of the passenger car after it assumed rectangular lines, and while a standard type was developing. In two-story cars of this sort the upper deck was most popular in fair weather as the lower floor was poorly lighted and ventilated. Such double-decked vehicles were not generally adopted. The cupola was very uncommon.

The man came back, his drawings were published, and America stepped over the threshold of a new age.

Forty years had elapsed since Oliver Evans asked Pennsylvania and Maryland for the right to use self-propelled steam carriages. Thirty-one years had gone by since the first application of the railway principle in America, at the Boston brick kiln. Fourteen years had passed from the day on which Evans offered to run a steam-engine on rails at the rate of fifteen miles an hour, while Stevens at the same time was urging the building of railroads by Congress as a national policy and advocating the construction of such a highway by New York State. Thirteen years had gone since Evans foretold a double-tracked, rock-ballasted railway over which men would journey between Baltimore and New York in one day, and in the cars of which they might sleep in comfort. Only seven years had slipped by since Stevens proposed a railroad from Philadelphia to Pittsburgh. The same period had passed since Dearborn placed before Congress his ideas for a railway train with cars big enough for thirty or more passengers, in which they might eat and take their rest while moving at twenty miles an hour.

Those are the landmarks of America's journey toward the modern railroad. Their significance, as an indication that this country was already pursuing an independent line of thought and would speedily have reached a material realization of the new transportation principle, even without Stephenson's later demonstration with the *Rocket* in 1829, scarcely seems to require further emphasis. But if there be doubt concerning the point then there still remains a comparison between the American attitude as already outlined and that assumed toward the subject in England until the year 1829.

The three most important early English books relating to railways were those of Tredgold, Wood and Lardner. Tredgold said:[1]

"Locomotives must always be objectionable on a railroad for general use, where it is attempted to give them a considerable degree of speed. . . . That any general system of carrying passengers would answer, to go at a velocity exceeding ten miles an hour, or thereabouts, is extremely improbable."

Wood's comment on the same phase of the question read:[2]

"It is far from my wish to promulgate to the world that the ridiculous expectations, or rather professions, of the enthusiastic speculator will be realized, and that we shall see engines travelling at the rate of twelve, sixteen, eighteen, or twenty miles an hour. Nothing could do more harm toward their general adoption and improvement than the promulgation of such nonsense."

And Lardner asserted that:[3]

"Carriages could not go at anything like the contemplated speed; if driven to it, the wheels would merely spin on their axles, and the carriages would stand stock still."

[1] "A Practical Treatise on Railroads and Carriages," 2nd edition, London, 1825.
[2] "A Practical Treatise on Railroads and Internal Communication," London, 1825.
[3] "Lectures on the Steam Engine," London, 1827.

266.—Probably in some respects a fanciful sketch. Yet many of the early cars were very short, highly decorated, and occasionally of unequal heights. The engine and tender are not impossible in general outline, and the splint-brooms attached to the locomotive for the purpose of sweeping the rails are genuine. They were often used; once in Pennsylvania during a plague of grasshoppers.

The serious English periodicals of the time reflected public opinion in similar strain. A typical utterance of the sort[1] contained this passage:

"What can be more palpably absurd and ridiculous than the prospect held out of locomotives traveling twice as fast as stage coaches! We should as soon expect the people of Woolwich to suffer themselves to be fired off upon one of Congreve's ricochet rockets as trust themselves to the mercy of such a machine going at such a rate. . . . We trust that Parliament will, in all railways it may sanction, limit the speed to eight or nine miles an hour, which we entirely agree with Mr. Sylvester is as great as can be ventured on with safety."

When the proposed Liverpool and Manchester railway asked Parliament for a franchise, during the same year of 1825, George Stephenson was summoned by the Parliamentary committee to be questioned concerning the velocity of which a locomotive might be capable. As Stephenson was about to testify, William Brougham, the railroad's own lawyer, warned him that if he discussed the possibility of any unusual speed, such as twenty miles an hour, he would "inevitably damn the whole thing, and be himself regarded as a maniac fit for Bedlam."[2] Stephenson permitted himself to predict a speed of twelve miles an hour,[3] members of the committee whispered their doubts of his sanity, and the application for a charter was denied.

England had then been building railways for nearly two hundred years, had made iron rails since 1738 and steam locomotives since 1804. Yet in 1825 the combined use of all three devices had suggested nothing to her public men or civil engineers save what has been indicated in the utterances just quoted. Even after the Stockton and

[1] In the "Quarterly Review" for March, 1825.
[2] Smiles' "Life of George Stephenson."
[3] The maximum velocity attained by his best and latest engine, just completed for the Stockton and Darlington road. The average working speed of. that locomotive was five miles an hour.

Darlington road was opened to traffic[1] the bulk of its motive power, for the moving of both passengers and freight, was furnished by horses. When one of its vehicles reached a down-grade section of the railway the horse would jump on a low platform built for the purpose at one end of the car, and so ride down to the bottom of the hill.

America, in considering the possibilities of the new locomotion system, stood on an equality with England as far as knowedge of the physical elements of the proposition were concerned. Neither possessed an overwhelming advantage. Each knew the railed track, the iron, and the steam-engine. If either can be said to have had a superior position from which to advance toward greater things—just before the general adoption and introduction of railways—then England was that one, for she had been aware of the railed-track device for a longer time and employed it more extensively. She had enjoyed a fuller opportunity to grasp its potentiality. Yet it was America which first saw—and demanded—the use of the whole value of the railroad idea. England, after nearly two centuries of railed tracks, eighty-seven years of iron rails and twenty-one years of locomotives, had progressed to the point illustrated by the Stockton and Darlington road and its methods. The possibility of further advance of consequence was unrealized in England; it was denied, after due consideration, by the men most competent to give judgment in such a matter.

America's less-experienced engineers were distinguished by one quality not possessed by their colleagues across the ocean. They had known of railed tracks for only thirty years, and had not employed iron rails or loco-

---

[1] England's first line for general business; opened in 1825.

motives at all. Yet to those three commonplace and material elements of mechanical construction, knowledge of two of which was theirs by hearsay only, they added a fourth and still more necessary component—imagination. Men like Evans, Stevens and Dearborn were accurately describing the railway and railway travel of the future in written words, and were planning the construction and equipment of railroads hundreds of miles in length, while yet the English had no conception of the possibilities that lay within the methods they had used so long.

Both countries were converging on the same historic event—the creation of practical railroads—along pathways which, though very different in themselves, were significant of the characters and processes of the nations employing them. Each reached the goal by its own method at substantially the same time as the other. Indeed, had it not been for the tremendous personality, remarkable mechanical ingenuity and persistence of the unlettered pit-engineer George Stephenson, it is altogether likely that America would have outdistanced England in the race. For it was Stephenson's solitary work, in opposition to which the influential body of his countrymen fought almost to the raving point, that pushed them, against their will and frantic resistance, over the remaining distance that separated them from success. Conservative England had moved toward the modern railroad by slow and almost imperceptible degrees for two hundred years. America took one mental leap and stood beside her.

It has been said the American contribution to the problem of railway creation was imagination. In reality it was something which, though intangible, was much more solid, substantial and valuable than that; it was the exer-

Drawn by J.W. Barber.

BOSTON.

The above shews the appearance of Boston as seen from the south-west, near the intersection of the Providence and Worcester Rail Road; the Rail House with its towering dome, and the Common appear in the central part. Bunker Hill Monument is seen on the extreme left.

Engraved by A. Willard and J. W. Barber.

267.—Two railway trains on the outskirts of Boston. The wheels of the farther train are placed outside the trucks; those of the train in the foreground are inside. From a drawing by J. W. Barber. Date, about 1839-1840.

cise of an ability existing from the first as a national trait, and which had developed at last into the quickness of thought so characteristic of this western people. It was a supreme manifestation of the same elemental quality that enabled the American of 1630 to behold the shape of a finished canoe in the trunk of the untouched tree. For seven generations the pioneer population of the new continent had been drilled, by stern conditions, in the importance of foresight, in the need of anticipating future personal necessities and in the duty of claiming the ultimate particle of value from any object.[1] Long years passed, and by and by came the railed track and the steam-engine. The consequences of their appearance here were inevitable. The American mind, trained as it had been, looked upon them and beheld the railroad as it was to be—as it must be, if the last vestige of its usefulness was to be extracted from the idea. And that determination was axiomatic.

So automatic was the mental process in question that the unknown, unrealized railroad of the future, even to its double track and ballasted roadbed, and its dining and sleeping cars, were described by Americans in the period between 1813 and 1819 in a way that was almost matter-of-fact. Such things were certain. They already existed except in the unimportant feature of concrete form. Although knowledge of the manner of making them did not happen to be available at the moment, that was a trivial detail. Nothing further was necessary but to devise or find out a practical method of building the contrivances, and to get permission and money for their construction.

---

[1] Scarcely any article was thrown away, for fear that at some future time, in an unexpected way, it might "come handy." When its day of active usefulness was done it was taken up into that museum of American household archeology, the attic. So deeply was the trait in question implanted in those early generations that its effects are still clearly visible, and until to-day the destruction of useless home rubbish often constitutes an agony.

The men who saw all this—who created the railway in the American fashion of seeing first and then compelling their hands to catch up with their ideas—set about the job of getting permission and the money, and did not stop until they had succeeded. They were men who, though unknown and unpreferred among their fellows, had a broadness of vision that enabled them to perceive and proclaim the relationship between this new transportation method and the country's future. The universal practise of anticipating necessities was by them shifted from its personal basis to a national one. Their part of the work was not done with transit, plumb-line, pickax and shovel. Tens of thousands could use those implements. All they employed was brains. By their endeavors, extending through only a few years, America overstepped the age-long process by which England had advanced, and plunged headlong into an effort to produce in material form the elaborate vision that hung, like a rainbow of promise, before the eyes of their fancy.

That was the pathway along which America approached the creation of her first railways, and the one whereby, ever since the period in question, she has proceeded in her march toward industrial and economic progress. She has anticipated necessity, and welded the stuff of dreams into mechanisms that seem endowed with reason. But in one respect the nation, in an imaginative sense, has gone backward in the handling of its natural and man-created riches. We have become wasteful and careless. Nature's prodigality and the creative ability of the people have wrought an insidious harm. No longer do we seek to extract the last ounce of utility from the things we possess. Of each unit of energy or material or opportunity we cast aside one-third, and it is lost.

One other general feature connected with the creation of the early railways of the country is deserving of mention. It has been seen that the men who first built them in imagination, and furnished the impulse which resulted in their actual construction, dealt with the subject mainly in terms of speed, length, and the conveniences of human travel. The new highways were to connect regions separated by hundreds of miles, over which people were to be conveyed at fifteen or twenty miles an hour in cars wherein they might also eat and sleep. The men of money, without whose help no progress could be made, shook their heads at this and saw only the possibility of using railroads for the moving of freight over short distances between existing towns and cities. That was the big purpose, from a capitalistic standpoint, for which the first roads were begun.[1] They were simply to be improvements over previous highways, designed for the transportation of mercantile commodities created by established communities. But little provision, or none at all, was made for the accommodation of human beings. Yet when the railways were opened for traffic, and solitary rattletrap passenger cars were devised or stage-coaches put on proper wheels for the sake of experiment, the passenger vehicles were overwhelmed, as they have been ever since.

The foresight and understanding of the men who built in terms of fancy were clearer than that of the ones who used nothing but metal and stone and wood. Railroads were not wanted solely as carriers of goods between cities. They were children of the spirit of conquest and the demand for wider, swifter movement, even though the financial nurses who coddled them were blind to their parent-

---

[1] That is to say, it was the purpose of the capitalists. True of England as well as of America.

age.[1] The railways also in due course came to anticipate necessity, rather than simply try to catch up with it, and though their efforts in that regard were sometimes misdirected, yet on the whole such endeavors have been of value, and have done much in aiding the people to strike root in regions otherwise impossible of permanent and flourishing settlement.

[1] In two appendices will be found tabular statements showing the organization, first use, length, and source of income of ninety-five early American railways, together with the relationship between their capitalization and cost of construction. It was passenger traffic, and not the carriage of commercial commodities, that gave the railroads a great majority of their income, saved them, and encouraged their future building and extension up to 1850 or later.

CHAPTER XLII

THE DREAM-BUILDERS SUPPLANTED BY MEN DESTINED TO PERFORM ACTUAL CONSTRUCTION WORK — EARLY POPULAR IDEAS ABOUT RAILROADS — HOW THE PEOPLE SHOWED THEIR INTEREST — CONTEMPORARY NEWSPAPER COMMENT AND PICTURES — THREE ASPECTS OF THE SUBJECT — OPINIONS ON THE PHYSICAL CHARACTER OF THE NEW DEVICE — HOW TRACKS WERE FIRST BUILT — MANY DIFFERENT GAUGES — A MISTAKEN NOTION REGARDING THE USE OF RAILWAYS AS HIGHWAYS — ITS RESULTS IN AMERICA — THE CENTER-POST DEVICE — AN INDIANA PREDICTION OF 1830 — RAILROADS AS MORAL INFLUENCES — A MASSACHUSETTS ROAD ASKS FOR SERMONS IN ITS BEHALF — ONE OF THE RESPONSES

THE work of Evans, Dearborn, Stevens, the Pennsylvania Society and others had not been in vain. Railroads had been discussed, advocated and described in their future form by a few Americans during a period of about fifteen years. Argument was now to be superseded in part by action, and railroads themselves were to appear and alter the character of the debate concerning them.

No sooner did it become apparent that actual physical creation of the new transportation device was at hand in this country than more interest in the subject which had so suddenly usurped attention was manifested by all sorts of odd methods. Crude representations of railroad loco-

914

motives and cars began to appear as decorative patterns on the dishes, china and glassware used by the people. Small metallic medals were struck in honor of the introduction of the railroad. The popular sheet-music of the period was occasionally embellished with pictures of steam-engines and cars. Even whisky bottles appeared bearing upon their sides crude designs and inscriptions commemorating the introduction of railed tracks. Nor was this manifestation of popular interest confined to the subject of railways alone. Pictures and all sorts of other representations of steamboats, stage-coaches and canal boats also multiplied at the same time, and hardly a household could be found either in the city or country whose possessions did not include various objects indicative of the feeling here suggested.[1]

This condition of the public mind was further shown by similar evidences appearing in the newspapers and books of the day. A picture of a railroad had been printed in a daily newspaper as early as March 7, 1826, when the *American Traveler,* of Boston, issued a full page broadside containing a view and description of the Hetton Railroad in England.[2] In the discussion of railroads contained in the broadside is the following:

"The acknowledged importance of Rail Road conveyance and the great anxiety existing in the public mind, respecting the relative value

[1] Examples of the wall-paper, medals, sheet-music and bottles here mentioned are reproduced elsewhere in these pages. The medal and wall-paper were issued about 1825 in celebration of the completion of the Erie Canal. The piece of sheet-music was engraved in celebration of the commencement of the Baltimore and Ohio Railroad, and was placed on sale in Baltimore on the 4th of July in 1828, when the building of the road was begun. The bottle which bears the inscription "Success to the Railroad" is also believed to have been made in the same year. It is "No. 1" in Barber's list of the eighty-six designs of historical American glassware thus far discovered. Of it Barber says: "Among the oldest forms of decorated glass bottles or flasks known to have been made in the United States is one which bears a relief design representing the first railroad. The device shows a horse drawing a four-wheeled car along a rail. . . . It is probable that this very interesting object was produced at the Kensington Glass Works, Philadelphia. . . . The character of the glass, the color, the shape and the peculiar mould markings point to such an origin." Barber's book is entitled "American Glassware Old and New." It was privately printed in Philadelphia in 1900.

[2] Reproduced on another page. It is, perhaps, the first picture of an actual railroad printed in America, and antedates the issuance of Strickland's book by about five months.

268.—Style of passenger car most frequently used during the decade from 1840 to 1850. The windows of this vehicle were not raised, but the entire panels were dropped bodily down into the sides of the car. Drawn and engraved by Alexander Robb.

of Canals and Rail Roads, as species of internal communication, must render any information concerning either of some interest; and if that information come from persons who have made the subject their particular study, and have given to the public the result of their faithful experiments, whether they tend towards establishing the one system or the other, they will be equally entitled to attention. . . .

"It may to many seem an object of surprise, that so simple and efficient a plan of moving carriages on a road has not been more generally employed; but it may be remarked, that though the idea of forming smooth surfaces for carriage wheels to roll upon, is not a modern one, still, until quite lately, there has been felt a great want of practical information on the subject, and consequently a lack of enterprise in our citizens, in entering upon the 'unbeaten path.' "

But very few other American newspapers of that date gauged the importance of the subject with such accuracy, or indicated by actions their appreciation of the public interest in it. Another newspaper of the East to print a similar railroad broadside was the *New York American,* whose page was issued on March 11, 1830. The *American's* broadside was devoted to an account of the locomotive competition held in England during the previous October[1] and was illustrated with pictures of two of the competing machines. Doubtless there were still other American papers that took occasion to comment on

[1] The entire first page of the paper was given to the matter, as news, though the event described had happened about five months before. Reproduced elsewhere.

269.—A train on the Hudson River Railroad, near the town of Hudson. Contemporary pencil sketch. Signature, Philip Doane. Date, about 1851.

railroads with equal prominence during the first three or four years after railway building on an extensive scale became assured in this country, but as a general thing the daily and weekly press — though in the aggregate giving a great deal of space to the subject — confined its activities to the printing of paragraphs and short articles.

Many of the books issued during those same years — especially such volumes as were devoted to description of the country — contained articles about railways, and sometimes the accounts were accompanied by illustrations.[1] A definition of railroads contained in an encyclopedia[2] of the period read:

"Railway.—A species of road or carriage way, in which the tracks of the carriage wheel being laid with bars or rails of wood, stone, or metal, the carriage runs with so much greater facility that one horse will perform the work of many. On some railways the wagons are moved by steam instead of horses. It is contemplated to make railways in various parts of the U. States. Many have been commenced, and several are already completed. Their utility and superiority over canals will, no doubt, cause general construction in most states in the U. States within a few years where the travelling is great."

While a majority of the people were thus thinking of railroads in their completed shape and were speculating about the future advantages they were so impatient to enjoy, the other and less numerous class of men then giving attention to the subject were concerned with problems relating to the physical character of railways and the best manner of their use after they had been built. Both in point of suddenness and of the revolutionary procedure which it entailed, the adoption of the railway idea to human movement and traffic no doubt constituted

[1] Two such articles from contemporary books are reproduced elsewhere. One of them is a description of the Baltimore and Ohio Railroad in its earliest days, accompanied by a wood engraving of a horse-drawn passenger car of that road. The other book illustration is a page that apparently shows a train on the Boston and Worcester road in Massachusetts, and the picture is accompanied by a printed description of the "most common apparatus for travelling on roads."

[2] "A Family Encyclopedia, or, an Explanation of Words and Things." By George Crabb, New York, 1831.

the most important alteration in established methods of performing certain work which mankind had yet undertaken. The last of the pioneers saw that here was an agency containing vast possibilities, while at the same time they admitted that the most desirable manner of employing the potentialities concealed in the new process must be discovered as they went along. Yet some sort of start had to be made, and much controversy arose regarding the proper things to do. Some thought one plan of building and use was best, and others considered a different method was preferable, but everybody, no matter what his opinion, was tolerably certain he was right. The old feeling of cock-sureness—developed by long contact with familiar economic problems whose well-known solutions had made such a mental attitude formerly excusable—was abundantly displayed.

During this widespread discussion of railroads all close consideration of the subject dealt principally with three phases of the newly arisen question: namely, the proper physical construction of railways; their precise character as highways; their social and economic influence. The debate naturally resulted in the appearance of a considerable literature devoted to the problem, and all the books about railroads published in America during the decade immediately following the commencement of railway building in the country contained numerous statements and arguments which—to our more modern thought—are curious and entertaining. The narration of some of these primitive methods of track building, and of contemporary ideas about them, will show the astonishing contrast that existed between the finished product of the former dream-builders and the actual plans that were adopted and applied by the men into whose hands were to fall the details of structural work. One of the earliest and least known of these American publications[1] began in the following words:

"The first thing to be determined in the formation of a Railroad is the kind of power that is to be employed on it, whether horses or steam engines. It is desirable not to use both kinds of power on the same road; . . . because the slow travelling of horses will present a serious obstruction to the free operations of locomotive steam engines, compelling them to frequently turn out and occasionally delay and inconvenience; . . . because the action of the horses' feet will throw dust and gravel on the rails, which it will be desirable to avoid on roads for engines. . . . A further reason is, that the dust thrown on the rails will be converted into mud in wet weather, and will materially diminish the adhesion of the wheels of the locomotive engine to the rails."[2]

The same authority advanced the argument that in creating a railroad designed for operation by horse-power it would be desirable so to build it as to secure a regular alternation of up-grades and down-grades. This expedient, he said, would enable the horses to jump aboard a car designed for their accommodation when the train was about to start down hill, thus saving the animals' strength and eliminating a waste of the motive power. In this connection he also remarked:

"A further advantage in travelling a gradually ascending and gradually descending road would be found in the carriage of passengers, and goods requiring speedy transportation. Travellers desire to go faster than a horse can travel with ease to himself, or profit to his owner, if the charges be moderate. By having the horses ride half the distance any admissible rate of speed for that portion of the distance might be had, so that the whole journey could be performed in less time."[3]

During his discussion of the proper method of laying a track the same authority declared:

"If the rails are not laid upon a foundation of sufficient firmness the supports soon settle unequally, so that the rails become undulating, re-

---

[1] "A Treatise on Rail-roads and Internal Communications. Compiled from the Latest and Best Authors. With Original Sketches and Remarks." By Thomas Earle, Philadelphia, 1830.
[2] Earle, p. 6.
[3] Earle, p. 17.

The "Baltimore and Ohio" whiskey bottle. Among all the many curious evidences of early popular interest in the subject of transportation the most strange, perhaps, was the designing of a whiskey bottle in celebration of the introduction of railways into America. Made of olive-green glass. Date, 1828-1830. American.

quiring a very irregular draught from the horses, and straining the wagons by the shocks they receive at the meeting ends of rails of different slope. . . . Where timber is scarce, and iron and stone abundant, it is considered advantageously to use rails entirely of iron, supported upon blocks of stone. Railways of this kind may perhaps be expensive, even in America, if steam engines are to be used. But where horses are to furnish the power it will generally be an important advantage to have a cheap work; and consequently wood, or wood and iron combined, will be preferred. . . . Locust or cedar wood is preferred for the sleepers as being slow to decay. . . . The wooden rails are of sawed timber. White oak is considered the best. They are of different dimensions according to the views of the proprietors, or the width of wagons to be used. Some are 3 inches wide by 5 in depth; some 4 by 6. . . .

"On some roads wooden rails without any covering of iron, except at crossing places and curves, are still used. Where the business of a road is small, and timber abundant, it may be expedient to save the expense of iron. In other cases iron plates should be used to protect the timber from wear, as well as to render the motion of the wagons somewhat easier. For this purpose plates of rolled iron are used, varying in dimensions from $\frac{1}{4}$ of an inch thick by $1\frac{1}{4}$ wide, to $\frac{1}{2}$ an inch thick by 2 inches wide."[1]

In speaking of the relative merits of single-tracked and double-tracked railroads the book written by Earle said:

"For the transportation of goods to a moderate amount, a single way will answer every purpose about as well as a double one. Engines can leave particular points at certain hours and arrive at other points at fixed hours.. . . For instance, take the distance between one of our Atlantic cities and Pittsburgh, suppose a distance of 320 miles. If trains or wagons were to leave each city every morning, and travel the distance in 4 days, meeting places would be required every 40 miles. If wagons should leave each city at both morning and noon, and arrive at both noon and night, the places of meeting would be every 20 miles, at fixed hours. . . . Arrangements of this kind are inconsistent with the beau-ideal of travel. The imagination delights in freedom from obstructions, and from the restraints of fixed rules. But we are compelled to submit, in practical matters, to the curb of reason."[2]

And finally, in discussing the relative value and cost of railroads and canals, the work here quoted observed:

"The engines are supposed to travel but 80 miles a day, half the distance without loads. From the experience of the English there is

[1] Earle, pp. 19-22.
[2] Earle, pp. 34-35.

reason to believe this is 20 per cent., too unfavorable an estimate. The prices of locomotive engines are probably put too high. They were sold in England five years since, at £600 for an engine weighing 6½ tons, since which the price is reduced. . . . Railroads may be used at least 11 months in the year: canals, in a northern climate, not more than 8 months. . . . The celerity of transportation is a great object in many cases. This can be effected on rail-roads, but not on canals. Certainty is another important object. Canals are very liable to interruption from breaches in the banks, or giving way in aqueducts, &c. News was received in one day, this season, of the stoppage of three lines [of canals] in Pennsylvania, viz., the Schuylkill, the Susquehanna, and the Alleghany. But rail-ways will rarely be interrupted, as in case of any accident to one track the carriages can turn on to the other track and pass the imperfect place."[1]

In connection with these observations on the physical character of a railway, as that character was generally seen in 1830, it may be well to indicate in convenient form the systems used in laying the tracks of some of the various early railroads of this country. The following table will show such details, together with the widths of the tracks in a number of cases:[2]

ROAD	Date	Length in Miles	Gauge in Feet and Inches	Cross-ties; Size in Inches	Wooden Rails; Size in Inches	Iron Covering of Rails; Size in Inches
Mauch Chunk (Pa.)........	1827	9	3.6	oak	4x6	⅜x1½
Schuylkill (Pa.)...........	1829	13	4.8½	oak, 12x12	4x7	½x1½
Mill Creek (Pa.)...........	1829	3	....	....	3x5	5-16x1¼
Schuylkill Valley (Pa.)......	1829	10	3.4	....	3x5	none[3]
Mt. Carbon (Pa.)..........	1829	7¼	4.8½	....	6x4	⅜x2
Baltimore and Ohio (Md.)..	1828	13	....	cedar,[4]	6x6	½x2
Quincy (Mass.)............	1826	3	5	granite	...	......
Charleston-Hamburg (S. C.).	1829	6	5	wood	6x10	......
Albany and Hudson (N. Y.).	1830	17	4.9	wood, 7x7	...	9-16x2½
Delaware and Hudson (Pa.).	1829	5	....	hemlock	6x12	......
Western (Mass.)............	1837	54	4.8½	wood, 7x12	iron	55 lbs.[5]
Long Island (N. Y.)........	1835	12	4.8½	cedar, 6x6[7]	iron	38 lbs.[6]
Erie (N. Y.)..............	1836	10	6	wood	iron	......

[1] Earle, pp. 103-105.
[2] The table is constructed from information contained in "A Description of the Canals and Rail Roads of the United States, etc., etc." By H. S. Tanner, New York, 1840; in Earle's "Treatise," and in other similar publications of the decade between 1830 and 1840.
[3] Covered with flat iron bars after a few months of use. Size of iron bars, ⅜ by 1½.
[4] Some of the ties first laid down were stone slabs. Other sorts of wood were also used. A variety of experiments was tried in the construction of the roadbed.
[5] Per yard.
Per yard.
Ties of stone were also used for several miles on this road.

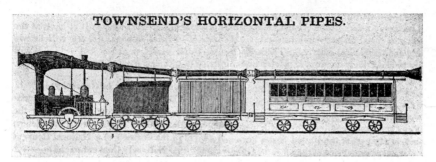

TOWNSEND'S HORIZONTAL PIPES.

270.—An American invention of 1847, designed to protect railroad passengers from the smoke and sparks of the locomotive. Nearly all the early engines used wood for fuel, and firebrands thrown out of the smokestack often burned the travellers' clothing. There is no record showing that Townsend's idea was put into practise. Published in the *Scientific American* of April 24, 1347.

It will be discovered from the preceding table that at least six different track-widths were used in building railroads during the first nine years following their introduction into America. The gauges so employed varied from three feet four inches to six feet, and there was not then, nor for more than thirty years after the commencement of the Erie road, any approach toward uniformity in the widths of this country's iron highways. For the first three or four decades of American railroad construction the distance between the rails of any track depended almost altogether on the whim of those in charge of its building. During all that time there was manifested no general appreciation of the relationship necessarily existing between uniformity of gauge and the utility of a continental railway system.

A number of pioneer American roads, embracing the earliest group laid down in Massachusetts and two or three in Pennsylvania and New York State, adopted the prevalent English gauge of four feet eight-and-a-half inches, together with the processes of track construction then most common in that country, including the use of stone rails and stone cross-ties, and eventually it happened that the track-width in question was adopted throughout the United States as a standard railroad gauge. But the final choice of that gauge in this country was not due to its employment by several of the pioneer lines of the western hemisphere.

Those primitive American roads which closely copied Stephenson's engineering practises naturally fell into the habit of utilizing dimensions introduced by him, but American railroad enterprises which were not begun or carried out under the sway of English example did not select the Stephenson gauge. They chose whatever track-widths appealed to them as most suitable for their own advantages. Often a gauge so adopted by American engineers approached very closely to the English standard; at other times it showed a wide divergence therefrom. Several of the pioneer roads of Pennsylvania were less than four feet wide. The building of the first railway in New York State—that between the towns of Albany and Schenectady—was not controlled by English advice nor did it obtain its first locomotive in England, and its gauge was fixed at four feet and nine inches. New Jersey's first pretentious railroad, the Camden and Amboy line, was projected by American engineers and business men not dominated by foreign opinion and it had a gauge of four feet and ten inches. The decision of the Camden and Amboy had so powerful an effect that a majority of the other New Jersey railroads for more than a generation adhered to the gauge last named. Those in charge of the railroad between Charleston and Hamburg, in South Carolina, decided on a width of five feet for their line, and the precedent thus set by the first of all such southern

271.—Picture of a train made about the years 1850-1855. The locomotive, however, belongs to a period about ten or twelve years earlier. Although it possesses a lamp headlight, it has no engineer's cab. The cow-catcher is also of a style obsolete a number of years before the appearance of such cars as the engine is pulling.

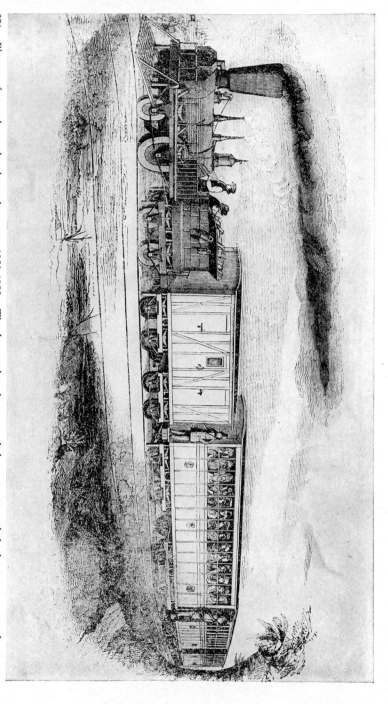

projects resulted in the establishment and use of an identical gauge throughout almost the entire South until after the Civil War. The Erie Railroad was built with a space of six feet between its rails, and so popular did that gauge become that its use by various other roads eventually extended as far westward as the Mississippi River and also continued until after the Civil War.

A full-page contemporary engraving,[1] elsewhere reproduced, shows several of the principal devices employed in building the roadbeds of a number of early lines. The four upper figures in the engraving depict the manner in which trestlework was built wherever it was desired to avoid the expense of earthen embankments through flat or marshy regions. This system of roadbed construction was extensively used by the Charleston and Hamburg Railroad of South Carolina. The four figures under discussion show the tracks of a similarly built railroad—that extending from Carbondale to Honesdale, in Pennsylvania. The trestlework built by the Pennsylvania road was about eight feet in width and seven feet high, and rested on continuous parallel foundations of broken stone. The rails were six inches in width and twelve inches high, and the top of each rail was plated with flat iron bars two-and-a-fourth inches wide and half an inch thick. The gauge of this railroad was five feet. Figure No. 4 in the engraving indicates the manner whereby ravines were crossed on trestlework. In such cases the timber structures stood on pillars of masonry erected at intervals across the streams.

The three lower figures of the engraving portray track construction methods employed on the railroad built and owned by the state of Pennsylvania between Philadelphia

[1] From Nicholas Wood's "A Practical Treatise on Rail Roads, Etc." Philadelphia, 1832.

and the town of Columbia. The central one of these three diagrams shows a deep trench filled with closely packed broken stone, in which was imbedded a ponderous row of granite rails that were a foot square and from five to nine feet long. On the inner edges of these stone rails were laid flat iron bars fifteen feet long, two-and-a-half inches wide and five-eighths of an inch thick. The iron bars were attached to the granite rails by means of square wrought-iron spikes three-and-a-half inches long and about one-third of an inch in diameter. The spikes were encased in cedar plugs, and the plugs were driven into holes drilled in the granite at regular intervals of eighteen inches. Much trouble was experienced, by all early roads, in keeping flat iron bars attached to granite rails while that method of track building prevailed, and various devices were tried by different lines in the effort to hold the bars in place. Melted lead was sometimes used instead of wooden plugs as a means of preventing the spikes from becoming loose.[1]

Figures 6 and 8 of the same series of diagrams show other systems of roadbed construction employed on the Philadelphia and Columbia road. They depict tracks made of large wooden timbers surrounded by masses of broken stone, and topped by iron rails that bore some slight resemblance to the rails used to-day. In these two cases the rails were held in place by cast iron arrangements called "chairs" weighing fifteen pounds each and placed about a yard apart. The chairs were attached to the wooden rails by means of long bolts weighing ten ounces each.

When flat iron bars were laid on wooden rails—

[1] The melted lead method of fastening rail spikes was adopted by the Philadelphia, Germantown and Norristown Railroad. See Wood's "Treatise," p. 512.

especially if the bars were thin—it was found that the weight of the trains often pressed the iron into the wood beneath, and in order to prevent this defect some of the roads put sheets of zinc on the wooden rails at the places where the ends of the iron bars came together.[1]

The first rails of the Camden and Amboy road resembled the ones of to-day more closely than had those of any previous American line. They were made of iron three-and-a-half inches high, three-and-a-fourth inches wide at the bottom and two-and-an-eighth inches in width at the top, attached directly to stone cross-ties by means of long spikes encased in wooden plugs and driven into holes bored in the granite. Such construction was soon discovered to be too rigid, and so an effort was made to give greater elasticity to the track structure by inserting thin strips of wood between the rails and the stone work on which they rested. But the wooden strips speedily went to pieces under the strain imposed on them, and eventually the Camden and Amboy, like all other pioneer roads, ceased to use stone in track making.

The early customs of New England, both with respect to the building of railroads and the method of their use, were adopted in large degree from corresponding ideas then prevalent in England. A pamphlet published in Boston in 1829[2] and dealing with the subject of railway making discusses the matter in this fashion:

"The labor of the horse may be relieved by providing a platform, placed on small wheels, on the long distances, on which the horse himself may ride. . . . This expedient, singular as it may seem to persons unaccustomed to observe the ease of locomotion on a railroad, is adopted with success on the Darlington and Mauch Chunk. And the horses eat their provender while they are returning to where their labour is to

[1] This expedient was employed by the Little Schuylkill Railroad in Pennsylvania. See Wood's "Treatise," p. 514.
[2] "Practicability and Expediency of a Railroad from Boston to the Hudson River."

be resumed. . . . An easy and convenient rate of travelling, with per-haps an average of about three miles an hour, and the journey [from Boston to Albany] may be accomplished in four days. . . .

"It will be found that an active horse may travel twelve or thirteen miles a day at a rate of nine miles an hour. . . . This power will be sufficient to draw, on a railroad of the description above supposed, a weight of 2½ tons, or a carriage with 20 passengers, with their baggage. On this assumption and estimate the cost of transporting 20 passengers between Boston and Albany, if the road is provided with stationary powers, [in the form of inclined planes to overcome hills] will be as follows:

16 horses travelling 12 or 13 miles each day, 50c.....	$8.00
2 men and carriage............................	3.00
	$11.00
Add 50 per cent...............................	5.50
For 20 passengers	16.50
For each passenger............................	82½ cents

"Or, if without stationary powers it would require 22 horses and cost per passenger $1.05, to which estimate add a toll tax of $2.00, and it makes a cost of $2.82 or $3.05 for conveyance from Boston to Albany in twenty-two hours."

One more example of the many ideas on railway build-ing and utility entertained during the first years of the new transportation method in America may be cited. It was contained in a letter published in the *Maine Farmer* newspaper of May 1, 1835. The communication—from some constant reader or old subscriber—read:

"Railroads have been found useful means of communication, and they are gaining favor rapidly with the community. They will be established, I doubt not, far more generally over the country than is now expected by most persons. This article is headed 'Rail Paths,' for I have in view rail tracks not so massy, solid and expensive as the railroads usually make. . . . Such solid and costly structures are not needed all over the coun-try; and lighter and cheaper roads will be sufficient. . . .

"Such paths may be used by locomotives propelled by horses. . . . Suppose that one of these machines, on proper wheels for a railroad, weighs 1200 lbs. and the horse in it weighs 800 lbs.; then he could not only move himself and his locomotive but a train of cars and their loads weighing 28,000 lbs. or 14 tons. . . . It may, therefore, be easily seen that a light rail road, sufficient to sustain at one point, or over a

272.—Two passenger trains of the same period. In this case the engines and cars are of contemporaneous creation, and represent the best existing equipment. Probably a scene on the Hudson River Railroad.

surface ten feet in length, 2000 lbs., will be adequate for all lines but the great routes of commerce and business.

"It is hoped that this subject will receive attention from those who are capable of studying the literary, religious and agricultural and commercial interests of the country. The writer has a conviction that not only may two great and distant centres of business be accommodated by rail roads, but that the system may be made to pervade our common towns, and extend its advantages even to the retired neighborhood."

Countless other books, pamphlets, arguments, and articles of similar character appeared in all the cities of the country, containing almost every conceivable speculation relating to the physical make-up and operation of a railway. Yet hardly one of these utterances was of appreciable value in shaping the after-history of the new transportation idea, and none of them suggested the future railroad half so accurately as those that had been made by Evans, Dearborn and Stevens years before. The so-called practical builders at first wandered far from the truth, and the initial railways of America bore little resemblance, either in their finished shape or usefulness, to the ideas of the men whose splendid visions they were designed to materialize.

Many of the first actual American railroad makers were also equally in error with regard to the economic character of the device after it was completed and ready for business. In considering the railed highway as a means of travel and transportation they adopted a mistaken idea originating in England, and in part established the American system on an erroneous economic basis. England at the outset considered that a railway was analogous in character to a "king's highway"; that is to say, the English thought that a line of rails suitable for the easy movement of vehicles was a public road which any man might use at will provided he built his wagon or car for that purpose. Before the introduction of railroads there had never appeared to the knowledge of men any method of general land transportation wherein the ownership and operation of the vehicles employed were vested in the same authority which owned and controlled the track on which those vehicles moved. So, since there was no precedent for the joint operation of both the road and wagons it was taken for granted in England—and for a few years in America—that the tracks of a railway and the wheeled cars moving over it had no very intimate relation with each other.

Several of the states entertained the notion that the new method of conveyance was to be merely a public highway over which any individual or company might run cars on payment of fixed charges or tolls. This was the plan first adopted by Pennsylvania. When that commonwealth built its state-owned railway from Philadelphia to Columbia there arose a public fear that the latest means of transportation might in some way fall into the hands of a monopoly, and so the state granted authority to no less than twenty different companies to run their

273.—Interior view of a passenger car of the best sort in 1852. Cars substantially identical with this composed the trains shown in the two foregoing illustrations.

horse-drawn cars over the road. There was no possibility of maintaining any schedule or regularity of traffic movement under such conditions, since the numerous wagons appeared on the tracks at any times suitable to the convenience of their owners. A kindred situation existed on other early lines.

The first ideas of Massachusetts were similar to those of Pennsylvania. In the early railroad charters granted by Massachusetts was included the following stipulation: "that a toll be and hereby is granted and established, for the sole benefit of said corporation, upon all passengers and property . . . which may be conveyed or transported upon said road, at such rates per mile as may be agreed upon and established from time to time by the directors of said corporation. The transportation of persons and property, the construction of wheels, the form of cars and carriages, the weight of loads, and all other matters and things in relation to the use of said road, shall be in conformity to such rules, regulations and provisions as the directors shall from time to time prescribe and direct, and said road may be used by any person who shall comply with such rules and regulations."

The attitude taken by those two states discloses the ideas probably entertained by a large part of the public during the first years when railroads were coming into existence on this side of the ocean. It was still supposed— by the majority—that they would be operated mainly by horse power, and that any one could run his wagons or cars on them if he did so in compliance with rules laid down by the company owning the road, or by the state if the new highway was a state enterprise. It required several years of actual experience, on railways at first used in that way, to bring about a realization that the vehicles of a railroad and the track itself were inseparable parts of one mechanism and could not be operated successfully under separate control. Those states and corporations which made an effort to conduct the business of their railroads in the manner indicated had no power over the owners or drivers of vehicles using the tracks, and were consequently unable to discipline them when they acted in a way that interfered with traffic.

Nearly all the first American roads were single-tracked affairs, and the only provision made by them for

THE CAR WINDOW.

274.—A glimpse of the past, seen through the window of a railway train. The early railroads, like the canals, followed the valleys of rivers when possible.

the passage of cars in opposite directions was the building of what were then called "turnouts." A turnout was a short strip of extra track a few yards or a few rods long, connected with the main line by switches at each end. Half-way between each turnout a large pole was set up near the rails, and this was called a "center-post." Whenever a car moving in its proper direction was met—before it reached a center-post—by another car travelling in the opposite direction, it was required to retreat to the last turnout it had passed in order to give right of way to the other vehicle. In the absence of any method of quick communication along the line, or between stations, this appeared to be the only practicable scheme for deciding which car should have preference over another, and numerous disputes and fights arose through its operation. A driver would hesitate to get very far from a turnout—

especially if the road was crooked and he could not see ahead for any distance—because he objected to returning in case he did not reach the center-post before meeting another vehicle. So he usually went very slowly until he got within sight of the timber goal and then whipped up his horses in a frantic effort to attain the coveted position before he encountered any opposition. If a driver who was coming the other way pursued the same tactics the two cars would be driven madly toward each other on the single track, each trying to get to the center-post first, and sometimes they met with a crash that disabled the horses or injured their drivers or the occupants. On a few occasions men were even killed by collisions brought about under the circumstances described. At other times there would be pitched battles between the drivers or the contrary-bound travellers, and considerable delays would necessarily ensue, much to the mental and physical anguish of the passengers who met defeat.

The foregoing conditions outline various popular ideas regarding the character of railroads as highways during the years of their introduction, and also suggest the experience of travellers who patronized such roads as were not equipped with locomotives from the first. There remains to be considered one other phase of the people's early attitude toward railways—their estimate of the social and commercial consequences destined to follow the adoption of the new contrivances.

Public opinion about that aspect of the subject was exceedingly diverse both in its scope and verbal manifestations. Most persons believed railroads would have a big effect on the social order and economic affairs; a few were of opposite mind. Doubtless, also, a majority of the people thought that whatever influence emanated from railways would be altogether excellent, but there were many who felt, and said, that the revolutionary system of movement in process of introduction would bring with it some results unfavorable to the country. There is always a considerable number of men who oppose important changes in established conditions of life. If that opposition is founded on an honest conviction that the proposed alteration is wrong in principle, or too extreme, or too rapid, then it is always useful to the permanent well-being of all the people, for such a belief tends to prevent unwise change and to retain an innovation within the realm of its greatest utility. But if such an opposition is not based on consideration of the comparative values of the old way and the new; if it is the expression of a fear that its possessor is about to be ousted from an unfairly won economic or social position, then the antagonism is either without effect or else works harm instead of good. For neither strength nor value can abide in such an attitude—either for or against change—unless its existence is founded on sincere belief untainted by greed. Whether or not the element of greed is present may sometimes be discovered by scrutiny of the worldly affairs of the objector, by studying the methods through which his existing position has been obtained, and by calculating the effect upon him of the condition he seeks to avoid.

The introduction of railroads did decidedly upset the previous methods of men in various ways and brought about radical alterations in their manner of doing numerous things. Many contemporary observers who foresaw the impending changes, and who awaited them with apprehension or delight, voiced their opinions at the time in letters to the newspapers, just as people do nowadays when the semi-weekly miracle is announced. One such

4.—GENERAL VIEW OF A NIGHT-CAR ON THE CENTRAL.

275.—A sketch published by *Harper's Weekly* in 1858. Although sleeping cars had appeared twenty years before, a large majority of the people who were compelled to travel by night did not look upon them as indispensable adjuncts to comfort.

communication of 1830, the apparent protest of a reader who "viewed with alarm," exclaimed:

"I see what will be the effect of it; that it will set the whole world a-gadding. Twenty miles an hour, sir!—Why, you will not be able to keep an apprentice boy at his work! Every Saturday evening he must have a trip to Ohio to spend a Sunday with his sweetheart. Grave plodding citizens will be flying about like comets. All local attachments will be at an end. It will encourage flightiness of intellect. Veracious people will turn into the most immeasurable liars. All conceptions will be exaggerated by the magnificent notions of distance.—Only a hundred miles off!—Tut, nonsense, I'll step across, madam, and bring your fan! . . . And then, sir, there will be barrels of pork, cargoes of flour, chaldrons of coal, and even lead and whiskey, and such like sober things that have always been used to slow travelling—whisking away like a sky rocket. It will upset all the gravity of the nation. . . . Upon the whole, sir, it is a pestilential, topsy-turvy, harum-scarum whirligig. Give me the old, solemn, straight forward, regular Dutch Canal—three miles an hour for expresses, and two rod jog-trot journeys—with a yoke of oxen for heavy loads. I go for beasts of burden. It is more formative and scriptural, and suits a moral and religious people better.—None of your hop skip and jump whimsies for me."[1]

But protests like this—even if they were genuine—could avail nothing when opposed to overwhelming popular desire. The step-lively microbe had slowly been multiplying until finally it was about to control and dictate the daily life of the people within whose thought it had long before found unsuspected lodgment. Only after the speed malady had run its destined course, generations afterward, was there to come a time when its dangers as well as its benefits demanded recognition; only after eighty years was it to be generally admitted that speed is not first among the advantages of movement; that safety, comfort and reliability of progress all take precedence over it in advancing the best interests of human society. The plodding citizens of those days did want to fly about

[1] From the "Western Sun," of Vincennes, Indiana, July 24, 1830. In view of the national temperament, and the manner in which this letter is phrased, it is easier to look upon the communication either as a joke or the product of a practised pen filched for the occasion than as the serious epistle it purports to be.

like comets. They did want to send their goods whisking away like sky-rockets. And they proceeded to gratify their desires, which grew as fast as they were satisfied.

It was believed by many, during the first days of railroads in America, that the new iron highways would exercise an appreciable and distinctive effect on the morals of the country. And over that question—just as in connection with their probable economic consequences—there existed a difference of opinion. A considerable number of men thought railroads would constitute an influence destined in some way to lower the prevailing standard of morality. That conviction was more noticeable in the East than elsewhere, and its existence in New England was visible for some time. The plea that railways were beneficial in a moral sense was sometimes employed in New England as a means of getting popular support for their creation, and the contrary opinion was advanced, on occasion, as an argument against them or their operating methods. Possibly the most conspicuous instance wherein a discussion of that sort took place was in connection with the building of the Western Railroad of Massachusetts.[1] The project was dragging a little in 1838 and the company, as one way of enlisting a larger public interest in it, appealed to the churches of the state and asked that sermons be preached on the moral effect of railways. This letter was sent out to the clergy of Massachusetts:[2]

"The Committee appointed by the Western Railroad Corporation, to assist the Directors in their application to the Legislature, for aid to finish the Road to the Western line of the State, have thought that the surest way to obtain their object would be to bring the importance of Rail-Roads before the whole people of our beloved Commonwealth. Its importance to our worldly prosperity we point out by an address circu-

[1] The Boston and Albany line. Chartered in 1833; begun in 1837; finished in 1841.
[2] In December of 1838.

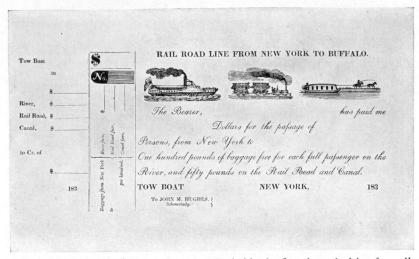

276.—Early railroad tickets and passes. Probably the first through ticket for railway travel used in America. Issued in 1831. It authorized the holder to journey from New York City to Albany by steamboat, thence over the Albany and Schenectady Railroad for seventeen miles to Schenectady, and then to Buffalo by canal boat. Printed in folio sheets containing three tickets to the sheet. Size of original, 9¾ by 5½ inches.

lated extensively throughout the State. But we are desirous to spread far and wide the Moral effect of Rail-Roads on our wide spread country. This, we think, can best be done from the pulpit. In this belief, we take leave, most respectfully, but earnestly, to ask you to take an early opportunity to deliver a Discourse before your Congregation on the Moral effect of Rail-Roads in our wide extended country.

"Trusting that the great importance of the subject to every inhabitant of this community will be a sufficient apology for asking your assistance in this great work, I have the honor to be, Reverend Sir,
"Respectfully your very ob't serv't,
"WILLIAM SAVAGE,
"Chairman of the Committee of Correspondence."

A number of sermons were delivered throughout the state in response to this request, and as a whole they indicated a pulpit belief that railways might become a beneficial moral factor in social affairs—or at least that nothing portentously bad need necessarily be expected of them. No doubt the committee was tolerably well satisfied with the result of its appeal. But the sermons were not unqualifiedly enthusiastic in their tone. There still existed in Massachusetts—and in other New England commonwealths as well—a considerable opposition to Sunday travel, and the prejudice in question cropped out in answer to the railroad's application for church approval. Much of the adverse criticism resulting from the letter was based on the proposed Sunday operation of railways, and in some of the addresses that feature of their policy was made the decisive issue which entitled them either to condemnation or endorsement. One of the sermons[1] which asserted that a railroad was either a good or a bad moral influence in accordance with its attitude toward Sunday observance said in part:

"The vision, however, is not one of unmixed brightness. . . . And among the causes for apprehension in the matter before us is the violation of the Sabbath, with which steam navigation and steam travel are connected, and judging from present appearances seem likely to be connected. The moral influence of Rail-Roads will be very much as it shall be made by the observation or violation of the law of the Sabbath. If this great method of locomotion, so distinguished that its introduction constitutes a new era in the history of the world, shall be so managed as to manifest due reverence for the God of the Universe and the institutions he has ordained, then its moral influence, it needs no prophet to foretell, will be good—eminently good. If, on the other hand, this distinguished improvement of the age shall be used in such a manner as to do dishonor to God and desecrate the institutions of religion which he has given to men, then its moral influence, as every one can easily see, must be evil—eminently evil.

"Livery stables not infrequently exhibit a scene of great desecration of the Sabbath. . . . No man who is worn down with worldly cares and labors may take the Sabbath for the purposes of recreation, and the mere recruiting of his physical energies to pursue the world again. . . . It would be much more reasonable that he should take a part of the week to recruit his energies for the Sabbath.

"It is the duty of the Stock-holder in any Company of the character mentioned, to raise the note of remonstrance against the desecration [of the Sabbath] which he deplores. . . . And as a last resort, when all

[1] That of the Rev. L. F. Dimmick, of Newburyport.

other means fail, or even before they fail, he can take the dividend which falls to him as the income of unrighteousness, and use it in the publication of Tracts and arguments for the correction of the very unrighteousness from which it flows.

"It may be proper here to remark that the lawmakers themselves are sometimes, perhaps, not sufficiently careful to observe their own statutes. Is it not the case that sometimes even they take the Sabbath to travel— and that to and from the very seat of legislation where the laws above recited are enacted? Do they consider the tendency of their proceeding? Will they themselves practice the very things which they prohibit in others as immoralities?

"Would not a Sabbath-keeping Rail-Road establishment be an honor to New England? . . . Sunday travellers are generally not happy men. It is deeply to be regretted that sometimes even professed Christians fall into this flagrant transgression.

"I have heard of an individual, sustaining some relation to the public conveyances of the day, and favorable to Sunday travelling, who professed to keep a list of all the Christians that went in his conveyances on the Sabbath, and threatened to publish them to the world. . . . Should not the Christian so live as to be free from the danger of exposure of this sort?"

So the controversies and discussions went on. Yet even while the impatient populace was thus arguing over the character of railroads, the best manner of their building and their probable influence, the new contrivance itself was taking visible shape before the eyes of the disputants.

CHAPTER XLIII

RAILWAY BUILDING BEGINS IN MARYLAND AND SOUTH CAROLINA — CAN A RAILROAD TRACK SUCCESSFULLY CROSS A GUTTER? — THE BALTIMORE EDITORS TRY A HORSE LOCOMOTIVE — OBJECTIONS TO THE SINGLE-MASTED METEOR — VON GERSTNER'S OBSERVATION — A NEWSPAPER ANNOUNCEMENT OF AMERICA'S FIRST PASSENGER TRAIN — THE TOM THUMB VERSUS HORSE POWER — CHARLESTON CREATES THE FIRST RAILWAY DESIGNED FOR STEAM — AMERICA'S PIONEER HOME-MADE LOCOMOTIVE — ITS EXPLOSION — LATER PRECAUTIONS OF THE DIRECTORS — THE FIRST NEW YORK STATE RAILROAD — OPPORTUNE PRESENCE OF MR. BROWN AT ALBANY — HE MAKES A PICTURE — ALL ABOARD FOR SCHENECTADY — SOME INCIDENTS THAT OCCURRED IN A TRIP OF SEVENTEEN MILES

WITHIN a few months after the issue of Strickland's book, in 1826, public meetings were called in various states and cities for consideration of the railroad question. Leadership in this popular movement was taken by Baltimore in Maryland, and Charleston in South Carolina.[1] The agitation in the two cities took place at about the same time,[2] and each outburst of interest resulted in the immediate commencement of a pretentious railroad. The work undertaken in South Carolina contained

[1] Both South Carolina and Maryland subscribed for several copies of Strickland's book.
[2] Early in 1827. The first citizens' meeting in Baltimore was held on February 12th.

some features of superior importance in their relation to the annals of American railway building and travel, but the more advanced ideas of the South Carolina enterprise resulted in a slightly later development of it. For that reason the events connected with the Baltimore project, and the primitive travel experiences of the people afforded by it, demand prior chronological consideration.

The public meetings in Baltimore found their con-

277.—First ticket of the New York and Harlem Railroad. Doubtless used for a short time only, on the first mile or two of track opened for traffic. The car is a representation of the original horse-drawn vehicles built for the road. Copper-bronze. Actual size. Die cut. Date, probably 1832. Circular pieces, made of silver-like alloy and bearing the same design, are also known. The round variety occasionally contains a punched hole, like some New York City stage-coach tickets of the same time.

sequence in the prompt appointment of committees, the preparation of charters, and the launching of the Baltimore and Ohio Railway by the Maryland legislature in March of 1827. A capital of one and a half million dollars was authorized for the road, which was eventually to be extended over the mountains to the Ohio River, and both the city and state were authorized to subscribe for its stock. "By this time," said one who had an active part in the work,[1] "public excitement had gone far beyond fever heat and reached the boiling point. . . . Parents subscribed in the names of their children. Before a survey had been made—before common sense had been consulted, even, the possession of stock in any quantity was regarded as a

[1] John H. B. Latrobe, in his pamphlet "The Baltimore and Ohio Railroad: Personal Recollections," p. 6. John Latrobe was counsel for the railway. His brother, Benjamin Latrobe, was an engineer in charge of construction.

provision for old age, and great was the scramble to obtain it. The excitement in Baltimore roused public attention elsewhere, and a railroad mania began to pervade the land."

The mania referred to by Latrobe was possibly a preliminary symptom of that approaching period of credit inflation and wide speculation which finally resulted in

278.—A later metallic ticket of the New York and Harlem Railroad. "Yorkville," on the reverse, indicates a northern district of the city to which the ticket holder was entitled to ride. The car here shown is probably identical with those portrayed in illustrations numbered 246, 247 and 248. Pewter. Actual size. Date, about 1840.

the panic of 1837. For several years after their introduction railroads were a chief subject of popular speculative interest, and an unbounded optimism led to the conviction that limitless riches were close at hand. That state of the public mind during the time in question ultimately operated to retard the widespread adoption of railways, for recovery from the resultant collapse of 1837 was slow, and not until about 1850 did railroad building begin to assume really extensive proportions.

Charles Carroll, the only surviving signer of the Declaration of Independence, laid the corner-stone of the Baltimore and Ohio Railroad on July 4, 1828, amid a most imposing civic demonstration and before one of the most enthusiastic multitudes that had assembled in the country up to that day. Every feature of the succeeding work was followed by the people with attention, and the various proposals of the engineers often aroused heated discussions and inspired long letters to the newspapers in approval or condemnation of the suggested plans. One of the most violent altercations of this sort arose from a proposition that the road be carried along Pratt Street, in Baltimore, which plan necessitated the crossing of numerous gutters at intersecting streets. A considerable faction of the public declared railroads must not try to pass such obstacles—that it was physically impossible for them to do so in safety. Finally one citizen wrote a letter suggesting that he saw but scanty prospect of building the road across the Alleghany Mountains if it could not be successfully carried over the gutters of Baltimore. Whereupon that particular dispute suddenly came to an end.

The first section of the railway to be finished extended from the city to Ellicott's Mills, a distance of some thirteen miles. In preparing one part of this roadbed two long parallel rows of holes were dug, each hole being two feet long and twenty inches wide. These were filled with broken stone, every individual piece of which was first passed through a small iron ring to test its size. Between each pair of stone-filled holes—and extending across the track—a narrow trench six inches in depth was excavated and similarly filled. Then cedar ties, or cross-pieces, were laid on top of the six-inch trenches. Near the ends of each tie, and just above the centers of the stone piers, notches were cut in which six-inch rails were laid, the rails themselves being pieces of yellow pine six inches square and from twelve to twenty-four feet long. These wooden rails were kept in place by wedges and spikes, and their outer edges were bevelled and covered with strips

of flat iron.[1] About seven miles of the track between
Baltimore and Ellicott's Mills were laid in this way and
the remainder of the line for the first thirteen miles was
somewhat similarly built. In some places the cross-ties
and rails were of huge stone slabs instead of wood. By
the spring of 1830 the section of the railroad here described was ready for business.

In the meantime several experiments had been tried on
the road in an effort to decide what motive power should
be adopted for its operation,[2] and one of those trials was
that of the second American locomotive, made by Peter
Cooper. Between July 4, 1828—when actual work was
begun—and the summer of 1829 the plans of those at the
head of the enterprise were largely governed by English
influence, and as a result its first section was built with
nothing but the employment of horse power in mind.[3]
During this first year of work on the Baltimore and Ohio
road it was not believed by the business men in control of
the matter that locomotives propelled by steam could
furnish sufficient power for a successful operation of the
new transportation device. Consequently they had prepared their roadbed and track in accordance with
practise then obtaining in England in building horse-
power roads.

But the general American public—notwithstanding
the opinions of British experts and those on this side of
the ocean who agreed with them—could not see any other
motive force but steam as the agency of future railroad
operation. There was in consequence a decided popular

[1] The strips of flat iron attached to the tops of the wooden rails in this case, and in
some other early American railroad construction, were placed at the outer edges of the
wooden rails because the flanges of the car wheels were at the outside of the wheels
instead of the inside, as at present.
[2] "In the beginning, no one dreamed of steam upon the road." Latrobe's "Personal
Recollections," p. 12.
[3] The competitive trial of locomotives by the Liverpool and Manchester road in
England had not yet been held. That important event took place in October of 1829.

Pass Bearer over **WEST PHILADA. RAILWAY** from **Blue Bell (Paschalville) to Third and Market.**

Treasurer P. & D. R. R. Co.

M'FARLAND & THOMSON, PRS. 311 WALNUT STREET.

279.—Pass issued by an early Pennsylvania road. The West Philadelphia line was a connection of the State-owned Philadelphia and Columbia. The granting of free travel privileges was carried to extreme lengths in Pennsylvania. Original printed on cardboard. Date, 1835-1840.

dissatisfaction with the nature of the work being done. The situation then existing and the conviction of the people are indicated in the following letter afterward written by Cooper.[1]

"At that time an opinion had become prevalent that the road was ruined for steam locomotives, by reason of the short curves found necessary to get around the various points of rocks found in their course. Under these discouraging circumstances many of the principal stockholders were about to abandon the work, and were only prevented from forfeiting their stock by my persuading them that a locomotive could be so made as to pass successfully around the short curves then found in the road."[2]

Cooper accordingly, in the summer of 1829, brought from New York a little boiler—about as big as a hot-water boiler attached to a modern kitchen stove—and set it up together with a correspondingly diminutive steam-engine, on a small four-wheeled flat car. Anthracite coal was the fuel employed. Using this locomotive, which from its size has come to be known as the *Tom Thumb,* he made a few trips of several rods in length on the rails then in place, and though the result did not satisfy him it was apparently sufficient to avert the withdrawal of the dis-

[1] To William H. Brown, under date of May 18, 1869; printed in full in Brown's "History of the First Locomotives in America," p. 109.
[2] A part of Cooper's interest in the matter arose from his ownership of a tract of land whose future value was believed to depend largely on the road's success.

affected stockholders. Cooper then undertook some improvements in his little engine, and eventually made with it a more pretentious test to be later described.

Another locomotive tried on the Baltimore and Ohio line before its formal opening was operated by a horse. The animal trod on a moving platform, from which power was transmitted to the axles. The inventor of this contrivance—and other people also—was enthusiastic over its possibilities, and after a private preliminary trial he invited the editors of the Baltimore newspapers, together with other guests, to enjoy his system of railway propulsion. The excursionists took their seats on benches that surrounded the horse, the animal was started and all went well until a cow, doubtless dazed by the rapid progress of civilization in her vicinity, ran into the contrivance and upset it. After picking themselves up at the bottom of an embankment the passengers organized a mass meeting on the spot and adopted resolutions appropriate to the occasion. Then they started back home on foot, stopping at intervals to amend and amplify the sentiments previously expressed. The local newspapers displayed an editorial bias unfavorable to the suggested innovation, and thereafter it was eliminated from consideration.

Another proposed method for early American railway travel was a sailing car, built by a prominent citizen of Baltimore named Evan Thomas. This vehicle was called the *Meteor*. Its body was a large bowl-shaped receptacle made of basketry in which the passengers sat. One of the visitors who travelled in the *Meteor* during its first trip over the Baltimore and Ohio Railroad was Baron Krudener, then Russian Minister to Washington, who himself trimmed the sails and manipulated the halyards of the railroad car. The Baron expressed himself as much pleased with the comfort and agreeable sensations connected with that manner of locomotion. As far as expense of operation was concerned the plan was an ideal one, the only apparent drawback being the unreasonable demeanor

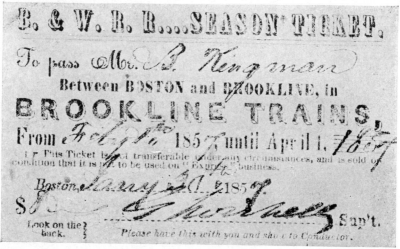

280.—Season ticket sold by the Boston and Worcester Railroad. Used by suburban dwellers in their daily trips to and from the city. The reference to "Express" business meant that the ticket holder must not carry parcels belonging to other people. Printed on blue glazed cardboard.

of the wind. In the course of a journey toward the west the motive power might nullify all the skill of the train crew and inexorably return the travellers to the spot whence they had started. To put the matter in a nutshell, it was found that the *Meteor* could only be depended upon for east-bound traffic, and could only make such trips when a stiff breeze came out of the northwest. And since it was even then recognized that a practical, smooth-working railway schedule providing for movements in both directions could not be drawn up on those lines, the inexpensive single-masted locomotive was abandoned.

A HISTORY OF TRAVEL IN AMERICA

As we look back from the pinnacle of to-day such ideas as these seem absurd, and the testing of them appears still more so, but the impulse behind them was not ridiculous. It was, on the contrary, invaluable. Such schemes illustrated the national method. They indicated an inventive spirit which at the outset of the railway era took a tremendous forward jump and thereafter resulted in the American creation of innumerable devices destined to universal adoption. America's predominant influence in shaping the outward form and enlarging the value of the new transportation instrumentality was recognized almost from the first by those whose practical experience and vision embraced the whole subject. When the Chevalier von Gerstner, a distinguished German engineer, was asked why he had come to America[1] to study railway development instead of remaining in England, he answered:

"That is the very thing I want to escape from—this system of England, where George Stephenson's thumb, impressed upon a plan, is an imprimatur which gives it currency and makes it authority throughout Great Britain; while here, in America, no one man's imprimatur is better than another's. Each is trying to surpass his neighbor. There is a rivalry here out of which grows improvement. In England it is imitation—in America it is invention."[2]

Von Gerstner's summary of the situation, expressed at such an early date, has since remained consistently true. Almost all America's railway methods have been of her own devising. Even at first she copied but little, and soon discarded nearly all the ideas so imported. Her rails, multi-tubular boiler, air brake, wheel trucks, locomotives, telegraph, dining cars, sleeping cars, and various other material features of her railroad system have been adopted by the rest of the world.[3] If America's contributions to

[1] While the railroad fever of the fourth decade was at its height.
[2] Latrobe's "Personal Recollections," p. 14. Von Gerstner made the utterance to Latrobe.
[3] The sleeping cars of some other countries, however, are superior to those of America. They are divided into compartments that afford a reasonable privacy to occupants.

951

the modern railway were subtracted from it, it would scarcely be considered as an indispensable feature of transportation.

By the summer of 1830 Cooper had made his contemplated changes in the *Tom Thumb,* and on August 28th of that year he ran it over the thirteen miles between Baltimore and Ellicott's Mills in an hour and fifteen minutes, or at an average speed of about six miles an hour. The return journey was made in sixty-one minutes, including a stop of four minutes for the taking in of water. On this occasion the little engine pushed in front of it a small car containing twenty-four passengers, who were thus the first representatives of the American public to be carried over rails by steam power. The trip had another aspect of importance at the time, for it also proved that steam could be used successfully on the road as constructed. This doubly momentous event in the early railroad history of the country was scarcely noticed by the newspapers of the day outside of the city near which it had taken place. One newspaper of New York City[1] mentioned it, nearly a month later, in the following paragraph:

"Railroad Cars.—The Baltimore Gazette mentions, that the first Rail Road Car, propelled by steam, proceeded the whole distance from Baltimore to Ellicott's Mills on Saturday last, and tested a most important principle, that curvatures of 400 feet radius offer no material impediment in the way of steam power on railroads, where the wheels are constructed with a cone, on the principles ascertained by Mr. Knight, Engineer of the Baltimore and Ohio Railroad Company, to be applicable to such curvatures. The Engineers in England have been so decidedly of opinion that locomotive steam engines could not be used on curved rails, that it was much doubted whether the many curvatures on the Baltimore and Ohio Road would not exclude the use of steam power."

This announcement of the first running of a steam passenger train in America was contained in fourteen

[1] The New York "Observer" of September 25, 1830.

lines of type placed at the bottom of the third column of the second page of the newspaper, and was printed without a head-line.

The achievement of Mr. Cooper, even if not fittingly received by the general public, did produce a striking effect in another quarter. It dismayed the stage-coach proprietors of the region, who beheld in it a menace to their own business and an ominous portent of the future. They could not with safety allow the people to gain an impression that this new travel method threatened the supremacy of stage-coaches, and one of the largest of the eastern firms of stage proprietors[1] therefore resolved to challenge the mechanical contrivance, and if possible demonstrate its inferiority as a vehicle of travel. So when Cooper took his engine and another load of passengers to the end of the road a few days afterward, a horse-drawn railroad car was also sent out to the same point on the second track[2] for the purpose of racing the locomotive back to the city. Cooper accepted the challenge, and when the word "go" was given both vehicles entered upon the competition, with the passengers of each hurling cries of defiance to those of the other. The big gray horse chosen to cast ridicule on the clattering mechanism sprang away on the instant and speedily obtained a lead of about a quarter of a mile. Finally the engine got up enough steam to move ahead, and thereafter gained slowly on its competitor until at last, after several miles, the passengers on the railroad car had the satisfaction of overhauling the wagon on the other track. The driver of the horse lashed his steed furiously, and responding with a still greater effort the fine animal for a time

[1] Stockton & Stokes.
[2] Two railroad tracks had been laid to Ellicott's Mills.

actually dragged his burden at a speed equally as great as that shown by the steam-engine. Then he slowly began to lag behind and victory seemed about to perch on the banner of progress. But the hope of those in the steam passenger car was destined to be blasted. Something went wrong with the locomotive, a leather band slipped from its wheel, and the engine lost its momentum. Cooper tried desperately to remedy the disaster, even injuring his hands in a foolhardy effort to replace the flapping band, but in vain. The horse recovered his lost ground, forged ahead for good, and finally won the race decisively.

Great was the exultation of those who planned to employ animal power on the railroad, and correspondingly deep was the depression of those who had pinned their faith to the strength of steam. Horse-drawn cars continued to be the only vehicles on the road until early in 1831. But by that time the success of locomotives elsewhere decided the company to adopt steam as a motive power, and on January 4th of the year named it published an advertisement in various newspapers offering four thousand dollars for the most efficient engine delivered for trial on the road by the first of the following June. A machine built by Phineas Davis of York, Pennsylvania, was the only one meeting the requirements of the company, which called for the pulling of fifteen tons of weight at the rate of fifteen miles an hour. This engine served as a model for those used on the road during several years thereafter.

The passenger cars built for the formal opening of the line[1] were large, open, wagon-like structures of cumbrous weight and uncouth appearance. They were equipped with roofs held up by stout timbers, and curtains

[1] May 24, 1830.

were provided which could be lowered for the protection of passengers in case of storm. These passenger vehicles were followed by others of decidedly more attractive appearance built on the general lines of the stage-coach, though considerably larger than stage-coaches and boast-

281.—A railway conductor's business card. Many conductors of long service and popularity became institutions on the roads they served. Rubber. Actual size.

ing an upper deck surrounded by a netting to keep people from falling off the top.

With the further construction of the road westward during ensuing years the locomotives and cars employed on it kept pace with improvements elsewhere throughout the country.

A little enterprise in Pennsylvania—through one incident that happened in 1829—had already acquired an importance in the history of early American railroads to which it was not otherwise entitled either by its size or general characteristics. This was the Carbondale and Honesdale Railroad,[1] extending for a distance of sixteen miles between the two towns named. It was chartered in 1826, begun in 1827 and finished in 1829. Its track ran for nine miles on trestlework, and also contained seven inclined planes. The line was built in connection

[1] The charter name of this road was the "Delaware and Hudson Canal and Railroad Company."

with some coal mines and was primarily intended to facilitate the transportation of their product. Immediately after its completion the road decided to make an experiment with steam power, and for that purpose obtained from England a locomotive named the *Stourbridge Lion,* which arrived in New York during early summer of the year named, and was soon afterward shipped to its destination and assembled by an American engineer named Horatio Allen. The *Stourbridge Lion,* operated by Allen, made a trial trip over the Carbondale and Honesdale Railroad on August 8, 1829, but was found to be so heavy that its employment on the trestles was unsafe, and it was never put into regular use. Nevertheless its trial trip constituted the first occasion on which a practical steam locomotive moved over a permanent railroad track on the American continent. After the *Stourbridge Lion* was discarded no further effort was made to use steam on the road, and the locomotive was offered for sale without avail. The engine was of nine horse-power and was calculated to haul a load of sixty tons at a rate of five miles an hour. It was about twelve feet long and weighed in the neighborhood of eight tons. The four wheels of the machine were made of oak surrounded by heavy wrought-iron tires, and on the front of the boiler was painted the head of a lion. After the engine was discarded it was placed in a little shanty beside the road from which it had been removed and there stood forsaken for more than a dozen years. It gradually disintegrated beneath the hands of curiosity seekers who carried away such parts of the mechanism as might be easily detached, and finally the remainder of the locomotive was sold for old iron.

Meanwhile a bill granting a charter for a railroad

282.—Railway schedules and time-tables. Four season time-tables of the Philadelphia, Germantown and Norristown Railroad. Showing commuters'
erasures, by ink or paper strips, of trains in whose movements they were not
interested. Actual size. Printed on white cardboard. 1847-1848.

between Charleston and Hamburg, in South Carolina, had become a law in December of 1827. Several citizens' meetings were held to discuss the subject immediately afterward; an amended bill in accordance with public desires was passed during the following month; and the final charter of the project was granted January 29, 1828. The company was organized on the 12th of the following May, and by January of 1830 some six miles of the road were ready. During the final weeks of 1829 and the first three months of 1830 it was the scene of experiments with horse locomotives and sailing cars similar to those on the Baltimore and Ohio line. The horse-power locomotive used once or twice on the South Carolina rails in 1829 moved at the rate of twelve miles an hour, carrying a load of twelve passengers. The employment of the sailing car took place before the road was open for regular traffic and appears to have been merely an impulse arising from impatience to travel on railroad tracks by any means whatsoever. One of the trips taken by such a vehicle was thus described in a local newspaper:[1]

"A sail was set on a car on our railroad yesterday afternoon, in the presence of a large concourse of spectators. Fifteen gentlemen got on board and flew off at the rate of twelve to fourteen miles an hour. . . . The preparations for sailing were very hastily got up, and of course were not of the best kind; but owing to this circumstance the experiment afforded high sport. . . . When going at the rate of twelve miles an hour and loaded with fifteen passengers, the mast went overboard with the sail and rigging attached, carrying with them several of the crew. The wreck was descried by several friendly shipmasters who kindly rendered assistance in rigging a jury mast and the car was again soon under way. . . . We understand it is intended by some of our seamen to rig a car properly and shortly to exhibit their skill in managing a vessel on land."

In September of 1829 Horatio Allen[2] was chosen to

---

[1] The Charleston "Courier" of March 20, 1830.
[2] The same civil and mechanical engineer who operated the "Stourbridge Lion" in Pennsylvania.

NEW-YORK & HARLEM
RAIL ROAD COMPANY.

SUMMER ARRANGEMENT.

On and after Thursday, June 10th, 1847, the Cars will run as follows, until further notice. Up trains will LEAVE the CITY HALL for

Harlem & Morrisiana.		Fordham and William's Bridge.	Tuckahoe, Harts Cor. and White Plains.
5 30 A. M.	2 P. M.	5 30 A. M.	7 A. M.
7 "	3 "	7 "	10 "
8 "	4 "	10 "	4 P. M.
9 "	5 "	11 "	5 30 "
10 "	5 30 "	3 P. M.	Pl'ville, N'castle, Bedf'd
11 "	6 30 "	4 "	Whitlockville, Cr. Falls
		5 30 "	7 A. M.
		6 30 "	4 P. M.

RETURNING TO NEW-YORK WILL LEAVE

Morrisiana & Harlem.	Fordham.	Wm.'s Bridge.	Tuckahoe.
			7 30 A. M.
7 05 A. M.	6 53 A. M.	6 45 A. M.	8 48 "
8 10 "	7 55 "	7 50 "	1 20 P. M.
9 "	9 09 "	9 03 "	5 52 "
10 "	12 23 P. M.	12 15 P. M.	*White Plains.*
12 35 P. M.	1 45 "	1 40 "	7 10 A. M.
2 "	5 08 "	5 "	8 33 "
3 "	6 15 "	6 08 "	1 P. M.
5 20 "	7 53 "	7 45 "	5 33 "
6 "			*Pleasantville.*
6 28 "			8 13 A. M.
8 05 "			5 13 P. M.

Newcastle.	Bedford.	Whitlockville.	Croton Falls.
8 A. M.	7 51 A. M.	7 45 A. M.	7 30 A. M.
5 P. M.	4 51 P. M.	4 45 P. M.	4 30 P. M.

The trains to and from Croton Falls will not stop on New-York Island except at Broome-street and 32d street. A Car will precede each Train ten minutes, to take up passengers in the city.

The morning Train of Cars from Croton Falls will not stop between White Plains and New-York, except at Tuckahoe, William's Bridge, and Fordham.

Stages for Lake Mahopac and Danbury, leave Croton Falls on the arrival of the 7 o'clock A. M. and 4 P. M. trains, and for Pawlings on the arrival of the 7 o'clock A. M. train.

Extra Trains on Sundays to Harlem and Morrisiana, if fine weather.

FREIGHT TRAINS leave the City Hall at 12 M. and at 7 P. M. Returning, leave Croton Falls at 7 A. M. and 9 P. M.

FARE FROM NEW-YORK.

To CROTON FALLS,	$1 00	To PLEASANTVILLE,	$0 62½
To WHITLOCKVILLE,	87½	To WHITE PLAINS,	50
To NEWCASTLE,	75		

G. F. Nesbitt, Stationer and Printer, corner Wall and Water-sts.

283.—Time-table of the New York and Harlem road, showing the train schedule for the summer of 1847. The southern terminus was at the City Hall. Extra trains on Sundays depended on the weather. Small broadside.

take charge of the construction work. Allen had recently been in England, and had observed the railroads there in use. He was already convinced that steam rather than horse-power was destined to be the future means of railway propulsion, and so insistently did he present his views to the South Carolina company that on January 14, 1830, its members unanimously decided their road should be built for the application of steam power and that mechanical propulsion exclusively should be employed upon it. The locomotive competition in England had taken place only three months before,[1] and it is accordingly probable that the South Carolina undertaking was the first railroad either in Europe or America formally to adopt the use of steam and pursue construction work in accordance with such a resolution. It is quite certain no other American railway had precedence of it in that respect.

By March of 1830 the South Carolina road had contracted for an engine which should be able to run at least ten miles an hour, and this machine, which was named the *Best Friend of Charleston,* was the first locomotive made in America for regular and practical use on a railway.[2] It was built in New York City, was shipped by ocean packet to Charleston in October of 1830,[3] and was placed on the road and operated in preliminary trials during the same year. The *Best Friend* ran off the track during a trial trip in November, but by the following month its performances had improved to such a degree that instead of moving at the speed de-

[1] It was concluded, and the prize awarded to the "Rocket," on October 14, 1829. That date was some months after Allen had left England, and after his opinion of steam power had been presented to the South Carolina company.
[2] A picture of the "Best Friend," together with a brigade of three cars propelled by it, is reproduced elsewhere.
[3] "The Charleston Courier" of October 23, 1830, contained the following paragraph: "Locomotive Steam Engine.—We understand that the steam engine intended for our road is aboard the ship Niagara which arrived in the offing last night."

THE UNITED STATES' MAIL LINE!

THE ONLY LINE
CARRYING THE GREAT MAIL!

DAILY TO THE SOUTH,

Via. Baltimore, Washington, Fredericksburg, Richmond, Petersburg, Weldon, Wilmington and Charleston, (S. C.) The Rail-Road from Weldon to Wilmington, (N. C.) being finished, and the whole Line in complete order, the Postmaster-General has ordered the following fast Schedule to take place from this date:

Leave Philadelphia, 1 A. M.—reach Baltimore 8 A. M.	96 Miles, in	7 Hours.
Leave Baltimore, 9 A. M.—reach Washington 12 M.	40 Miles, in	3 Hours.
Leave Washington, 12 M.—reach Fredericksburg 6¼ P. M.	70 Miles, in	6¼ Hours.
Leave Fredericksburg, 7 P. M.—reach Richmond 11½ P. M.	61 Miles, in	4½ Hours.
Leave Richmond, 12 P. M.—reach Petersburg 1¼ A. M.	22 Miles, in	1¼ Hours.
Leave Petersburg, 2 A. M.—reach Weldon 6⅓ A. M.	60 Miles, in	4⅓ Hours.
Leave Weldon, 7 A. M.—reach Wilmington 6¼ P. M.	161 Miles, in	11¼ Hours.
Leave Wilmington, 7 P. M.—reach Charleston 10 next day,	170 Miles, in	15 Hours.
	680 Miles, in 54 Hours.	

Whole time, from Philadelphia to Charleston, (all Stoppages included,)
60 Hours, or nearly 12 Miles per Hour ! ! !

☞ This route now offers to Travellers, advantages SUPERIOR TO ALL OTHERS—it has been built up at an, **expense of Six Millions of Dollars!** between Baltimore and Charleston, which it is believed is a guarantee that the Companies composing it are sufficiently interested to make and keep up THE BEST LINE between the North and South. To Strangers, it will be found particularly attractive, as it passes through the Seat of General Government, and in sight of Mount Vernon by day-light,—and generally through the most important part of the Country. Rail-Road Travelling is now well known to be the safest, most certain, and expeditious mode of conveyance; and in the commodious Cars on this route, it will be found equally as pleasant and comfortable as any other.

☞ This is the ONLY DIRECT ROUTE to the interior of Virginia, North and South Carolina, and the ONLY ROUTE connecting with the Greenville and Roanoke and Raleigh and Gaston Rail-Roads now completed to Raleigh, N. C., a distance of 103 miles from the point of junction with the Petersburg Rail-Road. From the Raleigh and Gaston Rail-Road, several Stage Lines now branch off to the West and South-West, into Tennessee, the interior of South Carolina, Georgia and Alabama.

☞ PASSENGERS intending to take this Route must leave Philadelphia (in the Train,) at 1 A. M. if they wish to go through without delay. At Baltimore, they step immediately from the Philadelphia Cars into the (Cars of the) Baltimore and Washington Rail-Road Company. At Baltimore, they pay through to Garysburg, (North Carolina,) where they take the Wilmington Rail-Road Cars.

☞ PASSENGERS for the *Raleigh and Gaston Rail-Road* pay through to Petersburg, Va.

☞ For further information and Through Tickets, apply at the Office of
STOCKTON, FALLS & CO.,
Adjoining the Philadelphia Rail-Road Office, PRATT ST., *Baltimore.*

284.—Establishment of rail communication between North and South. Schedule of the journey from Philadelphia to Charleston in 1840, which was made possible by the completion of several short railways. There were no through cars, and in making this trip passengers were transferred at 6:30 P.M., 11:30 P.M., 1:30 A.M. and 6:30 A.M., or four times in 12 hours. The average speed of 12 miles an hour was announced with pride.

manded by the road when the order for construction was given, it made about thirty miles an hour when travelling alone, and pulled four cars containing forty or fifty passengers at a maximum velocity of twenty-one miles an hour for a short distance.[1] The first formal employment of the *Best Friend* took place in January of 1831, about a year after the building of the road had been begun. As was customary on such occasions the celebration was festive in character, and one of its features was decidedly unusual. A brigade of cars was attached to the locomotive for a trip over the road and on one of them was installed a cannon belonging to the United States government, together with a group of artillery-men detailed for the purpose. While the train moved proudly along the rails the soldiers loaded and fired their gun in honor of the day and its significance. A contemporary account of the trip[2] said:

"On Saturday last the first anniversary of the commencement of the railroad was celebrated. Notice having been previously given, inviting the stockholders, about one hundred and fifty assembled in the course of the morning at the company's building in Line Street, together with a number of invited guests. . . . The first trip was performed with two pleasure cars attached, and a small carriage, fitted for the occasion, upon which was a detachment of United States troops, and a field-piece which had been politely granted by Major Belton for the occasion. . . .

"At about one o'clock she again started with three cars attached, upon which were upward of one hundred passengers. . . . At four o'clock the company commenced returning and all were safely landed at Line Street about six. The number of passengers brought down, which was performed in two trips, was estimated at upward of two hundred. A band of music enlivened the scene and great hilarity and good humor prevailed throughout the day."

Besides being the first railroad designed for the use of steam power, and besides being the first such line in America to build and operate a steam locomotive, the

---

[1] Various paragraphs in the Charleston "Courier" published during November and December of 1830 mention the use of the engine.
[2] In the Charleston "Courier" of January 17, 1831.

road was also the scene of the first locomotive explosion on record. This incident took place on the 17th of June, 1831, and was due to the action of a negro fireman who was assisting the engineer. The fireman was annoyed by the incessant sound produced by the escape of steam from the safety valve, and at length the harsh roar caused by the operation in question became intolerable to him. In an effort to abate the disturbance he sat down on a lever controlling the safety valve, and finding his posture had the desired effect he there remained seated until the engine blew up. A current account of this first of all American railroad accidents was thus phrased:[1]

"The locomotive 'Best Friend' started yesterday morning to meet the lumber-cars at the Forks of the Road, and, while turning on the revolving platform, the steam was suffered to accumulate by the negligence of the fireman, a negro, who, pressing on the safety valve, prevented the surplus steam from escaping, by which means the boiler burst at the bottom, was forced inward, and injured Mr. Darrell, the engineer, and two negroes. . . . The boiler was thrown to the distance of twenty-five feet, None of the persons are dangerously injured except the negro, who had his thigh broken."

The explosion and a number of other minor accidents resulted in the preparation by the company of the first set of rules to govern railroad traffic and provide for the safety of travellers. The action of the company was expressed by the following resolution:

"That in future not over twenty-five passengers be allowed to go on each car. That the locomotive shall not travel at a greater speed when there is attached:
"One car and passengers at fifteen miles on hour;
"Two cars and passengers at twelve miles an hour;
"Three cars and passengers at ten miles an hour;
"And that directions be given to that effect."

The Charleston and Hamburg road ordered a second locomotive in 1830, and it arrived at Charleston in February of 1831 and was soon afterward put into regular

[1] In the Charleston "Courier" of June 18, 1831.

operation. This engine was the second to be built in America for practical work, and was named the *West Point*. The explosion of the *Best Friend* had created among the Charleston people a feeling of uneasiness about the behavior of locomotive engines, and so when the *West Point* was put on the line for a trial trip the officials of the road strove to allay the nervousness of the passengers by a novel and effective expedient. Instead of placing the first passenger car immediately behind the little platform carrying a hogshead of water and wood for the engine, that position in the brigade was filled by a car on which was built a pyramid made of cotton bales. The cotton bales were securely fastened down by means of ropes, and they arose upward in the air as high as did the roofs of the cars which followed. The whole arrangement constituted a rampart interposing between the passengers and the engine, and was designed to prevent the boiler of the machine from flying back among the travellers in case it followed the example of the *Best Friend's* boiler. But the precautions of the railway officials did not even pause at that point. They also put a car containing a negro brass band immediately behind the cotton pyramid, and so the first regular passenger coach was third in the brigade as it finally started, with the other passenger vehicles attached in due order. To cap the climax of solicitude the mechanism of the engine was so altered as to make it impossible for the fireman to emulate the example of his predecessor, should he be so disposed. The trial trip of the *West Point* fulfilled all favorable expectations and was thus described by the Charleston *Courier* of March 12, 1831:

"On Saturday afternoon, March 5, 1831, the locomotive 'West Point' underwent a trial of speed, with the barrier car and four cars for passengers, on our railroad. There were one hundred and seventeen passengers, of which number fifty were ladies in the four cars and nine persons on the engine, with six bales of cotton on the barrier car, and the trip to the Five-mile House, two and three-fourths miles, was completed in eleven minutes. . . . The two and one-fourth miles to the forks of Dorchester road were completed in eight minutes. The safety has been insured by the introduction of the barrier-car and the improvements in the formation of the flange of the wheels. . . . The new locomotive worked admirably, and the safety valve being out of the reach of any person but the engineer, will contribute to the prevention of accidents in future. . . ."

Horse-drawn cars were never used in the regular traffic of the Charleston and Hamburg road, even in its earliest days. The success of its first two engines, despite the boiler explosion, was so emphatic that similar additional locomotives and cars were built for it as its rails gradually crept toward the West, and the experience of the road demonstrated at the outset the foresight of the man whose insistence had made it the first of all railways to be built and equipped for the use of steam.

While the events here related had been taking place in two of the southern states an almost equally important enterprise had been progressing in the interior of New York, amid a region memorable for a century and a half as the scene of significant steps in the history of American travel and traffic. As early as the year 1826 the New York legislature had granted a charter to the Mohawk and Hudson Railroad Company, and under its provisions work was begun in August, 1830, in laying out a road about seventeen miles long between the towns of Albany and Schenectady. Two inclined planes—similar to the one on the Pennsylvania state railroad near Philadelphia—distinguished the first New York railway, but these were of small length and the remainder of the distance traversed was over comparatively level ground. After a few miles of track had been laid two or three horse-drawn cars were operated on it, and these continued to run back and forth until the summer of 1831, at which time the entire seventeen miles of rails were in place. A knowledge of the success of the *Best Friend* in South Carolina had reached the men in charge of the Albany and Schenectady road, and so they decided to follow the course set by the Charleston undertaking. Early in April of 1831 they ordered a locomotive from the West Point foundry of New York—which had built the two South Carolina engines—and it was shipped up the Hudson River to Albany late in June of the same year. Their engine was named the *DeWitt Clinton*. After a number of preliminary trials without any burden the time finally arrived for a more pretentious demonstration, and August 9th was chosen as the date of the occasion. The trip made on that day by the *DeWitt Clinton* and its attached cars was, for several reasons, the most interesting journey ever undertaken by an early American railway train.

It so happened that on the appointed day there was temporarily sojourning in the town of Albany a man named William H. Brown. Mr. Brown was one of those itinerant silhouette artists who travelled about the country during bygone years, deftly cutting outline portraits of their customers from sheets of black paper. Brown was a master craftsman of his art, and in addition he was a man of intelligence and a close observer of the affairs of his time. Everybody in the city was discussing the approaching test on the railroad, and Brown heard the gossip. He had never seen a railroad or a railroad train, and putting aside his professional affairs—as he supposed—he joined the crowd that was trooping to the scene of the experiment. In company with many hundreds of others

DAILY
TO THE
SOUTH.
Via THE CHESAPEAKE BAY.

FOR NORFOLK, PORTSMOUTH,
AND CHARLESTON,
(Fare always the same as the Upper Route,)
IN THE SPLENDID STEAM BOATS,

ALABAMA,	Captain SUTTON,
GEORGIA,	Captain ROLLINS,
JEWESS,	Captain HOLMES,

EVERY AFTERNOON,
From the lower end of SPEAR'S WHARF,—BALTIMORE.

FOR
PETERSBURG & RICHMOND,
EVERY DAY, SUNDAY EXCEPTED.
PASSAGE, Meals found, ... TEN DOLLARS.

THIS IS THE QUICKEST AND MOST COMFORTABLE ROUTE,
GOING SOUTH.

☞ PASSENGERS have A GOOD NIGHT'S REST in the Bay—there are no Changes from Steamboats, Stages and Cars *in the Night*, as on the Washington route. *N. B. The Boat never leaves until the Cars from Philadelphia arrive.*

☞ CAUTION !!!—Passengers are requested to give no faith to the statements made at the depot in Baltimore, The WASHINGTON RAIL ROAD COMPANY rufusing to admit ANY AGENT into *their Depot*, but such as are connected with the *Upper Route ! ! ! !*

285.—Issued by a steamboat company that ran in opposition to the railroad route advertised in the preceding. Date, 1840. When using this route the traveller went to Baltimore by rail and thence to Charleston by water. Agents for the rival lines sometimes engaged in pitched battles for the possession of south-bound passengers in Baltimore.

he committed himself to the inclined plane with which the road began and was safely hauled to its top. There he beheld a throng of spectators who were pressing closely about the engine and brigade of cars as they stood ready on the track. The locomotive was a little affair about ten or twelve feet long whose principal features were its large wheels, lofty smokestack and central dome. At its rear was a platform built as a standing place for the engineer. Attached to the locomotive was a small flat car on which stood a couple of barrels of water and a pile of wood. Connection was made between the engine and water barrels by a leather hose. Following the water-and-fuel wagon were three passenger cars closely resembling stage-coach bodies, and each containing interior seats for six people. Additional seats at the outer ends of the cars provided accommodations for several more passengers on each vehicle. Five or six small flat cars were attached to the rear of the three passenger coaches, and these were equipped with plain wood benches. This was the appearance of the first steam railroad train assembled in New York State, and about which a crowd had gathered on the morning of that August day.

Brown alone, of all the multitude, had an appreciation of the historic importance of the thing he beheld. He took off his big flat-topped beaver hat, held it crown uppermost within the crook of his left arm, and made a careful drawing of the train on the back of a letter which he fortunately found in his pocket.[1] By the time this task had been completed the train was preparing to get under way and the passengers were taking their places. Brown himself fortunately secured a seat. When all the cars

[1] It should not be understood that he made the drawing on the back of an envelope. Envelopes had not yet come into use for mailing purposes. The sheet of paper commonly used for writing was folded up and sealed with wax. When opened it was about as large as a sheet of foolscap size.

were crowded to their utmost capacity the captain walked along the length of the train, collecting the fares of the travellers. Then he retraced his steps, climbed into a little seat attached to the rear of the water-and-fuel wagon and blew loud and long on the necessary tin horn. The train started.

It did not start all at once, but in sections. The tender was attached to the engine by a chain nearly three feet long made of three large links of wrought-iron; the first passenger coach was attached to the tender in a like manner; the second passenger coach was similarly connected to the first passenger coach; and so on down the train to the very last car. With the first forward jump of the engine the captain was nearly snapped backward out of his seat, but he seized a roof-support and luckily held on. The passengers in the first coach were unprepared for what was about to happen, and those sitting in the front and middle sections were projected backward and piled in a heap against the passengers at the rear. Those in the second car followed suit, and as the slack length of each chain was gathered up by the abrupt forward jerk the succeeding group of passengers was overturned. After the whole train was straightened out it rolled on in good order as far as smoothness of movement was concerned, but a new trouble then manifested itself.

The fuel of the engine, as has been suggested, was wood, and the smokestack soon began to belch forth big blazing sparks. These fell among the passengers. The damage done by them in the three covered coaches was not extreme, but the havoc they created on the crowded flat cars was sad indeed. Many of the travellers on the rear cars had carried their umbrellas, and those so equipped raised them for protection against the clouds of smoke and rain of fire. As a consequence all the umbrellas were soon in flames and were thrown overboard. Then the clothing of the passengers—a considerable number of whom were women—became ignited by the hot coals, and in a very little while the whole moving company resolved itself into a volunteer fire brigade, each member of which was belaboring the one next to him and trying to extinguish the conflagration in his neighbor's apparel. For a couple of miles, according to the stories of spectators along the track, the scene was one impossible of adequate description.

At this point of the interesting journey a further complication ensued. The train was approaching a spot where the locomotive's supply of water was to be replenished, and as it reached the tank the engineer threw a lever designed to apply the brakes and check the train's momentum. The mechanism worked to perfection. The water-wagon came up against the engine with a bump; the first passenger coach hit the tender with a crash; the second passenger coach flew against the first; and so on down the length of the train again, the resultant movements of the passengers being similar to those witnessed at starting, but in the opposite direction. As soon as the train was entirely stopped the travellers disembarked. The first thing they did was to put out the rest of the fires that still smouldered here and there in some coat or bonnet. The second thing they did was to tear down a farmer's fence, chop up the rails into appropriate lengths, and wedge them firmly between each two cars composing the brigade. This gave rigidity to the train, and after the engineer had taken on a fresh supply of water everybody resumed his place again with a heroism rarely duplicated, and the excursion moved on. The blazing sparks from

NEW SOUTHERN LINE,

ONE WEEK FROM NEW YORK TO NEW ORLEANS.

ONLY 36 HOURS STAGE TRAVELING!

WHOLE EXPENSE, $115.

BRUNSWICK & FLORIDA
LINE,

From Charleston to Mobile.

Via BRUNSWICK, TALLAHASSEE, PORT LEON, ST MARKS,
APPALACHICOLA, ST. JOSEPHS and PENSACOLA, viz.

From Charleston to Brunswick, Steamboat, - - 160 Miles.
" Brunswick to Tallahasse, Post Coach, - - 210 "
" Tallahassee to St. Marks, Rail-Road, - - 21 "
" St. Marks to Lake Wimico, S. boat, (innner passage,) 85 "
" St. Josephs to Mobile, Steamboat, - - - 215 "

This line will commence operations during October, leaving Charleston every
alternate morning, and arriving in Mobile in three and a half days, and
In New Orleans in Four Days.

PASSAGE TO MOBILE, (including meals,) $65.

☞ Seats may be secured in New York and Baltimore. ☜

The Steam Packets are of superior order, for safety and comfort. The
Stage Road is unsurpassed by any in the Union for evenness and firmness.
The whole Line is well appointed, and will soon be seen to be on the best
possible route for Northern and Southern Traveling.

Due notice will be given of the days of running and of other particulars.

Brunswick, Geo., 1840.

286.—A third announcement showing the facilities for travelling southward in
1840. It indicates that by means of railroads, steamboats, and stage-coaches
a man might go from New York to New Orleans in a week, at a cost of
only $115 exclusive of meals on the land portions of the trip. The pro-
portion of stage-coach travel necessary in any long journey was steadily
decreasing.

the dry pitch pine fuel still rained down on the excursionists, but they had acquired increased dexterity in dodging or handling them and the effects were not so bad. Such clothing as still remained to the travellers was ruined anyway, so the further visitation of fire was accepted with comparative unconcern.

The remainder of the trip to Schenectady was practically without incident except for the behavior of the live stock encountered in the progress of the journey. Nearly all the farmers of the surrounding region had gathered in their wagons and chaises at all favorable localities along the turnpikes to watch the first trip of the steam-engine, and at numerous places the roads had the appearance they presented at circus time or during a county fair. The country people did not know just exactly what was coming, and their horses had even less information on the subject. The only thought animating the two-legged spectators was to get as close as possible to the railway tracks in order to enjoy the show. It is needless to say what happened as the bedlam-on-wheels whirled past, headed by a mechanical monster vomiting fire and smoke. The effect of the apparition on the assembled countryside was later described in these words by a passenger who was on the train: "As it approached the horses took fright and wheeled, upsetting buggies, carriages and wagons and leaving for parts unknown to the passengers, if not to their owners; and it is not now positively known if some of them have yet stopped."[1]

On its arrival at Schenectady the train was welcomed by a crowd of several thousand people who inspected it

---

[1] Extract from a letter written by Judge J. A. Gillis, of New York State. Contained in full in Brown's "A History of the First Locomotives in America," pp. 183-5. Judge Gillis also describes the crashing together of the cars, the burning of the passengers' clothing and umbrellas and the use of fence rails to give rigidity to the train.

and the passengers with utmost interest. After a short interval it started again on the return trip to Albany, during which the intervening landscape was entirely devoid of horse-drawn vehicles. The events of the day were somewhat inadequately described by a local newspaper[1] in the following words:

"Mohawk and Hudson Railroad.—On Monday, August 9, 1831, the 'DeWitt Clinton,' attached to a train of cars, passed over the road from plane to plane, to the delight of a large crowd assembled to witness the performance. The engine performed the entire route in less than one hour, including stoppages, and on a part of the road its speed was at the rate of thirty miles an hour."

After Mr. Brown had got safely back to Albany he went at once to his hotel and there prepared a long strip of black paper out of which he cut in silhouette fashion an outline picture of the *DeWitt Clinton,* the tender, and the first two passenger coaches it had pulled on the trip here described. The artist performed his work with such fidelity and minuteness of detail that even the pictures of the passengers in the two cars were recognizable portraits of the men who occupied the seats. After leaving Albany Brown exhibited this silhouette picture of the Albany and Schenectady train to thousands of people in other towns, charging a small admission fee for the privilege of beholding it. At a later date he presented the original silhouette to the Connecticut Historical Society, where it still remains as an invaluable possession of that institution. Brown's picture, as made under the circumstances mentioned, is the best authenticated portrayal of an early American railroad train that has been preserved. It has been many times reproduced.[2]

The annoying features of travel by the new method

[1] The Albany "Argus" of August 11, 1831.
[2] One of the early lithographic copies of the original silhouette is shown on another page.

that were disclosed on the trip of August 9th were gradually eliminated, and on September 24 the road ran between the two towns a train containing numerous state officials and other dignitaries. A newspaper account[1] said of it:

"On Saturday, September 24, a numerous company, at the request of the president and directors of the Mohawk and Hudson Railroad Company, enjoyed a very gratifying ride upon the road. . . The party . . . did not leave the head of Lydius Street until nearly twelve o'clock. They then started with a train of ten cars, three drawn by the American locomotive 'DeWitt Clinton,' and seven by a single horse each. The appearance of this fine cavalcade, if it may be so called, was highly imposing. The trip was performed by the locomotive in forty-six minutes, and by the cars drawn by horses in about an hour and a quarter. . . . After dinner the company repaired to the head of the plane, and resumed their seats for the return to Albany. It was an imposing spectacle. It was a practical illustration of the great preference of this mode of travel and conveyance. The American locomotive started with a train of five cars, containing nineteen or twenty persons each, besides the tender, and never did 'Brother Jonathan,' as it was familiarly called, perform the trip in more beautiful style. It came down with its train in thirty-eight minutes, being at the rate of nineteen miles an hour; the last six miles were performed in fourteen minutes. The cavalcade with horses came down in sixty-eight minutes."

The little seventeen mile railroad between Albany and Schenectady, whose early endeavors were so picturesque, was destined to be the first link in a series of five or six small roads built westwardly from town to town through interior New York State during the next few years. By them it was eventually made possible for travellers to move all the way from Albany to Buffalo in railroad cars. At first the companies operating these several short roads were independent enterprises and did not manifest any especial desire to coöperate with one another for the convenience of their many patrons. Passengers in the cars were compelled to disembark at the

[1] Contained in the Albany "Argus" of Sept. 26, 1831.

end of each road and take passage on the next link of the embryonic system whenever its train chose to start. Eventually the insistence of the travelling public and a growing realization of the fitness of things brought about physical connection between these independent enterprises, and at last they fell under one corporate management and became known as the New York Central Railroad.

CHAPTER XLIV

MORE EXPERIENCES ON EARLY AMERICAN RAILWAYS —
MANNER IN WHICH A PENNSYLVANIA ROAD ACQUIRED
A LOCOMOTIVE — ACCOUNT OF ONE OF ITS TRIPS BY
A PEDESTRIAN PARTICIPANT — NEW YORK CITY'S
FIRST LINE — APPREHENSIONS OF THE PUBLIC —
PRECAUTION TAKEN TO SOOTHE THEIR FEARS — THE
RESULT — THE CAMDEN AND AMBOY ROAD — ITS
MONOPOLY OF TRAFFIC ACROSS NEW JERSEY — HOW
ISAAC DRIPPS BUILT A LOCOMOTIVE TENDER — THREE
NEW ENGLAND ENTERPRISES — NO STEAM TRAVEL
THERE UNTIL 1834 — ONLY SIXTEEN HOURS BE-
TWEEN BOSTON AND NEW YORK — PROTEST OF AN
OLD-FASHIONED TRAVELLER

DURING the year 1832 several other of America's
pioneer roads were sufficiently advanced in construction over parts of their routes to permit travel upon them.
Three of these lines were the Philadelphia, Germantown
and Norristown Railroad, in Pennsylvania; the New
York and Harlem road, in New York State; and the
Camden and Amboy Railroad, in New Jersey. The first
of these to be ready for public business was the Philadelphia, Germantown and Norristown road, which was
opened for six miles between Philadelphia and Germantown on June 6, 1832.[1]

[1] It had been chartered on February 12, 1831. The tracks did not reach Norristown
until August 15, 1835.

The first few miles of the line were operated for a short time by means of horse-drawn cars built according to the patterns then in vogue, although a determination had been reached soon after the road was chartered to use steam on it if that method of locomotion should prove practicable. The manner whereby the road obtained its first locomotive is an odd story, aptly illustrative of the methods prevailing in America during those early years of progress and experiment in independent railroad building. The city of Philadelphia—as earlier events had shown—was one of those communities whose citizens were always actively interested in all phases of the general subject of improved travel and traffic facilities. So in the year 1830, when public interest in railroads had attained a high degree of intensity, Franklin Peale, the proprietor of the Philadelphia Museum, decided further to enlighten the inhabitants of the city regarding the matter then uppermost in popular thought, and incidentally to coin popular curiosity into profit for himself. He accordingly resolved to exhibit a genuine locomotive in one of the halls of his institution, and set about obtaining an example of the apparatus in question. In furtherance of his idea he turned to a local business man named Matthias Baldwin. Baldwin's first knowledge of mechanics in any form had been gained as a jeweler and repairer of watches some thirteen years before. In 1825 he had extended his understanding of the mechanical arts by undertaking the manufacture of bookbinders' tools and such machinery as was then used in the printing of calico. He had even built a steam-engine for use in his shop, and the fact that Baldwin had actually made a workable steam-engine was the circumstance impelling Peale to approach him with a proposition to build a locomotive. Baldwin did build

977

a small model locomotive, which was duly installed in the museum on the 25th of April, 1831, where it pulled two diminutive four-seated passenger cars around a circular track,[1] and the public was thereby enabled to gratify its highest ambition by riding in a railroad train—such as it was.

Of course the little locomotive in the museum became at once the talk of the town, and when the incorporators of the Philadelphia, Germantown and Norristown road decided that they wanted a steam railway engine, they, in turn, went to Baldwin and gave him an order for one of them. The Camden and Amboy Railroad was even then being built, and it had already imported from England an engine known as the *John Bull*. Although the *John Bull* had not yet been put together, Baldwin went and examined it carefully, and then came back home and set to work. The result of his effort was the engine known as *Old Ironsides,* first of all such contrivances to be operated in Pennsylvania. It could hardly be expected that a railway locomotive constructed—as *Old Ironsides* was—by a man who had never done such a thing before, could be a very successful mechanism, and in the early stages of its existence it was not.[2] The history, appearance and performance of *Old Ironsides* were afterwards described by an assistant of Baldwin's in the following account:[3]

"The first really effective locomotive in America, says Mr. Haskell, in the Coachmakers' Journal, was built in Philadelphia, from a draught by Rufus Tyler, brother-in-law of the late Matthias Baldwin, of Philadelphia. Messrs. Tyler and Baldwin had formed a co-partnership and entered into business at the corner of Sixth and Miner Streets, Philadelphia, where the plans and patterns were made and the building of the

[1] The track was made of upright pine boards, covered with hoop-iron.
[2] The same thing was true of all early American locomotives built by men without experience in such work. They required numerous alterations.
[3] In the Philadelphia "Public Ledger," January 18, 1869.

CENTRAL RAILROAD,

FROM SAVANNAH TO MACON, GA.,
190½ Miles.

Passenger Trains leave Savannah daily, at......8 00 A. M.
  " " " Macon daily at.........8 00 A. M.
  " " arrive daily at Savannah at....6 15 P. M.
  " " " " at Macon, at......6 45 P. M.

This Road in connection with the Macon and Western Road from Macon to Atlanta, and the Western and Atlantic Road from Atlanta to Dalton, now forms a continuous line of 391½ miles in length from Savannah to Dalton, Murray county, Ga., and with the Memphis Branch Rail Road, and stages, connect with the following places :

Tickets from Savannah to Jacksonville, Ala.,...........$20.00
 " " " Huntsville, } Ala.,.......... 22.00
 " " " Decatur, }
 " " " Tuscumbia, Ala.,............ 22.50
 " " " Columbus, Miss., }.......... 28.00
 " " " Holly Springs, }
 " " " Nashville, Tenn., }.......... 25.00
 " " " Murfreesboro' }
 " " " Memphis, Tenn.,............ 30.00

An extra Passenger Train leaves Savannah on Saturdays, after the arrival of the steamships from New York, for Macon, and connects with the Macon and Western Rail Road ; and on Tuesdays, after the arrival of the Macon and Western cars, an extra Passenger Train leaves Macon to connect with the steamships for New York.

Stages for Tallahasse and intermediate places connect with the road at Macon on Mondays, Wednesdays, and Fridays, and with Milledgeville at Gordon daily.

Passengers for Montgomery, Mobile, and New Orleans, take stage for Opelika from Barnesville through Columbus, a distance of 97 miles, or from Griffin through West Point, a distance of 93 miles.

Goods consigned to Thos. S. Wayne, Forwarding Agent, Savannah, will be forwarded free of commission.

          WM. M. WADLEY, Sup't.

Savannah, Ga., 1852.

287.—Announcement of the Central Railroad of Georgia in 1852. Indicating the further growth of steam travel facilities in the South, the cost attendant on their use, the persistence of water travel to the North and the continued activity of the stage-coach.

iron horse commenced. . . . The wheels of the engine were made of wood, with broad rims and thick tires, the flange being bolted on the side. It was called 'Old Ironsides,' and was built in 1832. At eight o'clock in the morning she was first put in motion on the German- town and Norristown Railroad at their depot, Ninth and Greene Streets. She ran a mile an hour, and was considered the wonder of the day. On trial it was ascertained that the wheels were too light to draw the tender, and to obviate this difficulty we had the tender placed in front of the engine, which kept the wheels on the track. Mr. Baldwin, the machinist, and myself pushed the engine ahead until we obtained some speed, when we all jumped on the engine, our weight keeping the wheels from slipping on the track. The boiler being too small for the engine, steam was only generated fast enough to keep the engine in motion a short time,[1] so that we were compelled to alternately push and ride until we arrived at Germantown depot, where we rested. . . .

"At four o'clock we started on our return to Philadelphia, alter- nating riding and pushing in the same manner that we had come. Upon arriving at a turn on the road, at the up-grade, the engine suddenly stopped, when, upon examination, it was found that the connecting pipe between the water-tank and the boiler had been frozen, and the steam was all out of the boiler. It was then about eight o'clock, and was growing each moment colder. 'Necessity knows no law,' and so, after a short consultation, we made a summary appropriation of sundry panels of a post-and-rail fence close to the track, and started a fire underneath the pipe to thaw it. In a short time thereafter we had steam up and resumed our journey toward Philadelphia, arriving at the depot about eleven o'clock. Several successive trials were made during the following year; after each Mr. Baldwin added improvements and made altera- tions in the machinery. In about a year it was found that the grease had saturated the hubs and loosened the spokes, and they finally went to pieces, and were replaced by new ones."

The above-mentioned occasion, described long after- ward by a participant as that on which *Old Ironsides* was "first put in motion," does not appear to have been the first formal and public demonstration of the locomotive. Contemporary newspaper accounts of 1832 refer to a "first time" trial on November 23 that took place at a different time of day, and during which the engine went only half- way to Germantown and back again under decidedly different conditions. The account just quoted may refer

---

[1] The steam joints had been made by the use of canvas, covered with red-lead. This was an early English practise, which Baldwin had copied.

PENNSYLVANIA RAILROAD.

ARRANGEMENTS—1851.

FORTY-SIX HOURS TO PHILADELPHIA.
FORTY-FOUR HOURS TO BALTIMORE.

280 Miles Railroad—103 Miles Canal.

TWO DAILY LINES EXPRESS PACKET BOATS,

Exclusively for passengers.

TO PHILADELPHIA, BALTIMORE AND NEW YORK.

On the opening of Canal Navigation, two daily Lines, new **Express Packet Boats**, will leave for Johnstown, thence by Portage Railroad to

HOLLIDAYSBURGH,

There taking the NEW PENNSYLVANIA RAILROAD, two hundred and forty-five miles direct to

PHILADELPHIA.

☞ Time through, forty-six hours.

Fare to Philadelphia, $10. Fare to Baltimore, $9.75.

☞ The cars on this route are new, and of the most approved construction for comfort and safety.

☞ Packets leave every morning *precisely* at eight o'clock, and every evening at the same hour.

PASSENGERS FOR BALTIMORE,

on arrival of Cars at Harrisburgh, take the York and Cumberland Railroad, (now finished,) direct to that city, (84 miles.) Time, four hours.

☞ *No charge for handling baggage on this route.*

The increased speed makes this the most comfortable, safe and desirable route now to the Eastern Cities.

For passage or information, apply to

J. P. HOLMES, Agent, Monongahela House, or to

D. LEECH & CO., Canal Basin, Penn-st., Pittsburgh.

N. B. On the 1st of July, the PENNSYLVANIA RAILROAD will be finished at Lockport, Pa., which will shorten the time through six hours.

288.—The journey between Pittsburgh and Philadelphia reduced to 46 hours. Advertisement of Leech's Line in 1851. It started two express canal boats eastward each day. On arrival at Johnstown the passengers still had to use the Portage railway across the mountains, but at Hollidaysburg they left the state-owned system and transferred to the newly built Pennsylvania Railroad, which company had been chartered in 1846, and whose line had been finished to Hollidaysburg in September of 1850. The state canal from that town to Philadelphia had been abandoned by passenger traffic.

to a preliminary test. One local newspaper[1] of November 24th said:

"A most gratifying experiment was made yesterday afternoon on the Philadelphia, Germantown and Norristown Railroad. The beautiful locomotive engine and tender, built by Mr. Baldwin, of this city, whose reputation as an ingenious machinist is well known, were for the first time placed on the road. The engine traveled about six miles, working with perfect accuracy and ease in all its parts, and with great velocity."

Another paper[2] gave a still more detailed statement as follows:

"It gives us pleasure to state that the locomotive engine built by our townsman, M. W. Baldwin, has proved highly successful. In the presence of several gentlemen of science and information on such subjects, the engine was yesterday placed upon the road for the first time. All her parts had been previously highly finished and fitted together in Mr. Baldwin's factory. She was taken apart on Tuesday and removed to the Company's depot, and yesterday morning she was completely together, ready for travel. After the regular passenger cars had arrived from Germantown in the afternoon, the tracks being clear, preparation was made for her starting. The placing fire in the furnace and raising steam occupied twenty minutes. The engine (with her tender) moved from the depot in beautiful style, working with great ease and uniformity. She proceeded about half a mile beyond the Union Tavern . . . and returned immediately, a distance of six miles, at a speed of about twenty-eight miles to the hour. . . . It is needless to say that the spectators were delighted. . . . We rejoice at the result of this experiment."

While Baldwin was adding improvements to his locomotive during the first months of its career the road of which it formed such an interesting part displayed a proper solicitude for its welfare. It advertised in the newspapers that the engine would haul the passenger cars of the railway at certain hours if the weather was good, but that if it rained the cars would be pulled by horses. Sometimes it rained. But eventually *Old Ironsides* was transformed by Baldwin into an extraordinarily effective piece of machinery for that day, and in 1833 it ac-

[1] "The United States Gazette."
[2] The "Chronicle" of November 24.

HUDSON RIVER RAILROAD.
REDUCTION OF FARES.
NEW-YORK TO AND FROM
ALBANY & TROY

THROUGH FARES ON ALL TRAINS
Between Albany and New-York, $1.50

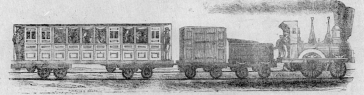

On and after Monday, July 12th, the Trains will run as follows:

GOING NORTH,
Leave New-York, from the office cor. Chambers Street and College Place, at

6 A.M. Express Train for Albany and Troy, connecting with Northern and Western Trains, stopping only at Peekskill, Fishkill, Po'keepsie, Rhinebeck, and Hudson. Through in 4 hours from 31st Street.

7 A.M. To Peekskill, stopping at all Way Stations.

8 A.M. Mail Train for Albany and Troy, stopping only at Manhattan, Dobbs' Ferry, Sing-Sing, Peekskill and all Mail Stations north.

9 A.M. To Peekskill, stopping at all Way Stations.

11½ A.M. Passengers and Freight to Po'keepsie, stopping at all Stations.

1 P.M. Way Train for Albany and Troy, stopping at Yonkers, Tarrytown, Peekskill, Cold Spring, Fishkill, New-Hamburgh, Poughkeepsie, Rhinebeck, Tivoli, Oakhill, Hudson, and Stuyvesant, and connecting with the Express Train leaving Albany at 6.30 P.M. for Buffalo.

2 P.M. To Peekskill, stopping at all Way Stations.

4 P.M. Way Train to Albany and Troy, stopping at Yonkers, Dobbs' Ferry, Dearman, Tarrytown, Sing-Sing, Peekskill, Garrisons, Cold Spring, Fishkill, New-Hamburgh, Po'keepsie, and all Stations north on signal.

4½ P.M. To Poughkeepsie, stopping at all Way Stations.

6 P.M. Express Train for Albany and Troy, stopping only at Peekskill, Fishkill, Po'keepsie, Rhinebeck, Hudson and Stuyvesant. Through in 4 hours from 31st Street, and connecting with Western Trains.

6¼ P.M. To Peekskill, stopping at all Way Stations.

7½ P.M. Emigrant and Freight Train for Albany and Troy, stopping at all Way Stations.

Leave Po'keepsie for Albany at
6¼ A.M. Stopping at all Way Stations.

GOING SOUTH,
Leave Troy Engine Station and Albany, viz:

Leave Troy	Leave Albany	
A.M. 5.45	**6 A.M.**	Way Mail Train for New-York, stopping at all stations where there are mails to be received and delivered.
A.M. 6.45	**7 A.M.**	Express Train for New-York, stopping only at Hudson, Rhinebeck, Poughkeepsie, Fishkill, Cold Spring and Peekskill. Through in 4 hours.
A.M. 10.45	**11 A.M.**	Way Train, stopping at Stuyvesant, Hudson, Oakhill, Tivoli, Barrytown, Rhinebeck, Hyde Park, Po'keepsie, Fishkill, Cold Spring, Peekskill, Cruger's, Sing-Sing and Dobb's Ferry.
P.M. 3.45	**4 P.M.**	Way Train, stopping at Stuyvesant, Hudson, Oakhill, Tivoli, Barrytown, Rhinebeck, Hyde Park, Po'keepsie, New-Hamburgh, Fishkill, Cold Spring, Garrison's, Peekskill, Cruger's, Sing-Sing, Tarrytown and Yonkers.
	4½ P.M.	For Poughkeepsie only, stopping at all Way Stations.
P.M. 6.	**6¼ P.M.**	Express Train, stopping only at Hudson, Rhinebeck, Po'keepsie, Fishkill and Peekskill. Through in 4 hours.
P.M. 8.30	**8¾ P.M.**	Night Mail Train, stopping at all stations on signal.

Leave Po'keepsie for New-York at

6¾ A.M. stopping at all stations above Peekskill, and at Cruger's, Sing-Sing, Tarrytown, Dearman, Dobbs' Ferry, Hastings, Yonkers and Manhattan.

8¾ P.M. Milk and Freight Train, stopping at all Way Stations.

Leave Peekskill for New-York at

5.50 & 6.30 A.M. Stopping at all Way Stations.

3½ & 6 P.M. Stopping at all Way stations.

Passengers will procure Tickets before entering the Cars. | Tickets purchased in the Cars will be 5 cents extra.
New-York, July 10th, 1852. | **GEO. STARK, Superintendent.**

289.—Broadside train schedule issued by the Hudson River Railroad in 1852. There were twenty-six trains a day on the line. The picture of a locomotive shows a curious form of the lately introduced engineer's cab. A growing desire of all roads to have passengers buy tickets instead of paying cash on the cars is indicated by the request at the bottom. Printed on blue paper.

complished the astonishing performance of running a mile in fifty-eight seconds—without any cars behind it—and two and a quarter miles under similar conditions in three minutes and twenty-two seconds. This was indeed an achievement for a self-taught engine builder, and it is not surprising that out of the results here narrated and the American spirit responsible for them there slowly grew one of the principal locomotive building establishments of the world. Several contemporary pictures of *Old Iron-sides* and of cars drawn by it are elsewhere reproduced in these pages, and a view of the station of the Philadelphia, Germantown and Norristown road is similarly shown.[1]

The second of the three roads already mentioned that were opened for business in 1832 was the New York and Harlem.[2] The work of building it had been begun during the previous year, and the first part of it to be finished was a short section of track about three-quarters of a mile in length extending southward from Fourteenth Street, in New York City.[3] Although this first division of the line was not dedicated to public travel until November 26th of 1832, it is evident that cars had been placed on the tracks a few days before the date named, since a local publication[4] mentioned the progress of the enterprise in these words on November 17:

"We were highly gratified on Wednesday last, as we were passing up

[1] As is likewise a picture of the Baldwin Works drawn by John Sartain about 1845, in connection with locomotives of the type then made by it and used in this country.

[2] Chartered on April 25, 1831.

[3] Additional sections were completed and used for travel as follows:
Between Fourteenth and 32nd Streets on June 10, 1833;
From 32nd Street to Yorkville, about 2¾ miles, May 9, 1834;
From Harlem to Williamsbridge, September 3, 1842;
From Williamsbridge to White Plains, December 1, 1844;
From White Plains to Croton Falls on June 1, 1847;
From Croton Falls to Dover Plains, December 31, 1848;
From Dover Plains to Chatham Four Corners, January 19, 1852;
The section extending southward from Prince Street to the City Hall was opened on May 4, 1839.
At Chatham Four Corners the road connected with the Albany and Westchester road.—Poore's "History of the Rail Roads and Canals of the United States of America, etc." New York, 1860. Vol. I (all published), pp. 287-288.

[4] "Railroad Journal." Vol. I, No. 47. New York, November 17, 1832, p. 737.

BEERS' TEMPERANCE HOTEL

THIRD STREET WEST,

North of Pennsylvania Avenue, and near the Railroad Depot,

WASHINGTON, D. C.

☞ PRICES TO SUIT THE TIMES. ☜

290.—Advertisement of a hostelry catering to railroad travellers and kept by a well-known temperance advocate of Washington. Date, 1851. Drunkenness was more common than at present, and travellers who objected to drinking and its attendant scenes preferred those few hotels where liquor was not sold.

the Bowery, with a view of the beautiful Cars of the Harlaem Railroad Company. We understand they were made by Miln Parker, coachmaker, of this city. They are spacious and convenient, being divided into three distinct apartments, each [apartment] amply large enough for eight, and can accommodate very conveniently ten persons—or twenty-four to thirty passengers inside; and, when we saw them, there were at least, we should think, an equal number upon, and hanging around the outside, the whole drawn by two fine horses abreast, at the rate of ten or twelve miles an hour. We admired their construction, and believe they are less liable to accident than most others we have seen, as the wheels are under the body. . . .

"We have now a specimen of Railroads in a busy, bustling street, and it will, we trust, satisfy those who have been apprehensive of danger from their introduction, that they are far more safe to the pedestrian than hacks and stages, as they pursue a direct, forward course, and usually at a uniform velocity.

"We consider this section of the Harlaem Railroad, now ready for use, the first link in a long line of railroad, which will, and at no distant period, connect this city with the far and fertile west, and we therefore wish to all who are concerned in it, success in the undertaking, a speedy completion of the work, and a liberal return for their investment."

In addition to the details of appearance mentioned by the article in the *Railroad Journal,* it may be said in description of the first cars on the New York and Harlem road that they possessed both springs and brakes. The springs were made of leather strips, riveted together in the manner used for making stage-coach thorough-braces. The brake was a friction-block, and was put in contact with the wheels by an arrangement which the driver operated with his feet. The driver himself sat on an elevated seat at the front of the car, just as the pilot of the stage-coach had done for many years.

During the building of the southern section of the road the location of a few miles of its track in one of the important streets caused apprehension in the public mind that numerous accidents would happen as the result of its operation. The officials of the road were naturally anxious to prove that any such alarm was groundless, and so they resolved that on the day appointed for the formal opening of the line they would give visible and conclusive proof that the heavy passenger coaches could be stopped almost instantly by the drivers, and that collisions between the cars and other vehicles need not be feared. The vice-president himself[1] took charge of affairs on the day of the opening and decided to run two cars along the tracks, one close behind the other, in order to produce a situation out of which a collision might result unless due care was exercised. But let it not be thought that it was his intention to have a mishap. He was arranging the stage and scenery, so to speak, for a dramatic proof that there need be no accident even under those conditions anticipated by the prospective travelling public. He chose for the driver of the first car one Lank O'Dell, a local character famed for his dexterity with the reins. The second car was entrusted to a hack driver. The passengers in the two vehicles were city dignitaries and other invited guests, of whom the mayor and members of the

[1] John Lozier.

city council rode behind O'Dell in the first car. Other municipal officials filled the second. At the appointed hour the streets were lined with enthusiastic citizens and away went the cavalcade.

O'Dell, in compliance with his instructions, urged his team into a sharp pace and the car containing the mayor and council bowled smoothly along, closely followed by its mate. Suddenly, at the appointed spot, O'Dell pressed heavily on the brake lever and brought his car to an abrupt stop. Vice-President Lozier instantly gave the agreed-upon signal which was to halt the second car also, but the hackman had become flustered over his temporary prominence as one of the central figures of the pageant, and instead of manipulating his brake he merely shouted "Whoa!" and pulled on the lines, just as he would have done if he had been sitting on his own hack. These precautions were insufficient to stop the heavy vehicle and the tongue of his car went smashing through the rear door of the one in front, while the mayor and council jumped off the front platform and climbed out of the windows. Nobody was hurt, and the procession was soon resumed.

New York City's first road was operated by horse power until about 1837, when locomotives were introduced on it and puffed their way through the streets of the town. The employment of steam on the road resulted in numerous accidents to pedestrians, and casualties of that sort soon came to be considered as inevitable. The somewhat callous sentiment of the time even looked upon such accidents as jokes, and the cartoonists made funny pictures showing the Bowery locomotives plowing their way unconcernedly through groups of men, women and children.

The New York and Harlem Railroad - because

some of its tracks lay in busy city streets — has often been considered as a street-railway in the modern understanding of that term. Such was not the fact. It was not built, and at no period in its history was it operated, as a railroad destined simply to carry city passenger traffic back and forth. As the *Railroad Journal* said in its article before quoted, the enterprise was considered "the first link in a long line of railroad, which will, and at no distant period, connect this city with the far and fertile West." It merely happened that the first of its trackage was laid in a city street, and it was no more a street-railway than were other similar early railroads in the highways of Philadelphia and other large communities, whether they were operated by horse power or by locomotives.

During the third and fourth decades no American city presented a problem of distinctively urban passenger movement that called for the creation of local railway facilities exclusively for its accommodation, although such a condition was slowly approaching. At that time all city passenger traffic along established routes was carried in stages and omnibuses.[1] The nature of the railroad tracks universally in use during the years under consideration made it impossible to build the sort of street railways ultimately destined for city traffic. The rails of those days — whether of wood or iron — stood up several inches above the surface of the ground, and the laying of such tracks throughout a city would have created serious barriers to all wheel traffic desiring to cross the thoroughfares so occupied. Street railways, as we understand them, could not exist until after the invention of

---

[1] Elsewhere is reproduced a scene in lower Broadway, New York City, showing the city stages which at that time occupied the place now held by street-cars. Examples of the metallic tickets used in connection with such city stage lines are also reproduced.

JULIUS KLINKER, NEW YORK, 1852. EDT...

MORS POPPEL, SCULPST.

291.—Conditions in New York City. Aspect of lower Manhattan in 1850. Castle Garden was on an island reached by a bridge. The church at the left is Trinity. Windows of adjoining office buildings now look down upon its spire. Engraved by Poppel from a drawing by the artist Julius Kimmer.

the low or sunken rail whose surface permits the use of cars while offering little interference to other street movement.

The third of the railroads mentioned whose opening for traffic fell within the year 1832 was the Camden and Amboy, which was chartered in 1830 and finished for a distance of fourteen miles between Bordentown and Hightstown on December 22 of 1832.[1] The principal historical interest attaching to this early iron highway lies in its economic relation to the people who used it, rather than in any curious or picturesque phases of its operation. For many years it held an unparallelled place in the transportation system of the country, and the main features of that position can best be outlined by quoting certain words[2] which dealt with it at the comparatively late date of 1860. The statement ran:

"This road is probably the most productive work of the kind ever constructed. It has paid dividends averaging nearly 12 per cent. annually for twenty-seven years, accumulating in the meantime a very large surplus. Its extraordinary revenues are in a great measure due to the monopoly it enjoys of the right of way between the cities of New York and Philadelphia. This monopoly was not created in the act incorporating the Company, but was subsequently purchased by a grant to the State of stock in the road to the amount of $200,000, and by an agreement to pay certain transit duties on persons and property passing through its territory. The parties connected with this work were not long in perceiving the value of the exclusive right of way across the State, which may be regarded as the key to the great routes of commerce and travel for the whole country, with the power to levy exorbitant tolls. The State became a willing party to the scheme, under the idea that it could thereby draw the means for supporting its government from citizens of other States, thus relieving its own from the burdens of taxation. Such a result has been gained. The State now derives a revenue of over $200,000 annually from transit duties and dividends on the stock

---

[1] One part of the track between Bordentown and Hightstown was opened for travel late in 1831, and the English locomotive named "John Bull"—previously mentioned in connection with Baldwin's work—was then used in pulling a passenger train for a few miles. This was the first locomotive and train operated in New Jersey. The road was completed between the towns of South Amboy and Camden, a distance of 61 miles, in 1834.
[2] From "History of the Railroads and Canals of the United States of America, etc." By Henry D. Poore. Vol. I. New York, 1860, pp. 377-387.

presented to it. The effect, however, has been to build up within it a power, to which, in all matters touching real or fancied interest, the Legislature itself is the subordinate one—no act being allowed to pass that body against the wishes of the Company. Such a relationship, however, cannot exist without serious injury to the moral and material welfare of the people of the State. It is fortunate that this policy of imposing a tax for the privilege of passing through its territory is confined to two States—New Jersey and Maryland—otherwise the internal commerce of the country might be almost entirely destroyed, and our States converted into hostile communities, intent only in plundering each other. . . . Although there is no doubt that the State of New Jersey has suffered vastly more than she has gained by the monopoly, the prospective advantages of a liberal policy, necessary to a full development of the energies and resources of the State, weigh nothing against an absolute payment of more than $200,000 annually. The total amount received into the State Treasury from transit duties and dividends on its stock, . . . has been $3,870,250. This Company makes no reports, except the meagre ones to the Legislature. It has published no general statement for twenty years past, so that nothing can be known as to the conditions of its affairs. All inquiries for information, even to the amount of equipment on the road, were refused. . . . The Company is the paramount authority in the State, dictating the legislation upon all subjects in which it has a real or fancied interest."

The Camden and Amboy road closely followed one of the travel paths across New Jersey that had been in use for more than a century and a half. Its first history was that of a trail through the forest over which men made the journey between New Amsterdam and Philadelphia, either afoot or on horseback, in four or five days. Then came the introduction of the "Flying Machines" and those improved sailing vessels designed to carry travellers from Amboy across New York Bay to New York City. Following the Flying Machine wagons came the regular lines of real stage-coaches, which gradually decreased the time necessary in passing between the two cities, and finally a railed-track and mechanical contrivance in its turn supplanted the stage-coaches.

When the Camden and Amboy company was organized it chose for its president a man named Robert

L. Stevens, son of the John Stevens whose still earlier prominence in the building of steamboats and the advocacy of railroads has already been observed. Robert Stevens was sent to England soon after the company came into existence, and while there he ordered a locomotive for the New Jersey road. This was the *John Bull*. It reached Bordentown late in the year 1831, and its various parts were there assembled into working order — after Baldwin had studied them — by a young American machinist named Isaac Dripps, who had been chosen by Stevens to take charge of the mechanical details connected with the operation of the road. Young Dripps had never before seen a steam locomotive either in dismantled form or ready for use, but he nevertheless succeeded in putting the *John Bull* together and running it. No tender had been bought for the engine, and to rectify this oversight Dripps built a small flat car and attached to its platform an empty whisky cask bought from a grocery store. Then he found it necessary to connect his extemporized water tank with the engine, and to accomplish this purpose he hired a Bordentown shoemaker to make a hose out of leather. When the tender was further equipped with a box full of wood the engine was ready for service. The first passenger cars on the Camden and Amboy road were of the type resembling three stagecoach bodies united into one vehicle, with entrance at the sides.

When the road had been finished between Amboy on New York Bay and Bordentown on the Delaware River, the traveller between New York and Philadelphia could make his trip in this manner:

By steamboat from New York City to Amboy, a distance of twenty-three miles;

NEW-YORK & ALBANY

RAIL-ROAD.

New-York, March 24, 1842.

SIR,—

Your attention to the subject of the following proceedings, is earnestly solicited, from the interest which it is presumed that you, in common with us, must feel in restoring and maintaining the prosperity of our City.

We believe that the immediate construction of a RAIL ROAD, between New-York and Albany, is absolutely necessary, to the Commercial and Landed interests of New-York,—and that such a ROAD can be constructed, as will not only secure to us the benefits of our heretofore unrivalled position, but will also produce a large income upon its cost to the Stockholders.

The enterprising citizens of Boston, have deemed it *their* interest, to expend upwards of nine millions of dollars, to effect a direct intercourse, over an almost impracticable country, between Boston and Albany, and thus compete with us, for the trade of the North and West. Less than one third of this sum, will construct a better ROAD between New-York and Albany : and only one million of dollars, towards this amount is required from this City. Can it be that New-York, with four times the population will not make the effort, to preserve the trade which our enterprising neighbors are seeking to divert,—and which if once diverted into new channels may never return to us.

292.—The Hudson River Railroad had been commenced in 1847 as a result of the agitation begun by this address, which was signed by thirteen prominent men of the city. It was finished and equipped in 1851, at a cost of $9,305,551, thereby connecting New York with the chain of little railways extending westward from Albany to Buffalo. All of these, whose capital stock amounted to $22,858,600, and the Hudson River line, were finally combined under one corporate ownership, and unbroken railroad trips from New York to Lake Erie became possible.

By railroad cars from Amboy to Bordentown, a distance of thirty-six miles;

By steamboat from Bordentown to Philadelphia, a distance of twenty-eight miles.

The road was soon afterward completed at its western end to Camden — opposite Philadelphia — and its eastern end was carried up to Jersey City, opposite New York, finally providing an all-rail method of conveyance across the entire width of New Jersey, after that path of travel had been consistently used by men in various ways for about one hundred and sixty years.

The following description outlines the conditions attending the use of this travel route after steam power had come into use over its whole extent:[1]

"The steam-boats depart from the piers in the Hudson River near the Battery, at six o'clock in the morning in summer, and at seven in the fall and in the cold season. . . .

"A busy scene ensues immediately after leaving the dock in New-York, from the crowding of passengers to the office window to pay the fare, $3.00, and to arrange for the seats in the rail cars; on this the comfort and pleasure much depend of a party of ladies or gentlemen, and this should, if possible, be attended to immediately, before or after starting, or even the day previous . . . as the hurry and press is at times on this occasion disagreeable. . . .

"On arriving at South Amboy, the cars and locos will be found in readiness on the wharf; the ascent soon enters a line of deep cutting through the sand-hills, and continues in a barren and uninteresting region to Hubertsville, Hightstown, Spotswood, and Centreville, 36 miles to Bordentown, on the Delaware River. . . .

"The cars make a pause at the depot on the banks of the Delaware, and a change of conveyance takes place usually to the steam-boat, down the river to Philadelphia, although the rail-road is continued on the east side of the river, 28 miles, to Camden. The change in the mode of getting on from Bordentown, for the remaining distance by water of 30 miles, will be grateful, and will, like the part just traveled on the rails, occupy about two hours and a half very agreeably. . . .

"The entire and direct rail-road route that is now completed between New-York and Philadelphia . . . pursues very nearly the old-established

[1] From the "North American Tourist." New York, 1839, pp. 352-357.

revolutionary stage route, avoiding all water or steam-boat transfer from the land, and vice versa, but, in four or five hours quietly taking up the traveler in one of the principal cities referred to, at either end of the rail-road, and setting him down and transplanting him in all possible ease and luxury at the opposite extremity, a distance of 94 miles. . . . The first or six o'clock line of passengers from New-York will arrive at Philadelphia at three o'clock P. M. by the steam-boat.

"The second route from New-York to Philadelphia, leading by rail-road through Newark, Elizabethtown, and New Brunswick, . . . passes very nearly along the line of the old post-road, more in the interior of the State than the first route, and reaching Philadelphia at an early hour in the afternoon, fare $4.00."

The builders of the Camden and Amboy road were not content with the monopoly of railway travel between New York and Philadelphia obtained by them from New Jersey and already described. The road sought to further fortify its position by gaining control of a competing canal and some turnpike roads extending east and west in its vicinity. The canal,[1] in connection with the Delaware and Raritan Rivers and Staten Island Sound, formed a complete inland water communication between Philadelphia and New York. It was begun in 1831 by a joint stock company which in the same year was united with the Camden and Amboy Railroad company, and under this general management the waterway was continued and finally completed in 1838.

The connection between the railroad company and the Delaware and Raritan Canal, and between it and certain of the turnpikes in the neighborhood of the railway, was thus described in 1838:[2]

"The Company have also been allowed to take the stock authorized to be raised for cutting a canal from the Delaware to the Raritan river, and have purchased out all the turnpike companies from the one to the other, and thus secured to themselves the monopoly of the transit business of every kind during the continuance of their charter (50 years).

"It is proper, however, to add that the State has reserved one thou-

[1] Called the Delaware and Raritan Canal.
[2] In "The Traveller's Guide." Saratoga, 1838.

sand shares of the stock, amounting to $10,000 [$100,000], and has received from the Company a guaranty for the payment of $30,000 annually."

Another reference to this first of all American instances exhibiting the greed, political methods and mismanagement of privately owned railways reads:[1]

"By the terms of the charter which prohibits the construction of any other road within five miles of the one now in use, this company enjoys a complete monopoly in the conveyance of passengers and merchandise between Philadelphia and New York. The number of the former is immense, averaging during the travelling season about one thousand daily."

The three earliest railways of consequence in New England were all Massachusetts projects. They were the Boston and Lowell, the Boston and Providence and the Boston and Worcester roads. Massachusetts and the rest of New England had been a little slower than some other parts of the country in accepting the value of the new transportation system as a proved fact, and were likewise equally deliberate in the building of such enterprises after they had been determined upon. Although all the railroads heretofore mentioned — together with several others — had been created either in whole or in part, and were in operation either by steam or horse power, it was not until late in March of the year 1834 that a steam locomotive appeared in that part of the country where the travel impulse of the people had been born and whence it had spread until a third of the continent's width had finally been overrun and settled.

But when Massachusetts did decide to go ahead she undertook three important works at practically the same time, and advanced with their building at such a uniform gait that all three were finished in three years and

[1] Tanner's "Description," p. 90.

were opened for business throughout their entire extent within a period embraced by twenty-two days. The first of the Massachusetts roads to be chartered was the Boston and Lowell company, which was legally born on June 8, 1830. Both the other roads obtained legislative authori-

TRAVELLING IN THE UNITED STATES.

RAILWAY CAR.—DETACHING THE HORSES.

293.—Meanwhile the New York and New Haven Railroad had entered New York City and was using the tracks of the Harlem Railway. Permission for the physical junction had been given by New York State in 1846, and the necessary track laying was finished in 1848. Passenger cars of the New Haven line were pulled through the city streets by horses, and assembled into a train on Fourth Avenue, near the southern end of the tunnel shown in illustrations 248 and 295.

zation during the following year; the Boston and Providence being chartered on June 22, 1831, and the Boston and Worcester on the following day. As has before been said, the opinion of England that steam power would prove unreliable on railed tracks was reflected in New England for about a year after a contrary belief had been accepted in South Carolina and perhaps in one or two other American states. The laws that created the Boston and Lowell and the Boston and Providence lines contained nothing indicative of the contemplated use of steam power upon them, and only in the charter granted to the Boston and Worcester road, on June 23, 1831, was the use of steam locomotives authorized. The act by which the Boston and Worcester company was brought into existence also contained a provision somewhat monopolistic in character in so far as that particular enterprise was concerned, for it provided that no other railway extending in the same direction should be built within five miles of the route allotted to it.

Construction work on the Boston and Lowell road was commenced November 28, 1831, and the building of the other two Massachusetts lines began in the latter part of 1832.[1] The lengths of these three railways as originally constructed were as follows:

The main line of the Boston and Lowell road .... 26.7 miles
The main line of the Boston and Providence road .... 43.50 miles
The main line of the Boston and Worcester road ..... 44.63 miles

All of them were exceedingly well made for that day and generation. Two of them, indeed, were altogether too well built, for the Boston and Lowell and Boston and Worcester enterprises used a great deal of stone as foundations for the rails, and the resultant structures were discovered to be entirely too rigid and inelastic for obtaining the best results in operation. The Boston and Providence company was fortunate enough to use wooden ties from the first, thereby escaping the necessity of much

[1] The first section of the Boston and Providence Road to be completed was that between Boston and Canton, fourteen miles, in 1834. The whole road was opened for public use on June 27, 1835.
The first division of the Boston and Worcester Road to be finished was that between Boston and Newton, nine miles, on April 16, 1832. The road was completed to Needham, 13½ miles, on July 3; to Hopkinton (Ashland), 24 miles, on September 20; and to Westboro, 32 miles, on November 15, 1834. The public opening of the whole line to Worcester took place July 3, 1835.

roadbed reconstruction. This good fortune on its part was due to the shrewdness of an engineer who had been sent to England to study the newly built Manchester and Liverpool road. He detected the track rigidity produced by the use of stone in the foreign undertaking and avoided a repetition of the same blunder when he came back home to take charge of the work under his direction. The method of roadbed making employed by the Boston and Providence company furnished another instance wherein America declined to blindly follow English precedent and profited by the employment of its own ideas. In discussing the building of this and other early American railways a native student of the subject[1] afterward said:

"They were all well-built roads, especially that to Lowell, in the construction of which the Manchester & Liverpool precedents had been so closely followed that the serious error was committed of laying the rails on stone blocks instead of wooden ties. It is, indeed, matter of curious observation that almost uniformly those early railroad builders made grave blunders whenever they tried to do their work peculiarly well; they also invariably had afterwards to undo it."

All three of the early Massachusetts railways at first used horse-drawn cars on such sections of the roads as were opened for travel over short distances, but on March 24, 1834, the Boston *Advertiser* contained the following news announcement relating to the road in progress toward Worcester:

"The rails are laid from Boston to Newton, a distance of nine or ten miles, to which place it is proposed to run the passenger cars as soon as two locomotives shall be in readiness, so as to insure regularity. One locomotive, called the 'Meteor,' has been partially tried and will probably be in readiness in a few days; the second, called the 'Rocket,' is waiting the arrival of the builder for subjecting it to a trial, and the third, it is hoped, will be ready by the first of May."

[1] Charles Francis Adams, Jr., in his "Railroads: Their Origin and Problems," pp. 71 75.

SCENE IN CENTRE STREET, NEW YORK CITY, DURING THE LATE SNOW STORM.

294.—In winter time the process of making up a New England bound train in New York City was often attended with much difficulty. A scene in Centre Street, while a dozen or more horses were trying to haul a passenger car past the city prison called "The Tombs." Same period as the foregoing.

The first trip performed by steam between Boston and Newton was probably made on April 7th, on which occasion the directors of the company and more than fifty passengers enjoyed the journey. The same newspaper described the event in the following words:

"The party stopped several times for various purposes on the way out. They returned in thirty-nine minutes, including a stop of about six minutes for the purpose of attaching five cars loaded with earth. The engine travelled with ease at the rate of twenty miles an hour."

So elated were the officials over this successful test of their rolling stock that a still larger party was invited to repeat it on the following day. About one hundred and thirty passengers then crowded the cars, and they appear to have been overloaded, for the iron bars by which the cars were held together continually kept breaking, and the return was not finished until night. After this mishap several weeks were spent in improving the equipment, and on May 15th a very successful excursion took place in which six cars, containing about twenty passengers each, were pulled from Boston to Newton and back without accident. The return trip consumed less than half an hour. Two trains for the accommodation of the public were put into operation on the following day, and regular railroad passenger service in New England, therefore, began on May 16th. The advertisements published in the daily newspapers by the Boston and Worcester road at that time made the following announcements:

"The passenger cars will continue to run daily from the depot near Washington St., to Newton, at 6 o'clock and 10 o'clock A. M ., and at 3½ o'clock P. M., and

"Returning, leave Newton at 7, and a quarter past 11 A. M., and a quarter before 5 P. M.

"Tickets for the passage either way may be had at the Ticket Office, No. 617 Washington St., price thirty-seven and a half cents each; and for the return passage, of the Master of the Cars,[1] Newton."

Seven passenger cars, thronged by two hundred people and drawn by the locomotive *Yankee* were moved from Boston to Hopkinton on September 20, and on November 15 the opening of the road to Westborough was similarly celebrated. On that occasion it was arranged for trains to start from each end of the road as far as completed, and they were to meet and pass each other at the town of Needham, but a strong wind was blowing from the east that day and so one of the trains — drawn by the *Meteor* — found it hard work to fight the gale and was much delayed. The other train adhered to its schedule and had no trouble in reaching Needham on time. There

---

[1] It thus appears that the functionary now known as the conductor was at first some-times called the "Master of the Cars."

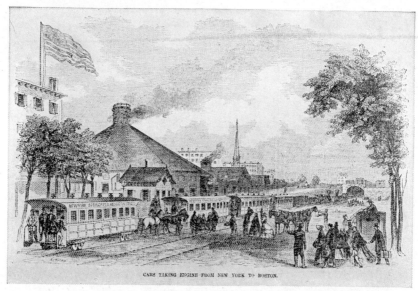

CARS TAKING ENGINE FROM NEW YORK TO BOSTON.

295.—Eventually all the cars, containing passengers picked up along the way, reached the designated place of assembly. Then the horses were unhitched, the cars were coupled, the locomotive was attached, and the completed train started on its northward journey. In the course of time a large passenger station called the Grand Central Depot was built on 42nd Street, at the farther end of the tunnel here shown, and the Hudson River and New Haven trains thereafter departed from it. These two railways were for many years the only ones which had access to Manhattan Island. All other roads were halted by the surrounding waters, and conveyed their passengers to the city on ferry boats.

it waited for a while according to the plan agreed on, but at last grew impatient and continued along the single track. After running four miles farther it saw the *Meteor* coming from the opposite direction and was compelled to stop and go back to Needham again. As a consequence of these unforeseen complications the train from Boston to Westborough required three hours to finish its journey.

The first train to go over the whole road from Boston to Worcester consisted of a locomotive and one passenger car, and the trip was made on July 3rd, 1835. That date was chosen in order that the public opening of the road might occur on the national festival next day, and on the Fourth of July each of the four locomotives belonging to the company made two round trips between the two cities, pulling eleven passenger cars behind them. More than fifteen hundred travellers availed themselves of the service offered during the first day of the road's operation for its entire length. The civic festivities invariably accompanying the dedication of such a work took place two days afterward, when a train of twelve cars drawn by two engines was run from Boston to Worcester carrying a distinguished company of more than three hundred people. The following contemporary comment on the completion of the enterprise was printed by a newspaper already quoted:[1]

"The road was opened on the 4th of this month. It has a single iron track, laid upon cross sticks of chestnut, oak, etc., laid upon rubble, but is graded in most places for two. . . . The road is 44 miles in length, and the usual passage is performed in 2½ or 3 hours, including stoppages. The cars having to stop at several towns, tends to prolong the time of the passage, though a few years since, 14 miles an hour would have been considered rapid travelling. The cars now pass each way three times a day, and their rate of travelling is so well calculated as to cause but very little delay at the meeting place in Framingham. . . . The price charged for passengers from Boston to Worcester on the Rail Road is $1.50—formerly by the stages $2.

"So great are the advantages gained, that already one of the principal dealers here [Worcester] has offered to lay a side track from the road to his own storehouse and unload his goods himself, for his permission. In fact, so great and so numerous are the advantages of rail roads, that it only requires one to witness their beneficial effects wherever they are constructed, to become convinced of their utility. . . . A person in business here informed me that he left Worcester one day in the 12 o'clock car—arrived in Boston—had 1¼ hour to transact his business—that he returned by the 4 o'clock car, and arrived here at 7 o'clock in the evening—thus travelling 88 miles in 8¾ hours;—whereas it formerly required one day to go to Boston, a second day was consumed there, and a third employed in returning. . . .

"Some of the passenger cars on this road are very elegant, and will hold from twenty to thirty persons. . . . The motion of the cars upon

[1] The "Maine Farmer," July 18.

the road is so easy that I saw a little child walking from seat to seat, as if in a parlor."

The first cars that traversed the Boston and Providence road from one end to the other moved over the line on June 2nd, 1835. It had been intended to make the trip by steam power, but the locomotive owned by the road could not be induced to run successfully and the two cars accordingly set forth behind horses. On the same day that witnessed the inauguration of railway travel between Boston and Providence there took place another important event in the annals of American travel.

THE JERSEY CITY FERRY BOAT, FROM NEW YORK.

296.—A New York ferry boat of the days when a majority of the people who entered the city were carried by such craft across the Hudson and East Rivers. The print suggests rashness on the part of numerous passengers, and small regard for their safety.

One of the purposes inspiring the building of the Boston and Providence road was a desire to lessen the time consumed in journeying from Boston to New York, and an arrangement had been made between that company and an enterprising steamboat proprietor named Cornelius Vanderbilt under the terms of which Vanderbilt was to run boats from Providence to New York in close connection with the service afforded by the new steam railroad. The steamboat man had fulfilled his share of the compact by the building of a new and splendid vessel called the *Lexington*,[1] and her first trip between Providence and New York was likewise made on June 2nd of 1835. Those Boston travellers who desired to catch the *Lexington* at Providence left Boston at two o'clock in the morning by stage-coach, embarked on the boat at Providence and arrived in New York at six o'clock, P.M. after a water trip of about twelve hours, having left Boston less than sixteen hours before. This was the swiftest passage ever made between the two cities up to that time.

As soon as the locomotive of the Boston and Providence line was put in good running order a schedule of traffic was adopted, and the hitherto extraordinary feat performed on June 2nd was in its turn eclipsed through the instrumentality of steam movement on land between the Massachusetts and Rhode Island cities. This method of journeying from New England to New York at once superseded the old manner of stage-coach conveyance and continued in use until Boston and New York were finally united by an all-rail route in December of 1848.

---

[1] The later destruction of this steamboat by fire on Long Island Sound, on January 12, 1840, was one of the most memorable American disasters of the sort up to that time. About 120 persons perished. In accordance with the custom of the period a lurid "Accident Broadside" of the calamity was at once prepared and issued for public sale. A copy of the "Lexington Broadside" is reproduced elsewhere .

That use of the new railroad was unpopular with some people, however, the following passage contained in the diary of a traveller[1] from Boston to Providence will show:

"July 22, 1835 . . . Five or six other cars were attached to the locomotive, and uglier boxes I do not wish to travel in. They were made to stow away some thirty human beings, who sit cheek by jowl as best they can. Two poor fellows, who were not much in the habit of making their toilet, squeezed me into a corner, while the hot sun drew from their garments a villainous compound of smells made up of salt fish, tar and molasses. By and by, just twelve—only twelve—bouncing factory girls were introduced, who were going on a party of pleasure to Newport. 'Make room for the ladies!' bawled out the superintendent. 'Come, gentlemen, jump up on the top; plenty of room there.' 'I'm afraid of the bridge knocking my brains out,' said a passenger. Some made one excuse and some another. For my part, I flatly told him . . . I had lost my gallantry, and did not intend to move. The whole twelve were, however, introduced, and soon made themselves at home, sucking lemons and eating green apples. . . . The rich and the poor, the educated and the ignorant, the polite and the vulgar, all herd together in this modern improvement in travelling. The consequence is a complete amalgamation. Master and servant sleep heads and points on the cabin floor of the steamer, feed at the same table, sit in each other's laps, as it were, in the cars; and all this for the sake of doing very uncomfortably in two days what would be done delightfully in eight or ten. . . . Talk of ladies on a steamboat or in a railroad car! There are none. I never feel like a gentleman there, and I cannot perceive a semblance of gentility in any one who makes part of the travelling mob. When I see women whom, in their drawing-rooms or elsewhere, I have been accustomed to respect and treat with every suitable deference,—when I see them, I say, elbowing their way through a crowd of dirty emigrants or low-bred homespun fellows in petticoats or breeches in our country, in order to reach a table spread for a hundred or more, I lose sight of their pretensions to gentility and view them as belonging to the plebeian herd. To restore herself to her caste, let a lady move in select company at five miles an hour, and take her meals in comfort at a good inn, where she may dine decently. . . . The old-fashioned way of five or six miles with liberty to . . . be master of one's movements, . . . is the mode to which I cling, and which will be adopted again by the generations of after times."

The opening of the first three Massachusetts roads completes in some of its features the picture of incidents

[1] "Recollections of Samuel Breck," pp. 275-277.

and experiences connected with travel by railway during the earliest years of that means of locomotion in America. It was inevitable that the employment of railroads in this country should first occur chiefly in those older and more thickly settled commonwealths that had also witnessed, in former days, the introduction of almost all methods of conveyance hitherto employed by the people in their movements. The first canoes, sailing-boats, dog-sleds and burden beasts had been employed along the Atlantic coast region two centuries before. Those vehicles had given way to the keel-boats, barges, pack-trains, arks, Conestoga wagons and Flying Machines, and by them the various scattered communities and their inhabitants had gradually been knit more closely together. Then came the periodic stage-coaches and the steamboats, and with their advent the people for a time believed the millennium of travel facilities had been attained. Up to that time only the covered flatboat of the interior rivers furnished a type of vehicle not beheld in active use in the East. Next came the canal and its packet-boats, destined to hold their sway but for a few years and in limited areas. Finally the steam railway had appeared, and with it a conviction in the public mind that the railed track and vehicles fitted for operation on it were destined to supplant all other methods of locomotion and transportation for a long time to come. Each previous vehicle-era had arisen in the East, reached its maturity there and gradually declined, only to be revived again in a region still farther to the westward during the years of its decay in the East. The railroad had come at last, and like its predecessors was fast fixing its grip on the older communities, whence it was in due course to follow the westward progress of all the devices it had dethroned.

CHAPTER XLV

THE records say that when the first train on the Mohawk and Hudson Railroad was ready to begin its
first public trip to Schenectady, carrying several car loads
of passengers, the captain felt impelled to announce the
impending departure by blowing a loud blast on a tin horn.
From time immemorial that had been the proper way to
start a passenger-carrying barge, a flatboat, a stage-coach
or a packet canal boat. The mere fact that a new method
of human transportation had come into use did not appear
to constitute any valid reason for an alteration in those
ceremonies that had always attended the commencement
of a journey in a public vehicle.

The occasion in question, as the story of that peculiar
day well indicates, formed one of the evolutionary links in

a long and interesting chain of railway development. When railroads first began to appear in America their actual builders had no comprehension of the extent to which the new device would be used for the purpose of public travel. In that respect the history of the early days of railroads resembled the similar annals of the canal period, although the use of railroads for human movement—in proportion to the degree of its anticipation—was destined vastly to exceed the similar utilization of the canal boat. Before the iron highways came into existence the usual stream of human traffic between the cities of Baltimore and Washington was composed of less than fifty people a day, but no sooner was a railway completed between the two towns named than it found itself obliged to provide accommodations for two hundred and fifty people each day. A similar experience befell every new road as soon as it was ready for use.

Before the opening of the rail route between Charleston and Hamburg, in South Carolina, the demands of passenger traffic between those towns had been amply met by a two-seated stage-coach which departed three times a week each way. After the two places had been connected by a railroad, and during the six months ending December 16, 1835, no less than 15,959 passengers made the identical trip by rail, and the aggregate cost of their tickets amounted to $53,819.66.[1] This was an average of more than two thousand five hundred passengers a month, in comparison to a movement of perhaps fifty people each month before the railroad was built. The number of passengers carried by the Baltimore and Ohio Railroad during the year 1835 was no less than 97,786[2]; al-

[1] H. L. Barnam's "Reply to the President of the Ohio and Indianapolis Railroad Company." Jeffersonville, Ind., 1837.
[2] Ibid.

though its tracks were then only sixty or seventy miles long and had no western terminus of population importance. During the one month of August, in 1836, the receipts derived from passenger travel by the newly opened and short steam line between the towns of Schenec-

297.—The shape of New York City, combined with its size, had already made the daily movements of its population an important problem which pressed for solution. Tens of thousands hurried southward at the same hour in the morning, and all rushed northward together again in the evening. The stages and omnibuses could not carry the throngs, and as early as 1840 there began a discussion regarding the feasibility of building an elevated railway through the streets. This is a pictorial suggestion of such a plan, published about 1842.

tady and Utica, in New York State, amounted to $43,676.91.[1]

Every new eastern railroad as it was completed furnished similar evidence of the existence of a desire for travel to which its creation gave an outlet. This was afterwards as true of the first railways of the interior as

[1] Ibid.

it had been of the East. A like experience of the early Indiana roads was thus described in 1852:

"The large and greatly increasing amount of travel upon the Indianapolis and Madison road is well understood by the public. In 1850 the number of passengers over that road was 64,986. In 1851 the number was 71,432. . . . The few weeks' experience on the Terre Haute road affords abundant evidence of what is to be the result when all the lines projected from Indianapolis are completed. Heretofore a nine-passenger stage coach each way, daily, was sufficient to accommodate all the travel between Terre Haute and Indianapolis; now the Rail Road is carrying 100 passengers each way, per day."[1]

This sure proof of the people's craving for a means of swifter travel was thus suddenly indicated with almost the violence of an explosion, and its influence upon railroads and their equipment was immediately visible. The crude tracks, engines and cars at first employed were obviously inadequate, and American ingenuity was taxed to meet the emergency.

None of the innumerable devices and conveniences used to-day in connection with railroad travel, or that now form component and indispensable parts of the cars and trains with which we are familiar, sprang full fledged and perfect into existence. Nearly all of them, on the contrary, had their origin in expedients devised by fertile brains as a result of the necessities disclosed by accidents or other unforeseen occurrences. The trip of the first train between Albany and Schenectady, for instance, demonstrated two things conclusively. It proved that railroad cars could not safely be connected by any method which enabled one of them to move independently of the others, even for a distance measured by inches. The bumpings and car collisions which took place that day due to the use of chains two or three feet long between the

---

[1] George H. Dunn's "Exhibit of the Lawrenceburg and Upper Mississippi Railroad Company," n. d. (1837).

various vehicles, showed that a train of cars must be considered as one mechanism, and that when movement was imparted to it or taken from it, the motion should be applied or diminished in a practically instantaneous manner along the entire length of the train. This particular forward step in the practical business of railway construction was discovered by the travelling public before it was realized by the railway authorities themselves, and the method that was taken by passengers in remedying the defect has been described. From that date—as rapidly as suitable processes could be devised—railroad cars were attached to one another by means that made the entire train a moving unit. The result was at first accomplished through connecting the cars by iron bars. But the iron bars sometimes broke, as happened on the Boston and Worcester road when the train was overloaded with people, and they were gradually made of still greater strength and so continued in use until the single-link coupler and coupling pin were invented. That plan in turn prevailed until an automatic locking device was designed for coupling purposes.

The few cars that had been provided by the first railroads for such slight passenger traffic as was expected proved entirely unequal to the demands made upon them. The earliest coaches were small in size and sometimes consisted of stage-coach bodies transferred to appropriate wheels. Others were specially built affairs resembling stage-coaches but somewhat larger in size, and still others were rough vehicles made of heavy timbers and lumber, possessing wagon beds which bore some faint resemblance to the lower structure of the Conestoga wagon. The flat roofs of the last variety described were supported by vertical timbers rising from the sides of the wagon beds.

BROADWAY RELIEVED OF ITS TRAVEL.

298.—A cartoonist's idea of an elevated railroad in Broadway, printed about the same time as the foregoing.

The first passenger car on the Baltimore and Ohio Railroad was a three-seated stage-coach body mounted on special wheels, with leather thorough-braces for springs.[1] This vehicle was used for a short time early in 1830, but was discarded in favor of a vastly improved car described in one of the local newspapers[2] in these words:

"The body of the carriage will contain twelve persons, and the outside seats and both ends will receive six including the driver. On the top of the carriage is placed a double sofa running lengthwise, which will accommodate twelve more. A wire netting rises from two sides of the carriage to a height which renders the top seats perfectly secure. The whole is surmounted by an iron framework and an awning to protect from sun or rain. The carriage, which is named the 'Ohio,' is very handsomely finished."

Such a car, pulled by two horses, is shown on another page. The early woodcut from which the illustration is made was drawn and engraved by the Philadelphia artist, Alexander Robb. It displays a coach containing about twelve persons on the inside, with a double sofa extending along the roof, as well as the wire net, iron framework

[1] This does not take into consideration a car "not unlike a country market-wagon, without a top," which was used for experimental purposes when only one mile of track had been laid down.—See Latrobe's "Personal Recollections," pp. 12-20.
[2] Baltimore "American," August 5, 1830.

and awning mentioned in the newspaper account here quoted. Several other early American woodcuts, lithographs and copperplate engravings, of dates from about 1830 to 1835, and which are reproduced elsewhere, show a very similar type of early passenger car. It is quite possible that the coach thus used on the Baltimore and Ohio Railroad in 1830 was adopted or copied on some of the other lines opened for traffic between the years named.

It is apparent from official records of the Baltimore and Ohio road that neither the car here described nor those that followed it during the succeeding year were equipped with springs, since the report of the chief engineer of the road[1] for the year ending with September 30, 1831, contained this comment:

"It has been found absolutely necessary to the comfort of the passengers that carriages used for their conveyance should be mounted on springs or on some equivalent elastic fixtures. The jars and concussions that destroy the comfort of the passengers become increased with a load of stone, minerals or agriculture or with any other loading having a less elasticity than persons, and although the articles of traffic may not be damaged, yet the effects upon the carriage and road will be injurious. The chief disadvantage to be apprehended from springs is their cost. . . ."

Two or three years after the first section of the Baltimore and Ohio Railroad was opened for traffic there appeared on it a passenger car resting on eight wheels. This was a large, rectangular, box-like structure with the upper-deck arrangement previously described, and with a ladder at one of the rear corners for the use of passengers in reaching the seats on the roof. It is probable that the vehicle was the first eight-wheeled passenger car built in the country,[2] and in later years the question of its priority

[1] Jonathan Knight.
[2] It was designed and constructed by the civil engineer, Ross Winans.

Elevated Railway, Ninth Avenue.

299.—New York City's first elevated railway, as it appeared when built, many years afterward.

in the feature named formed the basis of an important legal dispute which was eventually decided against the originator of the Baltimore and Ohio conveyance. Evidence was produced at the trial indicating that four-wheel trucks had sometimes been put under the little flat cars devoted to the hauling of granite on the private Quincy railroad, in Massachusetts, during the years 1826-27. So the idea of employing eight wheels instead of four as a support for the body of a railroad car had been in use before it was applied on the Baltimore and Ohio, although not for passenger traffic.

An early vehicle placed on the New York and Harlem Railroad, in 1832, was thus described by its builder:[1]

"The car consisted of three separate compartments, each compartment holding ten persons, and being entered by separate doors, on the

[1] John Stephenson. From the construction of this car there afterward grew a private car building enterprise that was identified with American railroad history for many years.

side, from a guard-rail. Seats were provided on top of the car for thirty more persons. The car was very much like the English railway coach, though it was considerably lower. It was hauled by a team of horses, the conductor remaining outside on the rail, rain or shine. The company for which it was built was called the New York and Harlem Road, running from Prince Street, on the Bowery, along the line of the Bowery to Fourteenth Street, thence along the line of the present Fourth Avenue to Yorkville and Harlem."[1]

The primitive horse-drawn passenger cars employed on the Camden and Amboy Railroad were of the general type designed for the New York and Harlem enterprise, as were also the conveyances on several other of the railways opened for traffic between 1831 and 1835.

The original passenger cars on the Philadelphia, Germantown and Norristown Railroad are illustrated in a contemporaneous picture elsewhere reproduced. They were of the familiar stage-coach appearance—although not actually stage-coach bodies placed on trucks for railway use—and were pulled by horses, since the road did not possess a steam locomotive at the time they were first employed. The unknown artist who engraved the lithograph copied herein anticipated the future when he introduced an engine into his picture, and he also depicted an English railway locomotive very similar in appearance to Stephenson's *Rocket*. This was the road for which Baldwin built *Old Ironsides,* and two contemporary pictures of Baldwin's machine also show that passenger cars of the stage-coach pattern were still used by the Philadelphia, Germantown and Norristown line after steam power was introduced on it. The close resemblance between the Baltimore and Ohio passenger car described by the Baltimore *American* of August 5, 1830, and those

[1] A car resembling the description here given is shown on the small metallic ticket or medal of the New York and Harlem Railroad Company illustrated in these pages, and also in a woodcut drawn and engraved by the artist, Alexander Robb.
Stephenson's coach for the Harlem road was no doubt contemporary with the one described in the "Railroad Journal" of November 17, 1832, and mentioned in Chapter XLIV.

of similar type shown behind *Old Ironsides* two or three years afterward, suggests that perhaps the Pennsylvania road bought some of its cars from the same man who made the Baltimore and Ohio vehicle, or else copied it. There were only two or three builders of railroad cars in America

300.—Omnibuses and street-cars. The American omnibus was a modification of the previous stage-coach, and first vehicle used in connection with the periodic transportation of city populations. Adopted by many large towns during the period between 1835 and 1855. New York City's previous stages were doubtless the first omnibuses. The street-car, which appeared in the sixth decade, was a modified omnibus adapted to the railed track principle.

during the years in question, and the one used on the Baltimore and Ohio, and here mentioned, was constructed at the shops of Richard Imlay, in Philadelphia. It is likely that Imlay also built the first passenger cars used on the Philadelphia, Germantown and Norristown line, since his establishment was so near at hand.

As soon as it became apparent that the people wanted travel accommodations in excess of those first provided, the railroad companies set about the task of meeting the demands made upon them. They began to build bigger cars, though often they adhered to the original stage-coach idea therefor. This result was obtained by retaining the old lines of horse-vehicle construction and making the larger and longer vehicle appear as though it were composed of two or three stage-coach bodies joined together.[1] The seats for the passengers were sometimes situated as before, and extended across the vehicle from side to side. The trunks, hand-bags and other luggage of the travellers were still carried on the roof, which in most cases was surrounded by a wire netting or stout wooden lattice work erected to prevent such articles from being jolted overboard. Another feature of the stage-coach which was adopted by makers of the early cars was its gaudy decoration. The railroad vehicles were similarly painted in bright colors, and were endowed with individual names emblazoned on their doors or panels. All cars belonging to the same company were painted in a uniform color scheme, to distinguish them from the property of rival owners operating on the same road. A few were further embellished by the use of national flags which flapped over their upper decks, or by the erection of small wooden cupolas. Two of these practises—the naming of cars and the uniformity of painting and decoration—have survived until the present day, but the use of flags and cupolas never became general and soon died out.

The stage-coach sort of conveyance was supplanted on the Philadelphia, Germantown and Norristown road by a longer vehicle on eight wheels, with end doors, a central aisle, and benches extending along the sides. At each end of this new type of coach was a very small room about five

[1] The cars for the New York and Harlem, and for the Camden and Amboy, were examples of this type.

STREET RAILROAD CAR, NEW ORLEANS.

301.—One of the primitive American street-cars. Some of them were of strange and curious architecture. This was operated in New Orleans about the year 1856.

BELLEW

feet long. One compartment was for the use of such feminine passengers as might wish to make changes in their apparel under conditions of proper privacy, and the other was equipped as a bar-room for thirsty men travellers. The railroad built two cars of this description, one of which was named the *Victoria* in honor of the new sovereign of the British Empire, while the other was called the *President*. They were probably put into service in 1837. Doubtless they were also the first railway cars in the world that embodied any features—except seats—which were designed with the comfort and convenience of travellers in mind.

For about a decade the construction of passenger cars varied according to the notions of those who owned them. Then they began to assume a general resemblance and to approach more closely to a standard form and arrangement, just as had been the case with stage-coaches and canal boats. The curved lines reminiscent of stage-coach bodies disappeared because of the greater cost attending their presence, and were replaced by the straight and angular lines that have since distinguished railroad cars of all sorts. The use of the upper deck for passengers continued for a short while, and the top seats on cars so built were often more popular, except during inclement weather, than the accommodations within. Side entrances were altogether abandoned. After these changes had been brought about there were no further important alterations either in the outward appearance or principal interior arrangements of the vehicles designed for human use except those consequent upon their slowly increasing size.

The seats of some of the primeval passenger cars were even more uncomfortable than the seats of stage-coaches in use at the same time, and this circumstance, in connection with the fact that few of the new rail-carriages were equipped with springs, made riding in them very uncomfortable indeed. Some of the car seats were at first merely smooth wooden boards without any backs. Such things as cushions or seat-upholstery were then unheard of. With the change in the form of the coaches and their increased size, however, came a corresponding alteration in the method of placing the seats. They were no longer built entirely across the car from one side of the vehicle to the other, but were broken into two rows separated by a long aisle extending from door to door.

When passenger cars had assumed a somewhat standard form—about 1838 or 1840—they usually measured from thirty-five to forty feet in length and had a width of about eight feet. The central aisle was quite narrow, and the double seats on each side of the passageway were so short that two people of adult size could only squeeze into them with difficulty. The roof of such a car presented a slightly concave appearance when viewed by the passenger from below, and its interior surface was scarcely more than six and a half feet from the floor. The doors at either end were exceedingly small, and there was almost no ventilation. Some cars of the 1840 type contained a small ventilating hole eight or ten inches in diameter in the center of the roof, and as time went on the use of flues slowly increased and three or four were built in the top of each vehicle and covered with tin to keep the rain out. Even the numerous windows along the sides of a car were often so made that they could not be opened. In such cases some of the flimsy wooden panels between the windows were raised instead, provided they had not become warped and immovable. During hot weather a long trip in a train so constructed was an uncomfortable experience, even though no accident or other untoward event befell the traveller. In cold weather the only means of heating the car was a huge iron stove at one end of it, into which the captain or the passengers frequently threw big pieces of wood from a box across the aisle. Fortunate

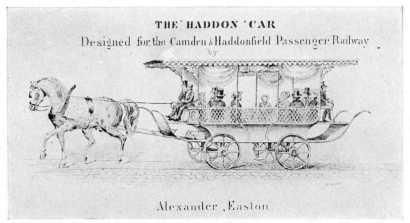

302.—A small, single horse street-car designed by Alexander Easton of Philadelphia.

was the man who on a day of freezing temperature succeeded in obtaining a seat near the stove. The fierce heat of the dry pine turned the iron to dull red, and the person who sat near it was bathed in sweat, while those in the center of the car and at its farther end were shivering with cold. But the passenger who had found an empty seat near the source of warmth was not fortunate in case the train met with disaster, for the construction of such a car with its big and red-hot stove were, in that event, the ingredients of danger not to be dwelt upon.

A night journey brought experiences equally poignant, although somewhat different in character. Both sexes had to make the best of their surroundings, and secure what rest they might while sitting erect in the narrow seats. A man hung his coat and waistcoat on one of the hooks along the wall, placed his feet on that part of the seat in front which was not occupied by the head of a fellow sufferer, reclined his own head on that part of his seat not occupied by the feet of the man behind him, and so awaited the coming of the morning. The womenfolk could not even do so much as this. They were limited to the removal of their bonnets and the closing of their eyes. During a night journey the cars were illuminated by two candles, one at each end. These were stuck in metal candlesticks fixed to the woodwork near the doors. After a number of years the roads discarded their candles in favor of a lamp of metal or glass that was suspended by means of chains or rods from the center of the roof.

About 1840—and on some roads shortly before that time—it became the practise to use iron to some extent in the framework of the seats, and to make them more comfortable by the employment of leather upholstery. Cars of this general description remained in universal use until the period of the Civil War, with almost no features of further improvement. Contemporary pictures of such railway equipment, showing both the outer and inner aspects of trains used about 1840 and thereafter, are reproduced in their appropriate places throughout the pictorial story.

The method of building the tracks of many early roads had a close relation to some of the incidents of travel which happened above them. It has been seen that for a time the rails on some lines were of wood, on which were placed thin strips of flat iron, and that the iron strips were fastened to the wooden rails by means of spikes. Now those spikes frequently became loose, thereby permitting the metal covering of the rails to get out of place. Often the loose iron strips would curl around the moving axles of a train overhead, or even penetrate bodily through the bottom of a passing car and bring it to a sudden stop even if none of the passengers within were injured by the intrusion. Accidents like this were not rare, and rather resembled in their character and effect the impalement of a flatboat on some western river by the sharp end of a sunken snag.

Every early brigade of cars employed on a road equipped with flat iron rails carried sledge hammers as part of its essential equipment, and whenever one of the rails worked loose and plunged through a car floor the big mauls were used to pound it back through the bottom of the car again. If this proved impracticable, then the part of the iron projecting into the car had to be laboriously filed off before the trip could continue. Whenever the engineer spied a loose rail on his own or an adjoining track he would stop the engine and the defect would be remedied before the journey was resumed.

For the first dozen years or more after the introduction of railroads there neither existed any way by which the position or safety of a train could be ascertained during its progress, nor any mechanical method whereby the captain could communicate with the engineer. It soon became evident that either or both of those things might frequently be urgently desirable, and so it came about that the men employed on the trains devised the first codes of railway signals. All systems of communication between the cars of a train and the engine were for a long time very crude. The cars on some early roads were equipped with ladders by which the captain might climb to the roof of his brigade and there shout at the engineer or throw something at him to attract his attention. If he did thus succeed in letting the engineer know he wanted to talk, the engineer would stop the train and find out what the trouble was. Many of the captains arranged signal codes requiring the use of their arms, hands and fingers. The waving of an arm in a certain way or the elevation

303.—Street-cars such as were first used in Boston. Except in their lesser length they closely resembled the steam railway cars of the time. Date, about 1856.

of a hand or a particular finger had a specific meaning, and if the attention of the engineer could be attracted he would usually act in accordance with the information conveyed to him.[1] But for a number of years the official relationship between the captain of the train and the engineer was not definitely fixed. Many of the men in charge of locomotives considered that their authority exceeded the power possessed by the captains and acted in accordance with such belief.

The change by which the captain acquired his supremacy over the engineer and all other members of the train crew was perhaps rather gradual in some parts of

[1] This sign language called into being by early necessities is still used, and has developed into a rather elaborate code.

the country, and may have depended upon various circumstances and conditions. But there was one event, happening in the childhood years of the Erie Railroad, which because of its peculiar character and wide notoriety undoubtedly had much to do with finally establishing the authority of the modern train conductor.

At the time in question the Erie operated only one train a day, and it ran back and forth for a distance of forty-seven miles between the Hudson River and a little town called Turner's, then the western end of the road. This train, which ordinarily consisted both of passenger and freight cars, was in charge of an engineer named Hammil and a captain named Ayres. It happened on several occasions that Captain Ayres wanted very much to stop the train, yet had no means of doing so. Hammil, in addition, was a stubborn chap who did not take those frequent backward glances over his brigade that were customary to men performing similar duties. At last Ayres was inspired by an idea. He bought a big ball of strong twine, and by means of staples he carried the rope from the rear car along the roofs of all the intervening cars to the engine, where he caused it to hang down directly over the platform on which the engineer stood. To the engine end of the rope he then fastened a stick of wood such as was used in the locomotive furnace. All this was done in the absence of Hammil. When the engineer reported for duty, ready to start his train as soon as the steamboat arrived from New York with the passengers, Ayres explained the new system to him. He told Hammil that if he should wish the train to be stopped for any reason he would yank on the string, which would cause the stick of wood to be lifted from the platform of the engine and fall back on it with a thump, and that if

Hammil at any time saw the stick jumping about he was to bring the train to a halt.

While the train was making its trip the captain decided to test his contrivance, but despite his repeated pullings on the cord there was no result. The brigade moved steadily on, and when it arrived at Turner's he found that Hammil had cut the string from off the stick. The engineer furthermore told the captain that he proposed to run the train without interference from any captain or anybody else. Next day Ayres tied a piece of wood on the string again and said to the engineer, "This thing has got to be settled one way or the other. If that stick of wood is not on the end of this cord when we get to Turner's you've got to lick me or I'll lick you." Ayres' signals during the journey produced no response, and as soon as the train came to a stop he ran forward and found the cord had been cut again. The captain thereupon took off his coat, climbed on the engine, knocked Hammil off the machine, jumped after him, and the desperate fight which then ensued settled once and for all the authority of a captain over an engineer on the Erie Railroad. After that combat the stick of wood remained in its place, and every time Hammil saw it hop from the floor of the engine and drop back again he stopped the train in accordance with the signal thus communicated to him. The story of this dispute spread among the other railways of the East, and within a few months all of them had installed signal cords on their trains. An iron weight supplanted the billet of wood on the engine, and at a still later date a bell was substituted for the piece of iron. Thus the bell rope came into use.[1]

An engineer, in his turn, often had need to commu-

[1] "How to Travel." By Thomas W. Knox. pp. 16 17.

nicate with the captain and other members of the train crew. Before the invention of the steam whistle he had tried different methods of accomplishing the purpose in view. One was the hoisting of a little flag on a pole set up on the engine, and the position of the flag would indicate the nature of the message. In case the engineer wished the crew to apply brakes to the train a great deal depended on the promptness with which the signal was detected, and a man was usually put on top of one of the cars during a trip in order that he might keep a constant eye on the engine. Another scheme available to the engineer for attracting the attention of the crew consisted in lifting the steam valve on the dome either with his hand or an iron rod. This action would permit the steam to rush out with a loud hiss, and the noise often served the purpose for which it was intended.

The first brakes on the cars were identical in principle with those that had long been used on stage-coaches. They consisted of stout blocks of hardwood, brought in contact with the wheels by means of levers operated by foot power. On the Newcastle and Frenchtown road, in Pennsylvania, the prompt halting of its first steam train was achieved in a manner still more archaic than this. When the locomotive was approaching a point at which a stop was necessary the engineer then shut off the power and sent a signal down the track by permitting steam to escape from the safety valve. Whereupon the negro roustabouts at the station would rush forward, seize hold of the engine and train with their hands, lean backward and dig their heels into the earth, and the station agent would thrust a fence rail between the spokes of a locomotive wheel. In that manner they could bring the train to a pause within a few yards.

Locomotives did not carry headlights for several years after the introduction of railroads in America. There were no such things. No night trips were at first undertaken, and the need for track illumination did not arise. The roads were so short that they could easily be traversed in a few hours, and the amount of traffic did not require their operation after daylight ceased. But when the

SCENE IN WINTER STREET, BOSTON, DURING THE LATE SNOW STORM.

304.—When heavy snow-falls made it impossible to maintain a service with the newly introduced street railways, the superseded omnibuses were brought forth again, placed on sled-runners instead of wheels, and pressed into use.

Charleston and Hamburg road had laid a hundred miles or more of track it became apparent that night travel would on some occasions be desirable. Horatio Allen, the civil engineer in charge of the line, realized that a man who was handling a locomotive in the darkness should be able to see the track ahead of him, and in order for him to do so it was obvious that a light must be shed upon the rails. Allen succeeded in solving the problem. He built a little square flat car, about five feet long, and arranged for attachment in front of the engine. On the car he spread a layer of sand several inches deep, and on top of the sand he built a fire of pine knots. The bonfire was so close to the front of the boiler that the flames were hidden from the eyes of the engineer, and their glare was thrown forward along the track. This headlight was put into use on the road, and required no further care for its operation except a frequent replenishment of fuel, which cost nothing.

Another circumstance that led to the use of railroads at night was the unexpected heavy passenger traffic which appeared as soon as the new travel method was brought into existence. The running of trains soon taxed the daylight resources of the roads to the utmost — because there were so few turnouts — and it was found desirable to conduct the freight traffic at night even on the short lines. The Charleston and Hamburg four-wheeled headlight was not generally adopted. It merely served as an incentive for further invention, and big lamps were soon attached to the front ends of night-running engines. Reflectors began to be placed behind the lamps about the year 1840, and with that device the locomotive headlight attained a form it was destined to keep for many years.

Locomotives, for a time, were made without cabs or other shelter for the engineer and fireman. Those appurtenances to the structure of a railroad engine did not come into use until about 1842, and were not adopted by all builders until several years after that date. Almost every early engine used wood in its furnace, and the fuel was carried on a little flat car immediately behind. It occasionally happened—on a long trip or because of some delay—that the supply of wood with which the trip was begun became exhausted. In such case the train came to a halt and the fireman and engineer, equipped with ax and saw carried for the purpose, dismounted and accumulated another stock of fuel from dead trees or fences in the immediate neighborhood. If wood was scarce in that vicinity and the delay threatened to be a long one, the passengers themselves joined in the work and aided in carrying the sticks back to the waiting engine.

The danger attending the issuance of sparks from locomotive smokestacks—so well illustrated during the first trip on the Albany and Schenectady road—was at once seen, though no means for abating it was discovered for several years. During seasons of dry weather innumerable fires were caused by sparks along the lines of various railroads, and it became necessary to hire many watchmen to patrol the tracks and extinguish incipient conflagrations in their neighborhood. Nearly all railway bridges were then built of wood, and a watchman was permanently installed on every structure of the sort, with several hogsheads of water convenient for his use. Finally an effort was made to prevent the emission of firebrands from the locomotives by covering the tops of the smoke stacks with wire screen, and this scheme, though it did not wholly remedy the trouble, proved so useful that it was generally adopted. A considerable number of small sparks and clouds of smoke still issued from the engine furnaces, however, and in 1848 an inventor named Townsend patented a method whereby the locomotive smokestack might be carried horizontally backward over the roofs of the cars, so that all smoke and sparks would issue at the rear of the train instead of at its front. The invention was illustrated in the *Scientific American* of that year and favorably noticed, but there does not appear to be any contemporaneous record of its adoption. Locomotives designed for burning coal instead of wood came into use a few years afterward, and the spark danger, in so far as it affected the travellers themselves, disappeared.

The origin of the sand-box on locomotives was due to a plague of grasshoppers in Pennsylvania in 1836.

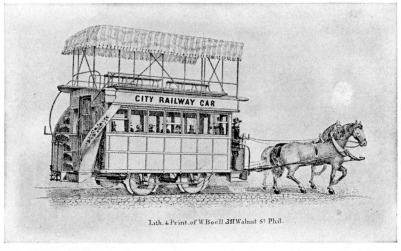

Lith. & Print. of W. Boell 311 Walnut St Phil.

305.—Another pioneer street-car designed by Alexander Easton. Similar two-story vehicles appeared for a time in various cities, but the street-car, like the barge, flatboat, stage-coach, canal boat and steam railway car, gradually assumed a settled and general type, and peculiar forms disappeared.

They covered the ground in myriads, and seriously interfered with the running of trains on the railroads then in operation. For a week or two the roads employed men to walk back and forth along the tracks and sweep the insects off the rails with brooms, but this expedient was unavailing, for no sooner were they displaced from one point than the little pests jumped back again after the track sweepers had passed. Scrapers were then installed on some engines and small brooms on others, but these attempts to remedy the trouble also proved useless, since the brooms were worn out in a short time and the contact between scrapers and rails made it necessary to run the trains at a crawling gait. Finally some genius whose name has been forgotten hit upon the plan of attaching sand-boxes to the locomotives in such a way that streams of sand should be automatically deposited on the rails in front of the wheels. The scheme proved an unqualified success, was adopted by other existing roads and used thereafter by all new ones.

At first there were no such things as time schedules and inexorably fixed moments for the despatching of trains. No road ran more than two or three brigades of passenger cars in each direction every day, and the starting times for them were often governed by the arrival of stage-coaches or steamboats from other towns. If the stage-coach or steamboat was an hour or two late, then the railroad train chose to await its arrival rather than make a trip without any passengers, or with only half the number to be obtained by the delay.

The passenger on a train never knew beforehand when he might reach his destination, and a person who was waiting for a train at some station along the line never knew when it would get there. A brigade of cars often departed from its starting-point at some usual hour provided conditions were favorable, but after it disappeared in the distance nothing could be known of its adventures until it came back again the next day. The employees situated at other places along the line knew when the train was theoretically supposed to start from the end of the road, but made no rash predictions respecting its visits elsewhere. One of the first methods employed to discover approaching trains was the setting up of lookout masts at the various stations, and when the time arrived at which a train might perhaps be expected if nothing had befallen it, the station master at that point would climb to the top of his pole by means of ladder-like cleats, take his seat in a little chair fixed at the top of the pole, and then peer down the track through a spy-glass. He would so continue to gaze for half an hour, or an hour, or two hours, as the case might be, or until he got tired and came back down to earth again. If at last he did detect the smoke of the approaching engine he shouted the glad news to the waiting people below, and thus they knew the train would probably be there within the next five or ten or fifteen minutes. If by any chance—through a pedestrian or stage-coach—knowledge had reached the station that something had happened to the train, a flag of some particular color was attached to the signal pole. By previous arrangement the meaning of such a flag was understood by all the patrons of the line, and so the news was heralded abroad.

A railroad company often announced the hoped-for movements of its trains in the advertising columns of the newspapers, but all the inhabitants of any town which boasted of a railway understood the circumstance governing its operation and knew when its trains expected to start as well as they knew any other fact of local consequence. About the year 1847, when business on a number of the principal roads had increased to such a point that a dozen trains a day were demanded in each direction, such roads began to issue regular printed schedules for the benefit of their patrons. Sometimes these printed announcements were in the shape of small pieces of cardboard,[1] and others were on larger sheets of paper called "broadsides." When issued in broadside form the time-tables were displayed in the post-offices, hotel lobbies, theaters, court-houses, and other public buildings.[2]

[1] Like those adopted by the Philadelphia, Germantown and Norristown road of Pennsylvania. A series of the little cardboard schedules issued by this line is reproduced elsewhere in their original size.

[2] Several such "broadside" schedules, dated between the years 1847 and 1852, are shown in these volumes.

CHAPTER XLVI

EARLY RAILROAD TICKETS — THE "BOOKING" SYSTEM —
ITS PRACTISE AT PHOENIXVILLE — THROUGH TICKETS
PREVENTED BY THE JEALOUSIES OF ADJOINING ROADS
— FREE PASSES APPEAR — ORIGIN OF THE MODERN
RAIL — DRIPPS INVENTS THE COWCATCHER — THE
FIRST PRIVATE CARS — SLEEPING CARS USED IN 1838
— THEIR CONSTRUCTION — THE TELEGRAPH EM-
PLOYED BY RAILWAYS — AMERICAN ROADS FREE FROM
SERIOUS FATALITIES FOR TWELVE YEARS — REASONS
FOR THE PHENOMENON — THE ACCIDENT PERIOD
BEGINS — POPULAR OUTCRY — ATTITUDE OF THE
PRESS — NEW YORK'S REGULATIONS OF 1856

THE early American practise concerning the collec-
tion of railroad fares and the issuance of tickets to
passengers varied greatly. A few of the pioneer roads
adopted the plan of printing tickets almost at once, while
others preferred different methods for collecting the
money paid by travellers who patronized them. Doubtless the first through ticket appearing in the country was
one prepared in connection with the operation of the little
seventeen-mile-long railroad from Albany to Schenectady
in 1831.[1] This ticket entitled its owner to transportation
from New York City to Buffalo, and was issued by the
joint arrangement of a steamboat company on the
Hudson River, the railway here mentioned, and a com-

[1] A reproduction of one of these tickets will be found on another page.

pany operating packet-boats on the Erie Canal. The ticket was a sheet of paper about ten inches long by five and a half inches wide. Although it called for only seventeen miles of railroad travel, its purchase carried the right to accommodations during a trip of some four hundred miles. A few other railroads issued paper or cardboard tickets in the later years of the fourth decade, and probably three or four made use of small metallic discs. These were of all sizes varying from that of a silver ten-cent piece to that of a half dollar.[1]

Those roads which did not at once adopt tickets pursued the method used in England, which was known as "booking" the passengers. Under this system the traveller paid his money at the railway station, and his name was thereupon written in a book kept by the station agent for that purpose. The Reading Railroad is the possessor of such a volume, used at the town of Phoenixville, in Pennsylvania, from the summer of 1838 until 1840. The first booking recorded in it was under the date of July 17, 1838, and for about a year the names of the various persons embarking at that place were duly set down. But after a time the exactitude of the clerk suffered a serious lapse, and he no longer identified the patrons of the road in his previous formal fashion. Instead of writing their names in his book he described them more briefly as "stranger," "lady," "whiskers," "friend," or "boy."

The style and form of the early railroad tickets varied according to the notions of the issuing company. Some of them—such as that printed in 1831 for the trip between New York City and Buffalo—were awkwardly large

---

[1] Examples of early metallic passenger tickets issued by railroads and stage-coaches are included among the illustrations.

sheets of thin paper. The metal ones were made in the semblance of pewter, brass or copper coins. But the most ordinary kind was a small oblong piece of cardboard containing merely the name of the company and the stations between which the traveller was to be carried. Very often it was glazed, and of some gaudy color such

Awful explosion on board the Helen Mc Gregor.

306.—Early American travel accidents and catastrophes. Explosion of the steamboat *Helen McGregor* at the Memphis wharf in 1830. The number of people who then lost their lives was never determined, but was variously estimated as being between thirty and sixty. It was the worst accident of the sort up to that time. From 1825, when numerous people refused to travel on steamboats, until the period of railway disasters during the sixth decade, the public sought, with no appreciable effect, to bring about a reduction of the danger which attended movements over the country in mechanical vehicles.

as red, yellow or blue. The introduction of consecutively numbered tickets—which were invented in Europe—did not take place in this country until about the year 1855, nor were they generally adopted until after the conclusion of the Civil War. Only a few of the large cities possessed pretentious passenger stations, and any intending traveller could embark upon a train, if he chose to do so, without buying or showing a ticket. In such a case he handed his fare to the captain. This condition of things resulted in a very large loss of revenues to the railroad companies through peculations, and soon after the year 1850 an effort was made by many roads to induce the purchase of tickets by passengers before they entered the cars. The method by which the roads sought to attain this end consisted in exacting a small amount in excess of the regular fare from those who paid in cash after the trains were in motion.[1] Several years after the Civil War the losses sustained by the railroads through the theft of cash paid to conductors became so serious that nearly all the principal lines of the country combined in the making of a secret investigation which disclosed the fact that an average of about two-thirds of all cash fares paid on the railroad trains never reached the coffers of the companies themselves. It was found that on some trips the conductors had received from twenty-five to seventy-five dollars in cash and turned in nothing at all. This revelation resulted in the establishment of the rule that no traveller could gain access to a train without first buying and displaying his ticket.

One reason that for a considerable time operated against the general adoption and use of through tickets lay in the jealousies of adjoining railroads and their refusal to coöperate with one another in the matters of uniform gauges and closely connecting schedules. Such was the situation over the route from Albany to Buffalo, in New York State, even after the entire distance between the two cities was spanned by railroad tracks. It was impossible to buy a railroad ticket from Albany to Buffalo

---

[1] The 1852 "broadside" schedule of the Hudson River Road, elsewhere shown, contains a request that passengers "procure tickets before entering the cars," and also states that "purchase on the car will be five cents extra."

CONVENT DU SACRAMENT.

307.—Explosion of the Mississippi River steamboat *Brilliant,* at Bayou Goula, in 1851. More than a hundred lost their lives. James Lloyd, in his *Steamboat Directory and Disasters on the Western Waters,* ascribes the *Brilliant* calamity to the common habit of using resin as fuel, in order to produce more steam and obtain greater speed. Four barrels of resin had been thrown into the boat's furnaces just before the explosion, and a fifth was about to follow them.

until the five or six railroads uniting those places fell under one control. The jurisdiction held by the captain of each train ceased when the end of his particular road had been reached. The progress of a train of cars beyond its own tracks and to the tracks of an adjoining road was for years virtually unknown, even though the thing was easily possible of physical accomplishment.

The habit of giving written or printed passes over railroads appeared about as promptly as the practise of issuing tickets. In Pennsylvania the distribution of free transportation had become widely prevalent at an early day, and the ownership of some railroads by that state resulted in the granting of free rides to every one in the commonwealth who had any semblance of reason on which he might base a request for such a favor and to a large number who did not. Of the pass-granting situation in Pennsylvania it has been said:

"The practice of giving train passes to politicians and other favored persons originated on the Philadelphia & Columbia Railroad and was carried to excesses never seen elsewhere. By the time the property went into the hands of the Pennsylvania Railroad Company every officeholder in Pennsylvania, from constable to Governor, held an annual pass on the 'State Railroad.' "[1]

Other distinctive features intimately connected with the operation of the modern railway and due to the American inventive spirit are rails of the type now in universal use, the cowcatcher, private cars, sleeping cars, and the telegraph. The modern rail, or "T-rail" as it is called, was designed by Robert L. Stevens in the year 1830. While Stevens was on his way to England, in the year named, to buy a locomotive for the Camden and Amboy road, he spent much of his time on shipboard in the Yankee habit of whittling, and since his thoughts were deeply engrossed in the subject of railroads his whittling operations followed the same trend. It occurred to him one day that a rail consisting of a line of flat iron bars was not necessarily the best track for locomotive wheels, and with his knife and a stick of pine wood he began to design possible substitutes for it. One of the models he thus shaped was the T-rail as it is now known, and on his urgent advice the Camden and Amboy company undertook to equip its road with rails of that description. At first the English iron mills avowed they could not possibly duplicate the wooden model which

[1] Sinclair's "Development of the Locomotive Engine," p. 109.

Stevens showed them, but he insisted that an effort be made to produce the desired pattern, and the task was eventually accomplished. Stevens' rails were laid by the New Jersey enterprise and proved so successful that other railways adopted them as the iron they had first used gradually wore out, until in course of time the rail pattern shaped by a Yankee jack-knife out of a pine stick superseded all others.

The cowcatcher device also first appeared on the Camden and Amboy road, and was an idea of the young machinist named Isaac Dripps — previously introduced. After Dripps had successfully assembled and put in operation the *John Bull,* which had been bought for the road in England by Stevens, he began to build locomotive engines himself, following the design of the *John Bull* in their general arrangement. During the first few weeks in which the Camden and Amboy line was operated it became apparent that wandering horses, cows and swine constituted a real menace to the safe movement of a railroad train, and Dripps devoted his ingenuity to the creation of an appliance that would enable an engine to sweep such an animal off the track. He built a low truck designed for attachment to the forward part of a locomotive, with its front end supported by two small wheels. Projecting about three feet ahead of the two wheels were several long, sharp pointed wrought-iron bars extending parallel with the track and about four or five inches above it. This formidable weapon, when pushed ahead of a locomotive, invariably impaled any animal that might be struck and prevented it from falling under the wheels of the engine. Such was the first cowcatcher, and its advantages were demonstrated a few days after its introduction. A big bull was hit by an engine thus fortified, and so firmly was he held by the metal prongs that the use of ropes and much force was necessary to detach him. The incident indicated that Dripps' cowcatcher as at first planned was even more efficient than was necessary, so the prongs were taken off and replaced by a heavy bar extending across the forward truck at a right angle to the rails. Subsequently

308.—Wreck of the Hudson River steamboat *Swallow*, whose appearance at the height of her popularity is shown in illustration No. 108. She ran on a rock, thirty miles below Albany, in 1845. Engraved from a sketch made by the artist E. Whitefield. A "Catastrophe Broadside."

this second form of cowcatcher was amended and the present variety came into existence.

Private cars were probably first used on the Massachusetts roads soon after their completion. They were of two sorts, one being simply a flat platform on which a domestic carriage or a stage-coach was securely fastened for the exclusive use of a family or party which desired to enjoy the sensation of a railroad ride without mingling with the other travellers. The other kind of private car was an ordinary railroad passenger coach chartered by private individuals for the occasion. The usual price for exclusiveness of either description was from five to twenty-five dollars — in accordance with the length of the journey — besides the regular fares for the persons so transported.

The first railway sleeping cars were adopted by railroads from canal packets and did not materially vary, in construction or outer appearance, from the vehicles used for ordinary journeys. Some of them could only be transformed into sleeping cars on one side of the aisle. The seats on that side of the central passageway designed for sleeping purposes were so built that they might be readjusted to form a lower tier of bunks, while two other tiers were arranged immediately above. The middle row of sleeping shelves was composed of wooden boards that lay flat against the side of the car in daytime and were lowered into a horizontal position at night, when they were supported by chains, or by small iron or wooden posts. The topmost line of beds consisted of a similar series of wooden shelves. Most of the early sleeping cars were equipped with three rows of bunks one above another, after the manner of the canal packets, and those who patronized them were perhaps even more cramped in their quarters than were canal passengers on a similar occasion. Only after a number of years was this arrangement discarded in favor of one providing for but two berths where three had existed before. Fifty to seventy-five cents, according to the length of the journey, was the price of a berth.

Sleeping cars were probably first utilized between Baltimore and Philadelphia, and their impending introduction to the public was discussed in an article printed in the Baltimore *Chronicle* of October 21, 1838. The newspaper said:

"The cars intended for night traveling between this city and Philadelphia, and which afford berths for twenty-four persons in each, have been placed on the road and will be used for the first time tonight. One of these cars has been brought to this city and may be inspected by the public to-day. It is one of the completest things of the kind we have ever seen, and it is of beautiful construction. Night traveling on a railroad is, by the introduction of these cars, made as comfortable as that by day, and is relieved of all irksomeness. The enterprise which conceived and constructed the railroad between this city and Philadelphia cannot be too highly extolled, and the anxiety evinced by the officers who now have its control in watching over the comfort of the passengers, and the great expense incurred for that object, are worthy of praise. . . . A ride to Philadelphia now, even in the depth of winter, may be made without inconvenience, discomfort, or suffering from the weather. You can get into the cars at Pratt Street, where is a pleasant fire, and in six hours you are landed at the depot in Philadelphia. If you travel in the night you go to rest in a pleasant berth, sleep as soundly as in your own bed at home, and on awakening next morning find yourself at the end of your journey, and in time to take your passage to New York if you are bent there. Nothing now seems to be wanting to make railway traveling perfect and complete in every convenience, except the introduction of dining cars, and these we are sure will soon be introduced."

Although the first commercial line of electric telegraph[1] had been built and put into use in the year 1844, it was not until 1851 that the device was adopted by a railroad as an aid in the conduct of its traffic. In 1848 a telegraph line had been built[2] and operated between New York City and Lake Erie, following generally the track of the Erie Railroad,[3] and in 1851 that railway began to avail itself of the telegraph in transmitting orders to its employees.

At that time the men who directed trains on the road were their own operators, and no central authority

[1] That between Washington and Baltimore, for the erection of which the Federal government granted to Morse and his associates the sum of $30,000.
[2] By Ezra Cornell.
[3] "Historical Sketch of the Electric Telegraph: Including its Rise and Progress in the United States." By Alexander Jones. New York MDCCCLII, p. 79.

LEXINGTON

309.—Burning of the steamboat *Lexington* on Long Island Sound in 1840. About 120 were lost. The fire occurred on a Monday evening, January 13, about sixty miles from New York. So primitive were the communication facilities of the country at that time, especially in winter, that the first rumors of the disaster did not reach the city until Wednesday. A relief boat started to the scene on Thursday, and on Saturday the newspapers were able to publish their "extras" with an account of the event. Another of the "Catastrophe Broadsides" that were hastily published after nearly every similar accident.

had knowledge of the whereabouts of all the rolling stock in active use. A telegraphic message coming over the wire for the information and guidance of a train conductor was received in the shape of dots and dashes printed on a narrow strip of paper. The translation of the message was a visual process. The symbols on the tape were read by the operator, who then wrote out the despatch and handed it to the man for whom it was intended. One day a conductor of the Erie line who was waiting at the little town of Addison for his train orders, noticed that the telegraph operator failed to look at the dots and dashes imprinted on the tape, but set down the words solely through his interpretation of the sounds made by the instrument. The conductor refused to accept or act upon orders acquired by him in such a manner. He further demanded that the instructions be copied from the printed symbols, in his presence, and reported the unprecedented conduct of the operator to the headquarters of the road. Fortunately the chief executive of the telegraph department recognized the importance of the discovery that electric tidings could be interpreted through their sound, and instead of being discharged, the unknown youth was promoted and became the first train despatcher in the world.[1] Within a few years thereafter all the railway lines of the country were equipped with telegraphic systems.

The acceptance of Morse's device[2] by Congress and the public, in the fifth decade of the century, illustrated the change — the awakening — that had taken place in the spirit of the people. Less than sixty years before the steamboat had been offered to the Federal government by Fitch without cost, for the common benefit. Only thirty years before Stevens and Dearborn had urged upon Congress the importance of railway building. But when Morse, in 1842, came forward with his instrument

[1] The operator who thus first read telegraph messages by sound was Charles W. Douglas, and the executive who recognized the value of the innovation was L. O. Tillotson.

[2] Morse's contribution to electric telegraphy did not lie in the discovery of scientific principles on which the process is based, but in the building of an improved mechanical contrivance for the employment of those principles. His relationship to the subject was defined by Professor Joseph Henry, of Princeton College, during the suit of Smith against Downing (Boston, 1850) in the following words:

"I am not aware that Mr. Morse has ever made a single original discovery in electricity, magnetism, or electro-magnetism, applicable to the invention of the telegraph. I have always considered his merit to consist in combining and applying the discoveries of others, in the invention of a particular instrument and process for telegraph purposes." (See "Evidence," p. 90.)

Smith, as a business associate of Morse, asked the court to enjoin Downing from conducting a rival telegraph line operating under patents issued to Royal E. House in 1848-9, on the ground that the House patents infringed on Morse's patents.

Morse's first caveat had been filed in 1837. The application for an injunction was denied. Much similar litigation was carried on for many years. In some cases Morse's requests for injunctions were granted.

Concussion of a passenger and lumber train of cars.

310.—Railroad collisions were at first called "concussions." This concussion occurred on the Portsmouth and Roanoke road in Virginia, in 1837, and the picture is one of the earliest published American illustrations of such a mishap. There was not, at that time, any method whereby a train captain could be informed concerning the whereabouts of other trains on the road.

to send human thoughts through space on a wire, over scores of miles in an instant of time, his reception was different from the one accorded to those other men. "To be sure," said the people; "why not? That's a useful contraption." The Federal lawmakers, though, were skeptical for a little while about the accuracy of the inventor's assertions and even had suspicions concerning his sanity. Senator Smith of Indiana, one of the members of Congress before whom Morse gave his demonstration in 1842, afterward wrote this statement about the attitude of himself and other Senators on the occasion in question:

"I watched his countenance closely, to see if he was not deranged. . . . and I was assured by other Senators after we left the room that they had no confidence in it."[1]

[1] "Early Indiana Trials: And Sketches," p. 413.

ACCIDENT ON THE BALTIMORE & OHIO RAILWAY

Hullmand & Walton, Lithog.

311.—An English representation of an American railway accident of 1853 in the Alleghany Mountains. Frontispiece to Alfred Bunn's "Old England and New England." Published in London in 1853.

In a further comment on the same subject and the results flowing from it, Senator Smith said:

"The privilege is not allowed even to genius in this world to inspect its own elements, and read its own destiny, and it is perhaps well for mankind that it is so. Could we lift the curtain which hides our future lives, and glance hastily at the misfortunes, the vexations, and the disappointments which await us, we should be discouraged from attempting the performance even of such deeds as are destined eventually to crown us with honor."[1]

The skepticism of Congress, so manifest in connection with the steamboat and the railroad, soon vanished in the case of the telegraph. The government appropriated thirty thousand dollars for the building of a trial line, and another forward step in national development was the result.

The first fatal accident due to the operation of a steam passenger train took place in connection with the first trip made by a passenger train in England. When the Liverpool and Manchester road was formally opened, on September 15, 1830, eight train-loads of distinguished guests and other persons were conveyed from Liverpool to Manchester, and during a pause in the journey one of the throng,[2] who had dismounted from his car, was run over and fatally hurt by the locomotive *Rocket*. Lord Brougham was present on the occasion in question, and in commenting on the accident the next day he said: "I have come to Liverpool only to see a tragedy. Poor Huskisson is dead or must die before to-morrow. He has been killed by a steam carriage. The folly of seven hundred people going fifteen miles an hour, in six carriages, exceeds belief. But they have paid a dear price."

The second fatal accident attending the operation of steam railroad trains was the explosion of the *Best Friend*

[1] "Early Indiana Trials: And Sketches," p. 414.
[2] William Huskisson, a member of the British Parliament.

locomotive in Charleston, a few months thereafter. The negro fireman who brought about the explosion by sitting on the safety valve succumbed to his injuries. Another fatality took place in Massachusetts two or three years afterward. It happened on an inclined plane of the Little Quincy road, and was due to the breaking of the rope which drew the cars up the hill. The cars fell back to the bottom of the incline, and one of the passengers was mortally hurt. This incident occurred during the building of the first three Massachusetts roads, and was one of the causes operating to prevent the introduction of inclined planes in connection with the New England roads then under construction.

Several other minor accidents characterized the operation of American railways during the earliest years of their existence, and a small part of them were attended with serious or fatal consequences. But speaking in a broad sense it may be said that the first twelve years of the history of American railroads—covering the period from 1829 to 1841—were distinguished by a most remarkable absence of heavy calamities. This condition of affairs was due to several causes. In the first place the average speed of trains during those years was slow— usually from ten to eighteen miles an hour. Traffic over the roads was insignificant when compared with the proportions it afterward assumed, and the average length of a journey was very short. There was scarcely any travel at night, and when a passenger train was run during the hours of darkness it was usually preceded by a pilot engine intended to discover whether or not the track was in proper condition. If a defect in the road did exist then the pilot locomotive, instead of the train itself, suffered the penalty.

Nearly all the accidents that did occur were due to one or another of four causes. They were either brought about by derailment, by the impalement of a car on a loose rail, by running into a stray animal, or by collision between two brigades of cars. Incidents like these were numerous and naturally resulted in much annoyance and delay to the travelling public, but it was seldom that an event such as described was attended by more serious effects. Even a collision between two trains running in opposite directions did not produce a memorable catastrophe during the first decade or more of railroad operation. A flimsy passenger coach of those years weighed less than one-tenth as much as a modern car, but the slow headway of the trains—though equipped with primitive brakes—made the operation known as "telescoping" practically impossible. Collisions in those days were called "concussions."

So the American public, for a period in excess of ten years, was gradually confirmed in the belief that really grave accidents were not to be expected in connection with railway travel. Perhaps in some degree this did not constitute an unmixed blessing. If an appalling railway calamity had occurred in America during the first decade of its railroad history it is reasonably certain that one consequence would have been a temporary check to the popular idea that iron highways were destined to supplant other methods of travel and transportation. But such a belief could only have been transitory in its effect and would gradually have worn away, whereas the unhappy event must assuredly have produced another thought whose consequences would have been more permanent and far-reaching. The occurrence of a great catastrophe during the first ten years of railway use would have emphasized, as no other circumstance could have done, the necessity of better standards in track building and rolling stock construction than those which then prevailed. No such disaster took place, and hence all American railroads, until well into the fifth decade, were so built and equipped that when the era of accidents did begin they were far

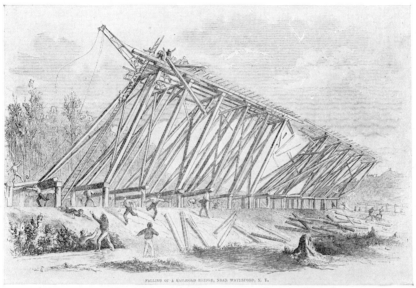

312.—Inadequate or flimsy construction methods characterized much American railway building prior to the Civil War. In this case a trestlework track could not stand alone.

more lamentable in their results than would have been the case if the rolling stock had been more substantial in character. This long continued immunity from disastrous mishaps in the formative years of America's railroad system had a still further and even more enduring effect. The use of flimsy standards of all sorts had become so firmly established, by the time the accident epoch began, that the numerous roads then in existence had invested large sums in equipment and found themselves—because of the expense involved—unable or unwilling to discard their rolling stock in favor of more substantial cars and to rebuild their roadbeds accordingly. So the early type of passenger coaches was retained, with only immaterial improvements, until long after the Civil War, and for more than thirty years the railroad history of the country was mournfully distinguished by a long series of unnecessary calamities.[1]

During the fifth decade railway accidents gradually grew both in number and in seriousness, and soon after the year 1850 they became so common and so doleful as to produce an almost national outcry for their abatement. The causes for the conditions existing after the year 1850 are easily to be seen. By that time traffic over the roads had swollen to such an extent that many more trains were in operation, and their speed had been much augmented. The average rate of movement of a passenger train during the period in question was perhaps twenty-five miles an hour, and on numerous occasions the speed developed was as much as thirty or thirty-five miles an hour. The multiplication of trains and their velocity had taken place without corresponding improvement either in the cars themselves or the roadbeds over which they ran. In other words, an attempt was made to accommodate a new generation of speed and traffic by means of an old and practically outgrown generation of rolling stock and roadbed. It is true there had been gradual increase in the size and weight of rails, and that the old signal posts had been supplanted by the telegraph, but the

[1] Some passenger coaches built thirty or more years ago, substantially identical with the type here discussed except in their greater capacity and consequent greater danger, are still permitted in operation. Their employment is morally indefensible, though still technically legal so long as it is not forbidden by laws similar to those statutes everywhere directed against the human use of unsafe buildings.

ACCIDENT ON THE CAMDEN AND AMBOY RAIL ROAD,

NEAR BURLINGTON, N.J

AUG. 29TH 1855.

313.—The Camden and Amboy wreck at Burlington, New Jersey, on August 29, 1855. Twenty-one were killed and seventy-five injured. Illustrating the small progress in car construction during twenty-five years. One of the last of the "Accident Broadsides."

mechanical improvements in the actual transportation vehicles themselves had by no means kept pace with public needs.

Accidents of all sorts—many being attended with loss of life—became so common during the years after 1850 that the illustrated newspapers of the time were constantly filled with illustrations of such events and with articles in reference to them. Nor was the travelling public entirely dependent on illustrated newspapers for a revelation of conditions then existing. So important did the matter of travel conditions become as a subject of popular discussion that numerous enterprising publishers issued what were known as "accident broadsides" after many of the tragedies attending travel by water and rail, and these broadsides—often printed in lurid colors—found wide and ready sale. Several special pictures of the sort are copied elsewhere in these pages, and a study of the ones depicting railroad accidents will disclose the character of the cars then in use and the scenes attending disasters in which they were involved.

The statements printed in the influential press of the day were as outspoken as the illustrations. One characteristic article is here reproduced in part, as a means of disclosing popular feeling and opinion during the most dangerous period of travel in America.[1] It read:

"Nobody's murders.—The railroads are insatiable. It is not enough that the cars should be the most dusty, noisy and wearisome of carriages . . . that the companies should absorb so much of the savings of honest

[1] This article was printed in "Harper's Weekly" of July 31, 1858, p. 483. It relates to an accident that had lately taken place on the Erie road. But it must not be presumed that the railroad thus discussed in "Harper's Weekly" occupied an unenviable position among similar enterprises, or that it was distinguished by any unusual excess in the occurrence of such events. The contrary was seemingly the case, for the Erie road appears to have been among those most infrequently involved in like catastrophes. The language here used by "Harper's Weekly" could with equal propriety have been applied —and at various times and by all the newspapers of the country was applied—to all the other important railroads then operating throughout the nation. The article is chosen as a typical newspaper utterance of the period because of its character as a general review of the whole subject of the dangers of railroad travel.

laborers all over the land, and never return a dollar in dividends—that the mercantile morality of the community should suffer such damage from stock speculations, and apparently respectable people come to shame by their inability to resist the temptation to swindle—all this is not enough, but every man who leaves the city by a train must cast a lingering look behind, in sober sadness, doubting whether the chances of a safe arrival are not entirely against him.

"The recent disaster upon the Erie Railroad has received very proper attention from the press; and it will very soon be time to organize vigilance committees for the protection of human life upon our railroads, by securing the prompt punishment of the persons directly and indirectly concerned. A train thunders along a down-grade around a curve above a precipice at the rate of forty miles an hour—a rail snaps—two cars are hurled off the track down the bank, and six or seven corpses and a score or so of maimed victims are taken from the ruins—the President or some other officer 'hurries to the scene of the disaster'—an inquest is held—the officers of the road swear that it was in 'good enough' condition—that the rate of speed was not unusual; that the same thing had been done a hundred times before safely; and as many other absurdities as occur to them—and a jury return, of course, that nobody is to blame. Nobody ever is. Boilers are bursting all over the country—railroad bridges breaking[1] and rails snapping—human life is sadly and foolishly squandered—but nobody is to blame. Boilers burst themselves. Rails break themselves. And it may be questioned whether the consequent slaughter of men, women and children is not really suicide.

"Take the Erie case, and look at it a moment.

"Suppose you can clearly free all the officers of the road from intentional guilt, and fix the fault upon the iron rail. There is no question that there was a flaw in the rail—that it was very poor iron. Now the makers of the rail, and the purchasers, should employ competent testers.[2] Considering the immense consequences, when rail iron is proved defective, the name of the house from which it is purchased should be widely advertised. In the present instance we learn that it was an English house. Let the public know what house, that if it be dishonest in its work it may be stigmatized; and if honest, that it may suffer the consequences of an oversight or of incapable servants. The makers of the rail are first to blame in this case, and then the buyers. . . .

"Why do the people submit to railroad accidents? Why not send representatives who shall insist that no railroad charters shall be granted except upon certain conditions of construction? Thus every road should

[1] An accident had taken place on the New York Central road a few weeks before, in which a railroad bridge near Utica collapsed under the weight of two trains and precipitated them into the stream beneath. A picture of this accident, as printed immediately afterward, is reproduced elsewhere.

[2] A noticeable increase in accidents due to imperfect or poor rails has taken place during the last few years and has attracted widespread attention. The article of 1858, here quoted, suggests that the problem in question has been calling for a solution for more than half a century.

ACCIDENT ON THE NEW YORK CENTRAL RAILROAD, NEAR UTICA, ON 11TH MAY, 18—

314.—In May of 1858 two trains on the New York Central road tried to pass each other on a double-tracked bridge near Utica. There was no collision, but the structure collapsed under the weight.

be carefully fenced along the whole route—where, upon high embankments, fences are impossible, there should be low walls, or the rate of speed diminished to an absolutely safe point—and after rails properly selected had been laid, the whole road should be garrisoned so amply that every inch should be inspected after the passage of every train by day and night.

"Of course it would be expensive—what of that? Fewer railroads might be built—what of that? Everybody knows that the first object of a projected railroad is not the advantage of any region of country, but of the stock-jobbers who originate the property and speculate in it. . . .

"The coroner's jury return that nobody is guilty of this last sad massacre. . . ."

The series of similar disasters happening throughout the country during the years after 1850 at last compelled a number of state governments to take official cognizance of existing conditions, and in several of the commonwealths an effort was made to form codes of operation under which railways might carry on their business with less danger to the public. One of the states so acting was New York, and in the year 1856 it drew up a series of rules for the purpose in question. The New York regulations exceeded two hundred and fifty in number, and as a whole they indicate the degree of care then demanded in the operation of American railway lines. They show that a train might expect to encounter an open drawbridge either by day or by night; that a difference of five minutes in time might without impropriety be recorded by the watches of conductors and engineers; that deviations from train schedules were only reported once a month; that recklessness on the part of engineers was to be presupposed; and that an engineer might run his train on the supposition that he would find another train out of its proper place at any point. Twenty paragraphs from New York's code of 1856 are here cited as examples of conditions still permitted at that day in the operation of the railroads of the country. They are as follows:[1]

1. "The Safety of Passengers is to be regarded as the highest and most important duty.
2. "All the operations of working, repairing or construction must be completely and entirely subordinate thereto.
3. "All rules, and the interpretation thereof and all contingencies where the rules do not apply, must be governed by the primary rule of safety to passengers.
38. "Flags are to be used . . . at drawbridges when open.
39. "Lamps are to be used for the same purpose after sundown.
75. "When on the road the train will be under the direction of the conductor.
98. "There shall be at least one Brakeman for every two passenger cars.
114. "No trains shall proceed towards a station where it expects to pass a train having a right to the road, unless it has ample time to arrive at that station strictly at or before the time, per time table, for the latter train to leave that station.

[1] From "Codification of Rules and Regulations for Running Trains on the Railroads of the State of New York." Albany, 1856.

118. "The five minutes, in this case, is intended to guard against a possible difference in watches.

122. "In no case shall a train leave the station unless its time shall be so arranged that it will not approach the forward train nearer than twenty minutes of the time of the forward train at any point between stations.

126. "Whenever a train is behind time, and a following train is liable to approach it nearer than twenty minutes, if between stations, a man with signals shall be left on the road.

135. "Trains that break down or have accidents between stations must immediately and always send out a man in each direction to a distance of not less than three miles, with signals.

138. "And the person in charge of a train under such circumstances must assume that there are trains approaching in both directions.

181—183. "Station masters must keep a record of the times of the passage of every train . . . and when any train is out of time, they must find out the cause of the irregularity and enter it on the record and make a monthly return of the same to the office of the Supt.

205. "It is the conductor's duty to check the enginemen when they run unsafely.

209. "Negligence or recklessness on the part of the engineman will be taken as a proof of the inefficiency of the conductor unless such conduct has been duly and distinctly reported on every occasion of its taking place.

229. "In case of accident the conductor 'may command the services of any freight, wood or gravel train, or hand-car on the road, either to forward his own passengers or to carry messages.'

238. "The engineman must invariably start with care, and see that he has the whole of his train before he gets beyond the limits of his station.

255. "He must always run on the supposition that at any station he may find a train out of place."

Shortly before the outbreak of the Civil War nearly all the illustrated weekly newspapers of the country suddenly abandoned their custom of printing pictures depicting fresh railroad accidents as they occurred, and to some extent they also modified the tone of their accounts of such accidents. Their articles became less severe in character. A somewhat similar phenomenon was also visible in the columns of the daily press, although many of the daily papers did not modify their previous position.

1060

Whether this phenomenon was due to a desire that the public be not further alarmed regarding the dangers then attendant upon travel, or whether it was in part due to a desire or influence of the railroads themselves, must now be a matter of speculation. Perhaps the altered attitude of the press at that time was caused by a combination of all the possible motives here suggested. The number of accidents slightly abated during the following years, and some time after the close of the Civil War began an era characterized by heavier rolling stock and betterment of roadbeds, and also by the employment of new mechanical devices in the shape of improved brakes and car couplers. These improvements contributed to a decrease in the calamities that had so unfortunately marked the development of the national railroad system during the previous twenty-five or thirty years.

CHAPTER XLVII

APPEARANCE OF RAILWAYS IN THE MISSISSIPPI VALLEY —
OHIO'S PIONEER ROAD — BUILDING A TRACK TO FIT
AN ENGINE — INFLUENCE OF THE "SANDUSKY" ON
RAILROAD HISTORY — THE FIRST STEAM TRIP IN
KENTUCKY — PROTECTING A LOCOMOTIVE FROM
SNOWFLAKES — INDIANA CONTRACTS THE FEVER —
JOSEPH BRUEN'S MIGRATORY RAILWAY — HOW IN-
DIANA GOT HER FIRST REAL ENGINE IN 1838 — IL-
LINOIS BUILDS A ROAD — THE STRANGE TRAIL ON THE
PRAIRIE — CHICAGO'S ENTERPRISE — THE TOWN FOR-
BIDS A RAILWAY TO ENTER ITS LIMITS — EARLY ROADS
OF THE SOUTHERN STATES — WORK OF CINCINNATI
AND ST. LOUIS — THE MISSISSIPPI FINALLY REACHED
BY IRON TRACKS — THE CELEBRATIONS OF 1857

WHILE the people of the East were aflame with
excitement over the new device between the years
1827 and 1835, and while they were enjoying the experiences heretofore described, a very different state of affairs
existed in the interior. The men of the states beyond the
Alleghanies were keeping themselves informed about the
progress of railroad building in the eastern commonwealths, and were looking forward to the time when they
also might enjoy the benefits that railroads would bring to
them. They even built a few miles of iron track previous to 1840, but such roads as did come into existence
in the West before the year named had no general effect

in altering social and economic conditions in that part of the country. All human movement and commerce, except an insignificant fragment, went on as before. And no part of the constantly swelling human tide that swept into the interior was affected by railways for many years. While the people of Maryland, South Carolina, New York, New Jersey, Pennsylvania and Massachusetts were riding behind their steam horses, the westbound population was still floating down the Ohio in flatboats and steamboats, or crawling over the face of the land in their wagons, canals and stage-coaches. A description of travel conditions as they existed in the West and on the way thither, during the first years of railroad building along the Atlantic coast, was written by Timothy Flint, a historian of the time.[1] He thus related the conditions referred to:

"On account of the universality and cheapness of steamboat and canal passage and transport, more than half the whole number of immigrants now arrive in the West by water. . . . They thus escape much of the expense, slowness, inconvenience, and danger of the ancient, cumbrous, and tiresome journey in wagons. . . . Immigrants from Virginia, the two Carolinas, and Georgia still emigrate, after the ancient fashion, in the southern wagon. This is a vehicle almost unknown at the north; strong, comfortable, commodious, containing not only a movable kitchen, but provisions and beds. Drawn by four or six horses, it subserves all the various intentions of house, shelter, and transport, and is, in fact, the southern ship of the forests and prairies. The horses that convey the wagon are large and powerful animals, followed by servants, cattle, sheep, swine, dogs, the whole forming a primitive caravan. . . . The procession moves on with power in its dust, putting to shame and uncomfortable feeling of comparison the northern family with their slight wagon, jaded horse, and subdued though jealous countenances. Their vehicle stops; and they scan the staunch, strong southern hulk, with its chimes of bells, its fat black drivers, and its long train of concomitants, until they have swept by.

"Perhaps more than half the northern immigrants arrive at present by way of the New York canal and Lake Erie. If their destination be

[1] In his "History of the Mississippi Valley": pp. 188-190.

the upper waters of the Wabash, they debark at Sandusky, and continue their route without approaching the Ohio. The greater number make their way from the lake to the Ohio, either by the Erie and Ohio or the Dayton canal. From all points, except those west of the Guyandot route and the National Road, when they arrive at the Ohio or its navigable waters, the greater number of families 'take water.' Emigrants from Pennsylvania will henceforth reach the Ohio on the great Pennsylvania canal, and will 'take water' at Pittsburgh. If bound to Indiana, Illinois, or Missouri, they build or purchase a family boat. Many of these boats are comfortably fitted up, and are neither inconvenient nor unpleasant

THE BOWERY LOCOMOTIVE, OR THE PLEASURES OF A RAIL-ROAD.

315.—The new system of locomotion was a fruitful subject for cartoonists. Their drawings, for a time, seemed to reflect the idea that the mechanism probably had privileges superior to human rights and convenience; that it was the duty of the people to escape, rather than the duty of the railroad to be careful. This cartoon followed the introduction of the locomotive into the streets of New York City.

floating houses. Two or three families sometimes fit up a large boat in partnership, purchase an 'Ohio Pilot,' a book that professes to instruct them on the mysteries of navigating the Ohio; and if the Ohio be moderately high, and the weather pleasant, this voyage, unattended with either difficulty or danger, is ordinarily a trip of pleasure. A number of the wealthier emigrant families take passage in a steamboat."

In addition to the various purposes and methods of west-bound travel here described by Flint, it should also be said that business men of the epoch whose interests took them to the West travelled thence by stage-coach or by steamboat. The stages and mechanical river craft of the interior continued to grow in importance as vehicles of movement even until the year 1845, which was some time after all the important centers in the region east of the Alleghanies were linked together by railroads.

Ohio's first iron highway was the Mad River and Lake Erie Railway, which extended from Sandusky to Springfield. The road was begun September 7, 1835, in the town of Sandusky, and by the year 1840 it had attained a length of thirty miles.[1] The first locomotive on the Mad River line was called the *Sandusky*. It had been built in Paterson, New Jersey,[2] for a little New Jersey road, but was bought by the Ohio enterprise and taken to the scene of its future labors by way of the Erie Canal and Lake Erie. The *Sandusky* was the product of an American mechanic named Swinburne, an employee of the Paterson locomotive works. The firm had brought over an English workman to design and build its engines, but the Englishman had failed in his attempt, and Swinburne volunteered to undertake the task. He made the *Sandusky* a success. It was the first locomotive west of the Alleghany Mountains,[3] and its arrival in Ohio was destined to have a more profound effect on the future railway history of the interior than was imagined by the company that had become its possessor. No rails had been laid when the *Sandusky* reached the town after which it was named, and as the company therefore found itself in the possession of a locomotive, but no tracks, it built the tracks

[1] Tanner's "Description of the Canals and Rail Roads of the United States," p. 212.
[2] By Rogers, Ketchum and Grosvenor, a firm that afterward became the Rogers Locomotive Works.
[3] The first practical, working locomotive. A diminutive model machine, hereafter mentioned, had previously appeared in Indiana.

to fit the locomotive. The gauge of the engine was found to be four feet and ten inches, and the gauge of the road was established accordingly. Nor did the influence of the *Sandusky* end at that point. Since the Mad River road was the first structure of the sort in the state, and was being still further extended, the legislature of Ohio passed a law

316.—Another cartoon of about 1840 dealing with the devastation caused by the running of railway trains through streets occupied by other traffic. A skeleton is in charge of the locomotive, and the engine bears grinning faces that are laughing at the joke played on the victims. The passengers are also unconcerned.

making the standard gauge of the state four feet and ten inches, to conform with the track already in place. The track-width introduced into Ohio in such a peculiar way was later adopted by other roads in adjoining commonwealths, thus adding to the confusion of gauges which afterward prevailed.

When the Mad River line was chartered in 1832 it was authorized to extend between Lake Erie and the Ohio River, and its course was specified in the law. The route in question was one that had been adopted nearly two centuries before, by French fur-traders and trappers, as the northern portion of their trail between Canada and Louisiana. The charter law also reserved to the state a right to buy the railway after forty years. That option was never exercised. Small box-shaped passenger cars were used on the Mad River road, and the people of northwestern Ohio were exceedingly proud of their project, but it was necessarily without much importance, except for local travel, until with the lapse of years it was extended and became linked to other parts of the growing Ohio system.

Meanwhile an ambition to possess a railway had seized the little town of Frankfort, in Kentucky, and it was advancing with a similar scheme at the same time that Sandusky was building the first Ohio road. There was no particular reason why Frankfort, far out in the Kentucky woods, should have a railroad, except that it had heard other communities were building them. And as a railroad even at that early day had to extend somewhere, in order that it might possess two ends and a time-table, it was decided to build the track toward the neighboring town of Lexington. Or perhaps it was Lexington which decided to build the road and chose Frankfort as the other terminus.[1] At any rate the undertaking was decided upon and was begun in 1834.[2] It is probable that all the engineering work performed in connection with the construction and equipment of the road was done without enlisting outside aid. The track consisted of flat strips of iron two inches wide, laid on limestone slabs. These stone rails were of irregular lengths, being from eight to fifteen

[1] Lexington, the eastern terminus of the road, was only a few miles from Boonesboro, where many of those who came into the interior over the first Wilderness Road had halted.
[2] And finished in 1839.

feet long, in accordance with the luck attending their quarrying and transportation. The strips of iron were secured to the stone rails by spikes that fitted into holes drilled in the stone. Melted lead was then poured into the holes around the spikes to prevent them from shaking loose. All this hard labor was soon found to be worthless, since freezing and thawing split the limestone. The original rails were therefore taken up and replaced by timbers.

There was at first no freight hauled on the road, and the pioneer cars built by the company were designed exclusively for passenger traffic. They were double-decked affairs, the lower compartment being reserved for women and children and the upper deck for men. Only about a dozen passengers—half of them below and the rest of them above—could find comfortable accommodations in a coach. The motive power during the first few months after the opening of the line consisted of horses, each vehicle being pulled by two animals. No steam-engine was brought from the East for a considerable time, and the first locomotive used on the road was a small machine made by a mechanic of Lexington. The engine tender was similar to the one made by Isaac Dripps for the *John Bull,* and the water hogshead was replenished from wells near the track at which the locomotive stopped when its supply ran low. Two timbers stuck out in front of the boiler, and to each timber was attached a broom made of hickory splints adjusted to brush the dirt off the rails as the engine moved ahead. The inaugural trip of the first locomotive on the Frankfort and Lexington road was intended by the company to be a long-remembered occasion, and it was. A considerable number of invited guests took their places on a line of little flat cars built for the event,

and the brigade moved off in good order, though at a very
slow speed. But when the train was approaching Frankfort a snow-storm began, and the engineer could not be
persuaded to continue the journey. He stopped the ma-

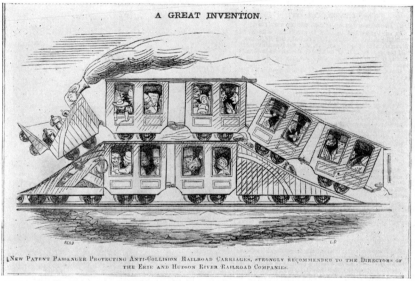

A GREAT INVENTION.

↓New Patent Passenger Protecting Anti-Collision Railroad Carriages, strongly recommended to the Directors of
the Erie and Hudson River Railroad Companies.

317.—Gradually a new feeling became apparent in the pictorial comment on collisions and other accidents, and the cartoonists, instead of making fun of
travellers or pedestrians who were killed, suggested that the railway companies find a way to lessen or prevent the growing number of accidents.
That viewpoint was thereafter maintained. A cartoon of about 1850.

chine under a shed to protect it from the inclement
weather, and those passengers who lived in Lexington had
to go back home by some mode of conveyance to which
a snow flurry did not constitute a menace. Although the
first locomotive of the road could move by its own power
and pull a number of cars behind it, it was not a success
and was abandoned. Horses were again employed and
continued in use until a more effective engine was obtained
some time afterward. By the year 1840[1] this railway had

[1] According to Tanner's "Description," p. 193.

been extended in a northwestern direction to the Ohio River near Louisville, had attained a length of more than ninety-two miles, and had cost about a million dollars. The Frankfort end of the road was distinguished for a time by a pretentious inclined plane no less than four thousand feet long, by which an elevation of two hundred and forty feet was surmounted.[1] The breaking of a rope on one occasion, and the consequent drop of a number of cars down the declivity, with serious consequences, resulted in the abandonment of the inclined plane and the conquest of the hill by a more tortuous route.

Although Indiana's first railroad—the Madison and Indianapolis line—was not begun until 1836, and not opened for use over any considerable part of its extent until 1838, an agitation in favor of railroads had begun in the state about ten years before. Governor Ray had contended for railed tracks rather than canals in 1827. In his legislative message of 1830 he had suggested the union of the Great Lakes with the Ohio River by means of a railway extending southward from Detroit through Indianapolis to Louisville. A year later he again urged consideration of the subject upon the legislature, and a committee of that body spent some time in discussing the practicability of the new transportation device as compared with the value of canals. During this same year of 1831 many of the people of Indiana obtained their first sight of a locomotive. It was not a big and practical engine like the *Sandusky*—which weighed four or five tons—but a miniature locomotive then being carried about the country and exhibited by an enterprising Kentucky showman named Joseph Bruen. Bruen moved his little engine from place to place in a Conestoga wagon, together with

[1] Ibid.　p. 193.

a diminutive passenger car and a few rods of portable track. When he reached a town of consequence he hired a man to help him take his railroad out of the wagon, and then he set it up and put it in operation, charging a small fee to such of the populace as desired to be moved by steam. Bruen's migratory railroad was a financial success, and his locomotive—although it really travelled much further in a wagon than on its own wheels—was the first machine of the sort in that part of the country.

No less than six railway charters were granted by the Indiana legislature in 1832, and about twenty-five more were bestowed before the first pretentious steam line was begun in the state. All these legal preliminaries, however, resulted in almost nothing. The private companies organized to carry out the many new enterprises could secure no capital for their proposed work. Only one of the roads chartered in 1832 succeeded in laying any tracks before 1836. The one exception was the Lawrenceburg and Indianapolis line, which was one-and-a-fourth miles long,[1] and was opened in 1834 with the usual Fourth of July celebration. The road had an embankment no less than ten feet high, another of five feet, and a cut five feet deep. It also boasted of two curves and two bridges. Its rolling stock consisted of one car, built at an expense of $222.12½, and a horse of value unknown. The total operating expenses incurred on the day of the opening were $12.62, and the net receipts were $60.00, which sum was immediately given in the shape of a dividend to the owners of the road, much to their gratification. As many as forty or fifty people crowded into the car for each of its trips, and the horse was found able to draw the load —for a very few yards—at the rate of nineteen miles

[1] The construction cost was about $1900.

1071

an hour. Doubtless the highly satisfactory gross receipts of the day would have been still larger had not the motive power succumbed to exhaustion. A barbecue also distinguished the occasion.[1]

More than four years intervened between the auspicious event just described and the opening of the Madison and Indianapolis road in 1838. The last-named enterprise was part of the ambitious but ill-fated scheme of public improvements upon which Indiana had entered in 1836.[2] The first part of the line to be built was a section of twenty-two miles between the towns of Madison and Vernon. Some idea of its physical characteristics and intended method of operation may be gained from the following contemporary statement:[3]

"The location & Plans of the road have all been adopted to the exclusive use of steam as the motive power. Of the propriety of this there can be no doubt. The cost of the horse path is thereby saved, the delay and confusion arising from the simultaneous use of both steam and horse power will be avoided, the character of the road elevated by the greater dispatch in the conveyance of passengers. . . . In the use of the rail roads constructed by the State it will probably be best for the State to furnish the motive power, leaving the cars for the conveyance of freight and passengers to be furnished by individuals or companies, from whom the State will exact the proper toll for the use of the road, and for the motive power."

The physical features of the roadbed were somewhat unusual. Two parallel trenches were dug, and in them were placed timbers about twelve inches wide and eight inches thick. Cross-ties were then laid on top of the two rows of timbers, at intervals of three feet. The cross-ties were eight inches wide and six inches thick. On top of the cross-ties were laid T-rails of the type first whittled by

[1] These features of the Lawrenceburg and Indianapolis road and of the formal opening thereof, were contained in a "Report" transmitted by the company to the legislature, dated December 5, 1834, and signed by James Blake, president pro tem.
[2] It was one of the roads chartered as a private corporation enterprise in 1832, but no work was done by the incorporating company and it became a part of the public improvement plan undertaken by the state.
[3] "Report of the Principal Engineer." December 5, 1837.

HOW TO INSURE AGAINST RAILWAY ACCIDENTS.
Tie a couple of Directors upon every Engine that starts with a Train.

318.—In course of time the new idea became more pronounced, and by the middle of the sixth decade the cartoonists, reflecting a slowly formed public opinion, were bluntly demanding that those in charge of the railways give heed to the duties resting upon them and administer the lines with more thought for safety and proper service, or else suffer the consequences of their negligence and greed. A cartoon of the last-described sort. Date, about 1858.

Stevens out of a pine stick. The rails were three-and-a-fourth inches high and came from England, where they were bought at a cost of eighty dollars a ton.

The locomotive of the road had been made in Philadelphia by Baldwin, and had been started to its destination on a sailing vessel by way of the Delaware River, Delaware Bay, the Atlantic Ocean, the Gulf of Mexico, and the Mississippi and Ohio Rivers. It never arrived. The ship bearing the important mechanism was lost at sea, and the time for the opening of the road drew near without anything to open it with. Confronted by this emergency the directors of the railway sought for another engine that might be brought to the scene in time, and discovered that the near-by Frankfort and Lexington line had a machine which it was willing to sell. It may possibly have been the one built by a Kentucky mechanic and brought to a halt under a shed to protect it from the snow-storm. At any rate the Madison and Indianapolis road bought the Kentucky locomotive, and it was somehow taken from Frankfort to Louisville. There it was loaded on a river ark, brought up the Ohio River behind a steamboat, unloaded on the shore of Indiana, hauled up a hill on the Michigan Road[1] by a multitude of oxen, and finally placed in triumph upon the awaiting rails. It was still able to move on its arrival, and in November of 1838 conveyed an excursion back and forth over the nine miles of track then finished. Among the guests of the occasion were the Governor of the state and many other officials. This event, rather than the much earlier Fourth of July celebration of 1834, is commonly reckoned as the commencement of Indiana's railroad history. Eighteen miles of track had been completed by April of 1839, and ten more miles were finished while the enterprise was still under state ownership. The twenty-eight miles built by Indiana cost $1,624,603. When disaster overtook the state's public improvement plan the road was for a time leased to a private company which operated it on a percentage basis, but the lessees were not pleased with their bargain and returned

---

[1] It is a strange incident of history that Indiana's first steam railway locomotive should have been dragged to the scene of its employment over a highway built by permission of the Indians.

the railway to the commonwealth. A second transfer to another company was effected, and finally by state aid the track was finished to Indianapolis in 1847. The road remained under joint ownership of Indiana and the operating company until 1852, when the state sold its interest and enacted a general railroad law under the terms of which competing lines might be built in opposition to any railroads then existing.[1]

The interest displayed by Ohio, Kentucky and Indiana, and the actual commencement of railroad construction in those states, had its inevitable effect on Illinois. At that time the revenues of the state were scarcely sufficient to meet the ordinary expenses of government, yet the people decided to begin railroad building on a rather extensive scale. The legislature of 1837 was the one that framed Illinois' prospective undertaking. Stephen A. Douglas was a member of the body, and he advocated state ownership of whatever new traffic routes were built. But his ideas regarding the extent to which the state should commit itself in the financing of such works were more conservative than the aspirations of his colleagues or the public. Douglas advocated merely the building of two railways and one canal, together with the improvement of the Illinois and Wabash Rivers. His plan was rejected, and in February of 1837 the legislature committed the state to the creation of more than one thousand three hundred miles of railroad, together with the improvement of various rivers and the laying out and improving of various turnpikes. The works thus proposed called for the expenditure of more than ten million dollars.[2] No

[1] Cottman's "Early Railroads of Indiana" gives much detail concerning the financial, political and economic history of the Madison and Indianapolis enterprise and other early roads of the state.

[2] Tanner, in his "Description," p. 197, gives the sum as $11,315,099 for the projected railroads alone.

319.—The railroads of the Mississippi valley and their effect. An early Kentucky railway train. Probably on the Lexington and Frankfort line, which was begun in 1834. Length of road, 28 miles. Date of engraving, 1837.

important canal system such as had been undertaken by New York, Pennsylvania, Ohio and Indiana was begun by Illinois.

Only one of the railroads authorized by the act of 1837 was actually finished by the state itself. This was the line from Meredosia to Springfield. Work on several of the others was commenced, but the financial panic made it necessary, almost at once, to call a halt in the plan that had been outlined. Track laying on the Meredosia and Springfield road was begun in May of 1837. The rails consisted of timbers to which thin flat strips of iron were fastened by spikes. A locomotive had been ordered by the state[1] immediately after the legislative act was passed, and it was shipped by water, being taken up the Mississippi and Illinois Rivers to Meredosia, which place it

[1] From Rogers, Ketchum and Grosvenor, of Paterson.

reached in September. It was put on the tracks and first operated on November 8th. The road was finally completed to Springfield, a distance of fifty-eight miles, in the spring of 1842.

Meantime a second locomotive, called the *Illinois,* had been obtained from the Baldwin works and was in operation. Trains were run from Meredosia to within a short distance of Springfield by March of 1842, and a Springfield newspaper[1] stated that "the cars ran from Jacksonville, 33½ miles, in two hours and eight minutes, including stoppages. It is believed that the distance can be passed over in an hour and a half." It is apparent, therefore, that the speed then obtained was about fifteen miles an hour. The schedule on this first railroad of Illinois provided for a train three times a week in each direction.

So scanty was the population served by the road that it could only be operated at a loss. Several annoying accidents, doubtless due to the archaic nature of the track, contributed to the misfortunes of the undertaking. The engine frequently jumped the rails, and so discouraging did the whole situation appear that one day, after an accident, the locomotive was left where it stood beside the track, and there it remained deserted for many months. Eventually it was bought by an enterprising individual who equipped the wheels with tires no less than two feet in width, and undertook to use it on the ordinary dirt roads of the neighborhood and across the prairie itself. The machine did make one overland trip between Alton and Springfield in its altered shape, but during most of the journey its deliberate movement was due to the persuasion of a yoke of oxen. The tracks it left excited the

[1] The "Journal," of March 18.

No. ___ to 8199 inclusive. 100 DOLLARS PER SHARE.

LEXINGTON AND OHIO RAIL ROAD COMPANY.

This is to certify, That *The City of Louisville* entitled to *Two Thousand* Shares of Stock of the above Institution, upon which Dollars per Share have been paid, which Stock is held subject to the conditions of paying the remaining Instalment according to the provisions of the Charter, and of forfeiture in case of non-payment; and transferable only at the office of said Company, by the said *City of Louisville* personally, or by Attorney.

WITNESS the Seal of the said Corporation done at Lexington, State of Kentucky, and the Signature of the President and Treasurer, on the *28th* day of *December* in the year 1835.

Thomas Smith President.

A. O. Newton Treasurer.

320.—The City of Louisville's certificate showing the municipality's ownership of 2,000 shares of stock in the Lexington and Ohio Railroad Company. Face value, $260,000. Several states owned railroads in the early days of railway building and numerous cities acquired a stock interest in the enterprises through subscription to them or in exchange for privileges granted. Date, 1835.

amazement of some travellers who came across them soon afterward, and so interested were they in the strange trail that they followed it to discover by what sort of creature it had been made. They found the locomotive where it had been abandoned by its latest owner. It was never again moved from the spot where it had been forsaken until it was dismantled for the metal it contained.

Even the schedule of three trains a week had been

abandoned after the final mishap, and the road was no longer operated. The legislature authorized its sale in 1847, and it was then acquired by eastern capitalists who altered the course of the line at its western extremity and opened it again for traffic in 1849 under the name of the Sangamon and Morgan Railroad.[1]

Chicago's first railway was begun in 1848. In that year the town had a population of some eighteen or twenty thousand, and a number of business men of the place resolved on the building of a railroad which should cross the northern part of the state to Galena on the Mississippi River. Construction work was begun in June of 1848 on the western edge of the corporate limits of Chicago, since the municipal officials refused to permit the railroad to enter the city. The men behind the enterprise had intended to use T-rails of the Stevens sort for their road, but the comparatively slender financial resources of the small town at first proved more powerful in shaping the physical character of the roadbed than did the enthusiasm of its projectors. Despite every endeavor they were unable to obtain sufficient funds to satisfy their desire for an up-to-date track, and so they contented themselves with some old-fashioned and second-hand strap-rails that had formerly been used and discarded by a railroad in the East. The rails were shipped by the Erie Canal and the lakes to Chicago, and there put into place. Next came the problem of a locomotive, and again the company was hampered by lack of money. It could not afford to buy a new engine, so it secured one that had been built by Bald-

[1] According to "James' Rail Road and Route Book for the Western and Southern States," Cincinnati, 1853 (p. 55), the road then had its western terminus at the town of Naples, on the Illinois River, several miles south of Meredosia, and its length had been reduced to fifty-four miles by the change made in its course.
An article dealing with this early Illinois railway, embracing the incidents here given and other facts concerning it, appeared in "Potter's American Monthly," July, 1879. The author was A. A. Graham.

win in 1836 for the road between Schenectady and Utica, in New York State. After several years of use by its first owners this engine had been sold to a new Michigan railroad,[1] by which it was christened the *Alert*. The Galena and Chicago road in turn bought the *Alert* from the Michigan corporation, and it was shipped to the third scene of its diversified labors by lake. When it arrived at Chicago the company was confronted by another embarrassment. Since the local government refused to allow the road to enter the town, the company found itself in the possession of a track on one side of the municipality and a locomotive on the other, with no practical way of bringing them together. But the authorities modified their opposition to railways in some degree and finally permitted the laying of a temporary track from the terminal of the road to the Chicago River, and by that means the engine, which was renamed the *Pioneer,* arrived at its final home. The other original rolling stock of the Galena and Chicago line consisted of half a dozen second-hand freight cars that were also obtained from the Michigan road. With the equipment so obtained Chicago's first railway was opened for business, and it was successful from the start. The excellent showing made by the early operations resulted in obtaining enough funds to push the road westward to the town of Elgin, which was reached in 1850.

The quaint *Pioneer* was fortunately preserved after its period of usefulness was ended, and to-day it reposes safely in the Field Museum of Chicago where it receives the veneration of these later generations.[2]

Michigan's earliest active interest in railroads was dis-

---

[1] Destined later to become the Michigan Central.
[2] The "Pioneer" is one of the earliest American-built locomotives that has been preserved. Its history, as above outlined, was traced by Angus Sinclair, and told by him in his "Development of the Locomotive Engine," pp. 362-366.

321.—Picture of a railroad train used by the bank of Tecumseh, Michigan, on its bank notes in 1833. Engraved by Rawdon, Wright and Hatch, of New York. The engine has a sharp-pronged cow-catcher, running on little wheels. Such a device was employed by Isaac Dripps, of the Camden and Amboy road, in 1832, and the engravers appear to have seen or heard of it. The iron bonnet on the smokestack was intended to arrest blazing embers, and was one of the schemes tried on some loco-motives as a result of the first trip of the *De Witt Clinton*.

played several years before a state government was organized. In 1832 the Legislative Council of the territory passed an act creating a corporation known as the Detroit and St. Joseph Railroad Company. It contained the following provisions:

"Said corporation, hereby created, shall have power to construct a single or double railroad, from the city of Detroit to the mouth of the St. Joseph river, commencing at Detroit, and passing through, or as near as practicable to the village of Ypsilanti and the county seats of Washtenaw, Jackson, Calhoun, and Kalamazoo, with power to transport, take and carry property and persons upon the same, by the power and force of steam, of animals, or of any mechanical, or other power, or of any combination of them."

The act also provided that the road should be completed within thirty years, and the state reserved to itself the right to purchase the railway at its first cost plus fourteen per cent. interest thereon. This road, which finally came to be known as the Michigan Central, was not begun for several years, but its construction was eventually undertaken, and by 1840 it was in operation to Ann Arbor, a distance of forty-four miles.[1] Its western terminus was later shifted from the point originally specified by the act of 1832 to a little settlement known as New Buffalo, located in the extreme southwestern part of the state. New Buffalo was for a time the western end of the road, and two steamboats departed thence each day to Chicago. By the use of these steamboats and the Michigan Central road in the West, and the chain of railroads through central New York State, it eventually became possible to travel from New York City to Chicago in about three-and-a-half days.

But the first Michigan road was not the one incorporated in 1832 and just mentioned. The first railway

[1] Tanner's "Description," p. 215. The road was finished in 1849.

operated in the state was a little road called the Erie and Kalamazoo, which was thirty-three miles long and extended from Toledo, in Ohio, to the town of Adrian in Michigan. A picture of an early—and perhaps the first—train on the Erie and Kalamazoo is given in these pages. It shows an engine named the *Adrian,* and one of the most peculiar passenger cars of which any graphic record has been preserved. In its panels, windows and façade the car conveys a slight suggestion of the ecclesiastical architecture of the Middle Ages, and indicates that the germs of art and originality had already appeared in the region where the vehicle was built.

The enterprises thus far enumerated tell of the first westward spread of the railway in the northern states during the fourth decade of the century. Wisconsin was still a sparsely settled territory, and its only internal improvements consisted of a few dirt roads and trails through the woods. The situation then existing in Wisconsin was described in 1840, by an authority already quoted, in the following words:[1] "With the exception of some surveys, authorized by Congress, nothing has been done in this section of the United States, in the way of canals or railroads." Numerous other small railways, and several having a length of a hundred miles or more, were built and opened during the fifth decade in the region north of the Ohio. Cincinnati, which was at that time the principal city of the Middle West, had its eastward outlet through a railroad extending northward to Sandusky, where the east-bound line of travel was reached.

The further spread of railways in the South remains to be considered. That part of the country, though not so restless as the North and more sparsely inhabited,

[1] Tanner's "Description," p. 220.

probably did a little more railroad building between 1829 and 1845—in proportion to its resources and population—than did the North. The early activities of South Carolina and Kentucky have been outlined. Virginia was another state displaying considerable enterprise during the fourth decade. One of the first iron highways of the Old Dominion was the Chesterfield Railroad, a line extending for about thirteen miles westward from Richmond.[1] This road was begun in January of 1830 and finished during the summer of 1831. It was primarily designed as an outlet for some coal mines, but also carried a little local passenger traffic. The Richmond, Fredericksburg and Potomac Railroad was thus described in 1840:[2]

"It is 61 miles long, and when extended to the Potomac . . . will be 75 miles long. . . . The superstructure is of the ordinary wooden rail, plated with iron, in general use in the south, and recommended on this and most other southern roads by the cheapness of timber and motives of economy. When the travel on this road, which is increasing very rapidly, shall have become larger, the company will probably find it to their advantage to lay down heavy iron rails the whole length of their road."

Among the further pioneer enterprises of Virginia described by Tanner were the Petersburg and Roanoke road, a plate-rail line fifty-nine miles long that had been built at a cost of eight hundred thousand dollars; the Greensville road, eighteen miles in length, and others that gave the state a railway system of more than three hundred and sixty miles by 1840.

North Carolina chartered the Wilmington and Raleigh[3] Railroad in 1833, and by 1840 it was in operation

[1] Its eastern terminus was really at the town of Manchester, across the James River from Richmond.
[2] In Tanner's "Description," pp. 162-163.
[3] Although by the original charter, this road was to extend from Wilmington to Raleigh, as its name indicated, an amendment to the act of incorporation in 1835 authorized it to change the location of its northern terminus. Hence its anomalous name, for as finally built it did not approach within fifty miles of Raleigh. It was begun in October of 1836 and finished on March 7, 1840.

for a hundred and sixty-one miles between Wilmington and the town of Weldon on the Roanoke River, where it connected with the Petersburg and Roanoke road of Virginia. Another of the early North Carolina roads was the Raleigh and Gaston, thirty-five miles of which had been finished by 1840. The Virginia and North Carolina roads were eventually connected on the south with the Charleston and Hamburg road previously described, and on the north with the railways of Maryland, Delaware and New Jersey, and thus a north-and-south route by rail along the Atlantic seaboard eventually came into operation.

Georgia had begun to build two pretentious lines before 1840. One of these—the Georgia Railroad—began at Augusta, at the head of navigation on the Savannah River. The town of Hamburg in South Carolina lay directly across the river from Augusta, and Georgia's early railroad system was thereby linked with that of South Carolina, since Hamburg was the western end of South Carolina's first road. The Georgia Railroad by 1845 had reached the northwestern corner of the state and connected with the early lines of Tennessee. Its first fifty-seven miles consisted of the familiar wooden rails topped by strips of flat iron, but throughout the remainder of its course the road was built, from the first, with improved T-rails having a weight of forty-six pounds to the yard. The other important early Georgia work was known as the Central Railroad. It began at Savannah and extended to Macon by a rather irregular route that followed the windings of the Great Ogeechee River. About eighty miles were finished by 1840, and its entire length of one hundred and ninety-three miles to Macon was in use a few years thereafter. Both passenger and

322.—A train on the Erie and Kalamazoo Railway, Michigan, in 1836. The passenger car, which deviates in marked degree from prevailing lines and was doubtless made in the West, somewhat suggests a large hencoop whose design was affected by the Gothic influence.

freight trains were in successful operation for a short distance north of Savannah as early as 1838, and by the final months of 1839 its passenger traffic had assumed respectable proportions.[1]

No extensive railroad building could take place in Georgia, Alabama or Mississippi during the period in which Indian nations owned and occupied large parts of those states. Georgia was the first of the three commonwealths to undertake pretentious schemes of the sort after the Indians had departed into the West, and Alabama and Mississippi followed her example a few years afterwards, as did Louisiana also. Mobile and New

[1] Tanner's "Description" (p. 176) gives the number of passengers carried by the road during the three months ending with Oct. 31, 1839, as 2,310, whose aggregate fares amounted to $5,244.85. During the same period its freight receipts amounted to $20,232.25. On the early railroads of the South the passenger traffic during the first few years of their operation did not constitute so large a proportion of the total business as was the case on the northern roads.

Orleans took up the question of rail communication with the North at a comparatively early day, and were stimulated in their efforts by the enterprise of Charleston and Savannah. Those two communities became united by rail with Chattanooga in 1849. Mobile undertook a road northwestward through Mississippi soon after the departure of the Indians, and New Orleans, by means of a route through Mississippi that eventually penetrated Tennessee and Kentucky, finally became connected with the Ohio valley by an overland line. Mississippi's first roads, however, were on the west side of the state and extended eastward from the great river that forms the western boundary of the commonwealth. The most important of these were short railways that touched the river at the towns of Vicksburg, Natchez, St. Francisville and Port Hudson. Their importance as links in the slowly developing modern travel system of the country was almost negligible until the sixth decade, during which period the South became still more active in rail installation. In that decade the hitherto isolated roads of the South were gradually joined by intermediate constructions, just as the scattered roads of the North were being similarly connected. Nearly all the early southern railroads followed the example of the Charleston and Hamburg line in the matter of gauge, and were five feet in width.

There were no railways west of the Mississippi River in 1849, and it was not until the year 1857 that a traveller could be carried from the Atlantic coast to the Mississippi River by power supplied by steam locomotives. Cincinnati and St. Louis had observed with concern, for about ten years, the growing importance of the east-and-west path of rail communication that led from New York by way of the Mohawk valley to the south shore of Lake Erie, and thence through southern Michigan to Chicago. The two cities accordingly resolved to build a road from the Ohio metropolis to the growing Missouri town which should become a worthy rival of the more northern route when used in connection with the railways that were approaching Cincinnati from the East. A road had indeed been projected between Cincinnati and St. Louis as early as 1832, during which year a charter had been obtained and some money subscribed. But at that time the plan failed to command sufficient support and was soon abandoned. It was revived in 1848, however, through a charter granted by Indiana, and Ohio's legislature passed an act in its behalf during the following year. Illinois — the third state to be crossed by the road — gave its permission for the undertaking in 1851. The important link in the national communication system which grew out of these three enactments was the Ohio and Mississippi Railroad. Surveys were begun in 1848, ground was broken in 1852, and twenty-six miles of rails extending westward from Cincinnati were in use on April 2, 1854. Then followed a period of financial embarrassment, and it was not until three years later that the line approached completion throughout its whole length.[1]

In the meantime the Baltimore and Ohio Railway had been slowly progressing westward despite difficulties of various sorts. It had reached the town of Wheeling, in Virginia, in 1853. By its use a traveller could then go from Baltimore to Pittsburgh in forty-four hours, and could reach Cincinnati by stage-coach in about four days more. If he were on his way to St. Louis he then crossed Indiana by stage-coach to Vincennes, whence he pro-

[1] It had a gauge of six feet.

ceeded over the Vincennes-St. Louis stage route on which periodic overland travel in the interior was first established.

Virginia[1] had refused to allow the Baltimore and Ohio Railroad to enter her territory except on condition that

EMIGRANTS' LINE.
FROM BALTIMORE TO WHEELING & PITTSBURG,
IN FORTY-EIGHT HOURS ! ! !
BY THIS LINE, PASSENGERS LEAVE BALTIMORE EVERY
Morning and Evening.

☞ This Road is **91 MILES nearer** to **Wheeling, Cincinnati, Indianapolis, Cleveland, Columbus, Ohio, Kentucky, Michigan, Indiana, Illinois, and Missouri,**—pleasanter, quicker; and **$1 less than any other line ! ! !**

☞ A reasonable number of Pounds of BAGGAGE will be allowed—all *Extra Baggage* will be forwarded for $1 50 per 100 pounds, and a Receipt given for its delivery. Apply at the Office,

42 FELL STREET, FELL'S POINT,

To **ABRAHAM CUYK, Agent** for Stockton, Falls & Co., and Balt. and Ohio R. R. Co.

323.—Travel to the interior in 1850. An advertisement issued conjointly by the Baltimore and Ohio Railroad and a stage-coach company. The railway did not reach Wheeling until 1853, and previous to that time travellers transferred to the coaches of Stockton, Falls and Company when they came to the place where the rails stopped. Thence they continued in the stages. "Emigrants," in the advertisement, meant Americans moving to the West.

the town of Wheeling should be made its western terminus. But the Baltimore and Ohio wanted to build westward by a more direct path, and desired to reach the Ohio River at a point considerably to the south of Wheeling. Virginia eventually saw she had made a mistake, and so in 1851 she had authorized the building of a road from Parkersburg, on the Ohio, that should connect with the Baltimore and Ohio at the town of Grafton. Such a road[2] was begun in December of 1854 and was finished late in 1856. It was practically a direct western extension of the Baltimore and Ohio, and by mutual agreement[3]

[1] Which then, of course, also included the present state of West Virginia.
[2] It was at first known as the Northwest Virginia Road.
[3] Under date of December 27, 1856.

its operation was undertaken by the senior enterprise. Thus there came into existence a rail route from the Atlantic to the Ohio River at Parkersburg, while at the same time another road was being laid down between Cincinnati and St. Louis. Only an iron link across southern Ohio still remained necessary in the ambitious scheme of joining the eastern coast and the Mississippi River. The requisite link was supplied by the Marietta and Cincinnati Railway, which was also finished in 1856.

The almost simultaneous completion of these three connecting railroads attracted country-wide attention, and the three lines themselves decided to coöperate in an elaborate celebration designed to commemorate the conquest of the eastern part of the continent by steam power. It was resolved to run a series of trains from Baltimore to St. Louis, making the trip in four days, with pauses at the principal towns and cities along the way. All the well-known men of the country were invited to become the guests of the three railways during the journey, and many of them accepted the invitation. The letter sent out by the Baltimore and Ohio road to its invited guests read thus:

"Sir:—The Ohio and Mississippi Railroad, uniting Cincinnati and St. Louis, will be formally opened on Thursday, 4th of June next. The Marietta and Cincinnati Road, which connects Cincinnati with the Ohio River near the western terminus of the Northwestern Virginia Branch of this company's road, will also be opened on Tuesday, 2nd of June.

"It is proposed to celebrate at the same time the opening of the branch road of 104 miles in length,—which unites the Baltimore and Ohio line at Grafton (100 miles east of Wheeling) with Parkersburg on the Ohio (96 miles below Wheeling), and which forms an important link in the direct line between Baltimore and Cincinnati and St. Louis.

"You are respectfully invited to make one of the company on this occasion, and to participate in the joint incidents and ceremonies attendant upon the trip."

The other roads issued similar invitations, and the party which set forth upon the journey consisted of distinguished business men from all sections of the country, city officials, editors, governors, members of Congress, cabinet ministers, and diplomats accredited to the government at Washington. Elaborate festivities marked the arrival of the trains at Marietta, Chillicothe, Cincinnati and St. Louis. Governor Salmon P. Chase of Ohio met the excursionists at Marietta, and the address delivered by him on that occasion contained the following passages:[1]

"Three distinct periods seem to mark the progress of intercommunication between the eastern and western—western once, but western now no longer—sections of our country. Our fathers were glad to avail themselves of the Indian trails and buffalo paths on land, and of canoes and broadhorns upon the water. . . .

"But the days of canoes and broadhorns, of Indian trails and buffalo paths passed away; steamboats made their appearance on the rivers, canals furnished new channels of water communication, and turnpikes and macadamized roads facilitated intercourse by land. Over the Alleghanies and westward as far as Springfield, in Ohio, the National Road was built for the accommodation of the traveller and the emigrant, and to secure the means of prompt communication in times of peril. The traveller on this road may still see, standing by the wayside not far from the city of Wheeling, a simple monument which commemorates the services of Henry Clay in the creation of this then important bond and ligament of union between the Atlantic States and the interior. The monument will crumble, the road itself may be deserted and forgotten, but the name of Clay will live while patriotism is honored and genius finds a shrine in the hearts of men.

"Turnpikes and macadamized roads, rivers and canals still supply indispensable facilities of intercourse. But a third period has begun.— The railroad and the telegraph now assert their claims to pre-eminence as the most important means of rapid communication, and the most beneficial agencies of progress. . . .

"To-morrow you will be received by the Queen City of the great Central Valley. . . . There a greater wonder awaits you. The Ohio and Mississippi Railroad, forming still another link of the American Central Railway, stretches away still westward; and the iron horse,

[1] Governor Chase's words, as here quoted, are taken from the text of the speech in Smith's "Book of the Great Railway Celebrations of 1857," pp. 174-176.

impatient of delay, is eager to bear you on beyond the ancient limits of the Republic, where the memories of the Crusades and of French empire and of French civilization are perpetuated by the name of St. Louis.

"There you may pause; but the Railroad, the Locomotive and the Telegraph—iron, steam and lightning—the three mighty genii of modern civilization—still press on, and, I venture here to predict it, will know no lasting pause until the whole vast line of railway shall be complete from the Atlantic to the Pacific. . . ."

In response to the welcome of Governor Chase the Federal Secretary of State, Louis Cass, made answer.

"Fifty-one years ago," he said, "I represented this county in the legislature of the State. At that session Fulton and Livingston presented a petition asking for an exclusive right to navigate the waters of the State by steam, and offering as a consideration to employ boats which should be propelled up the Ohio at the rate of four miles an hour. To us, who had seen nothing descend the river but the unwieldy flat-bottomed boat, and nothing ascend it but the heavy barges, poled by almost naked men, and employing six months in a trip from New Orleans, the proposition seemed so impracticable as to approach the ridiculous, and unworthy of our consideration, and we wisely rejected it. And so you see that if the result had depended upon our action, the magnificent enterprise of steam-navigation would not now be startling us with its grand achievements.

"I have just passed over the railway traversing the mountains dividing the East from the West, a work which Rome never equalled even in her palmiest days, and during the whole passage my memory turned back to other days and scenes. I have traversed heretofore the whole distance from Washington to St. Louis by this route. I travelled on horseback, and it was a painful journey of many days." [1]

Cincinnati greeted the excursionists with congratulatory addresses, parades, banquets and a display by the fire department in Market Square.[2] Cincinnati was the first American city to employ steam fire engines, and several examples of the newly invented apparatus were assembled in the plaza to demonstrate their power by throwing torrents of water into the air for the edification of the strangers from the East. During the performance some firemen lost control of a hose, and the power-

[1] Smith's "Book of the Great Railway Celebrations of 1857," pp. 177-8.
[2] Now Fountain Square and Government Square.

ful stream was directed into a carriage containing Secretary of State Cass and Governor Chase. A contemporary picture of the celebration at Cincinnati is embraced in the pictorial story.

The arrival of the trains at St. Louis, about midnight of June 4, was greeted by the thunder of cannon,

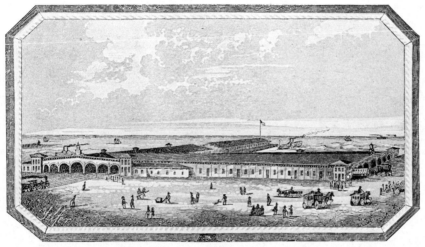

324.—Cleveland's railway station in 1854. The town then had about 37,000 people, an increase of some 36,000 since 1830. Six railroads, having an aggregate length of nearly 700 miles, already met there, and Cincinnati could be reached by an unbroken rail journey in nine hours. The trip to Philadelphia consumed but a day and a night.

the discharge of fireworks and the illumination of the city. The ceremonies on the banks of the Mississippi extended over a period of several days, and all the states and cities of the Middle West sent delegations to express their gratification at the completion of the work. During the following month official representatives of the interior states, and delegations from the principal cities and towns of the Mississippi valley made a return visit to the East, and were similarly entertained by the cities of Washington and Baltimore. On the arrival of the travellers from the West at Baltimore the mayor of that city[1] welcomed them by an address in which occurred the following passages:

"If we go back to the early explorations of Christopher Gist and Daniel Boone, not a century ago, we find the Indian watch fires burning upon the sites of what have since become prosperous and thriving cities. At the time of Wayne's treaty, about the year 1800, the whole Miami country with the exception of Cincinnati was an undisturbed wilderness, and at the same period the population of that great city did not exceed seven hundred and fifty inhabitants. In 1828, before the effect of her internal improvements began to be felt, her white population had barely reached a limit of twenty-five thousand souls.

"Until within the last quarter of a century the progressive energies of our people had scarcely found a vent in those efforts of power and development which have since resulted in so many stupendous works of skill and enterprise, which stand forth in every State as enduring characteristics of the age. Steam, gentlemen, is the active agent to which we are indebted for this new impetus which has been given to the march of improvement. . . . The voice of the locomotive is heard in the valleys and upon the hilltops; it has driven before it the redman of the forest; it has surmounted obstacles heretofore deemed to be impregnable, and has raised its shout of triumph amidst the repose of centuries."[2]

Governor Chase of Ohio responded on behalf of the West to Baltimore's welcome, and called attention to the historical relationship which existed between Maryland and the states of the former Northwest Territory. He said:

"The very existence of the State of Ohio and her sister States of the old Northwest, with their present dimensions and institutions, is due in no small degree to the persistent determination with which Maryland, during the Revolutionary struggle and at its close, insisted that the vast domain west of the Alleghanies was in fact, and of right ought to be, the common property of all the United States, and not the special property of any particular State. It was at Cumberland, in Maryland also, that the great National Road began; that first practical conquest of the Alleghanies, forever identified with the name and memory of the patriot statesman to whom his grateful countrymen are now rearing

---

[1] Thomas Swan.
[2] Smith's "Book of the Great Railway Celebrations of 1857." Part 2; pp. 62-63. The Baltimore celebration took place July 18th.

another monument amid the green fields of his beloved Ashland. And now you have made us your neighbors, and invited us into your midst by the great Railroad over which we have come hither. . . .

"No one, Mr. Mayor, who thinks at all of the westward progress already achieved by the railroads which form this American Central Line, can help anticipating the time when it shall reach the Pacific. How many years ago was it that Oliver Evans declared that the child was already born who would go from Baltimore to Boston in twenty-four hours? Many then thought him crazy. He only thought himself bold. But his anticipation lagged far behind the reality. As I was borne along, day before yesterday, from our State Capital to this city, in twenty-two hours, over great rivers and lofty mountains . . . I thought of Oliver Evans, and wondered how old is now the man who shall yet go from Baltimore to San Francisco in five days by rail. Perhaps it was a little presumptuous, but I did actually fancy myself hurled along, with shriek and puff and clatter, through the defiles of the Rocky Mountains, across the plains of the Great Basin, under or over the rugged summits of the Sierra Nevada, until the Bay of San Francisco flung back under my eye the glances of the sun. I hope, Mr. Mayor, I shall have the pleasure of meeting you at the celebration of the opening of the Atlantic and Pacific road, to which I trust the people of California will invite us all."

With the completion of the steam highway between Baltimore and St. Louis the Atlantic coast region and the Mississippi River were connected by rail. After the iron tracks had reached the great river of the interior valley, extensive railway construction toward the West paused for a time as though to gather strength for the final effort that was destined to carry it for the remainder of the distance across the continent. Active interest in a proposed railroad to the Pacific had been visible for more than a decade, but seven years were still to elapse before the plans for a trans-continental road were to assume concrete form and make its building an immediate certainty.

CHAPTER XLVIII

GENERAL VIEW OF TRAVEL CONDITIONS EAST OF THE MIS-
SISSIPPI JUST BEFORE THE GREAT OVERLAND RUSH TO
THE FAR WEST — A CONFUSING AND CHAOTIC HODGE-
PODGE OF STAGE-COACHES, STEAMBOATS, CANALS AND
LITTLE RAILWAYS — ONLY TWO WEEKS REQUIRED FOR
AN EXTENSIVE TRIP IN THE REGION — MORE SYMP-
TOMS OF IMPROPER RAILWAY PRACTISES APPEAR —
FRAUDS COMMITTED ON TRAVELLERS — COSTS OF
VARIOUS JOURNEYS AND THE TIME CONSUMED BY
THEM — CONDITIONS IN THE SOUTH AND MIDDLE
WEST — FROM BALTIMORE TO NEW ORLEANS IN
SEVEN DAYS, BY MEANS OF FIVE RAILROADS, TWO
STEAMBOATS AND TWO STAGE-COACHES, AT A COST OF
$62.50

BY the year 1848 about half of the continental width
had been overrun and permanently settled by the
white race. All that part of the country from the Great
Lakes to the Gulf of Mexico, and from the Atlantic coast
to the western part of Missouri was occupied by established communities and an active, restless, rapidly growing population. Nearly a hundred little railroads, from
five miles to a hundred and fifty miles long were scattered
over the eastern states and a score or more of similar roads
were likewise in actual operation in Ohio, Kentucky,
Indiana, Illinois, Michigan, and the interior commonwealths of the South. The navigable streams of the East

were dotted with steamboats, and nearly six hundred such craft[1] were busy on the Ohio, Mississippi and other interior rivers. These were being blown up, burned, sunk by snags or otherwise destroyed at the rate of a hundred or more a year, and were being replaced just as rapidly. A thousand stage-coaches ceaselessly rolled over the turnpikes between the cities and towns. The nation's facilities for communication had so multiplied and increased in excellence that with good luck a traveller could make any ordinary long journey in a week's time, and but little more than two weeks were necessary, under favorable circumstances, in accomplishing the most extensive trip possible within the limits of the country just defined.

If a man wanted to wander from upper New England to the farthest edge of Missouri, for instance, he could get to New York, Philadelphia or Baltimore by stage-coach and sailing-boat in four or five days, and to Pittsburgh by rail, canal and stage-coach in three days more. He could then reach St. Louis on a steamboat in four days, and by the end of the second week be nearly at his destination, having perhaps made the trip across Missouri on horseback. Such an expedition was about the most protracted that could be undertaken at the time within the settled limits of the country. A traveller could go from Philadelphia to New Orleans over the eastern route by means of railway cars and stage-coaches in a week, at a cost of $94 exclusive of food and lodging, or by way of Pittsburgh and the rivers in nine or ten days, for $36. Land conveyances were popular, notwithstanding the cheapness of water transportation, because they were believed to

[1] According to the list embraced in James Hall's "The West; Its Commerce and Navigation": Cincinnati, 1848.

325.—The completion of each new railroad which extended a little farther toward the Mississippi was the occasion of a public celebration. Ticket to a reception given in Meadville, Pennsylvania, in honor of two foreign capitalists who had helped to build an American railway.

offer the traveller a considerably better chance of getting to the end of his trip without loss of life or limb. The countless accidents to river boats caused many people to avoid them altogether.

The effects of the disastrous panic of ten years before had disappeared, and the country was prosperous. Fifteen or sixteen years of experience with railways had been sufficient to prove their value, and money was preparing to venture bravely in the iron highways. An era of extensive railroad building was about to begin, and many enterprises of the sort were being organized in every occupied part of the republic. But there was no more financial delirium; no new "railroad craze" exciting the public as a mass. Though the results of the crash of 1837-1838 had vanished its memory still remained as a warning, and some of the new highways were planned and pushed forward in a more practical way than had characterized similar work in the former period of inflated credit and wild popular speculation. The bulk of the people not only saw the urgent need for better railway facilities, but also recognized the need of sanity in their creation.

At about this time, however, there likewise appeared the first outward symptoms of an unfortunate condition that was destined to become much more prominent as the years went on, and that has injuriously affected the railway system of the country since the period mentioned. Although the people as a whole had cast out their mania and viewed the subjects of railroad construction and administration with saner eyes, a small but influential portion of the population did not follow their example. Those avaricious men who represented, in the economic and political affairs of their day, the influences which these later times have come to define as "predatory wealth" and "special privilege," were beginning to recognize the opportunities that would lie within their grasp if they could control so vital a portion of the nation's industrial fabric as the railways were obviously destined to become. They caught glimpses of the power that would be theirs if they built, operated and manipulated railways as gigantic weapons, rather than as agencies of public benefit which would methodically aid in the creation of new wealth through the operation of those processes they were primarily designed to perform.

To characters so warped, and to able minds so inclined, the lure was irresistible and the result was sure. Thus began the extensive practise of building railways with the object of acquiring money through their construction rather than by their later efficient operation. One common method by which this purpose was attained was for the originators of the enterprise—acting as its directors—to award to themselves (separately organized as a construction company) a contract for the building of the line, paying to themselves for their work as contractors the amount obtained for the capital stock bought by the public. A considerable part of the sum so appropriated would then be diverted from its legitimate use, and inferior equipment bought with the remainder. Thus the road would not only start upon its career with a debt greater than the value of its assets, but would also be compelled to use part of its earnings each year indefinitely thereafter to pay interest on money never employed in its creation. In order to meet obligations thus dishonestly placed upon it, a road so built would be compelled to fix its rates for service at a higher point than should have been the case. Out of practises such as these there later grew the widespread railway habit of issuing large dividends of new capital stock for which the issuing roads received no recompense.[1] Such issues still further increased the debts of the companies, added more interest charges to their yearly burdens and resulted in additional advances in the rates they were compelled to charge as the price of their services.

Another external symptom of the deep-seated disease which attacked the railways of the country was the practise, long universally followed by their owners and manipulators, of granting secret concessions to favorites. This purpose was achieved through the bestowal of their service at a reduced price, or for no price at all. Those who were not so unfairly favored had to bear the burden.

[1] A process that eventually came to be called "cutting a melon."

A third manifestation of the malady sometimes consisted in the dishonest manipulation of railways through their combination; a process designed to create one big and new company unit out of two or more small pre-existing units. Such an operation was often accompanied by intricate financial practises, obscure to the lay mind, but which usually had one common result. The new railroad company thus evolved nearly always found itself weighed down by a greater debt than the sum of all the previous debts of its constituent parts, and the amount represented by the discrepancy was the profit of the avaricious ones. The public did not object to the physical and operating amalgamation of such railroads as were involved in unifications of the sort, for such unions of previous separate, short and often hostile lines were exceedingly desirable and advantageous in so far as they contributed to more expeditious or safer transportation facilities. In that respect they improved railroad travel and traffic as much as the removal of a sand-bar and a thousand snags improved the navigation of a river. But the people did look askance at the mounting debts, unrepresented by a corresponding increase in assets, and at the greater annual interest obligations which they had to pay in the shape of correspondingly larger charges for service.

And, finally, a fourth symptom of the disease incurred by the railways through their contact with the special privilege of former days was their enforced and corrupt association with the political affairs of the republic, and of its states and cities.

The possibilities that lay in all these things were glimpsed at an early period, and tests made by the discoverers demonstrated the soundness of their judgment.

A long continued carnival of wrong then began, and the result is familiar history. An unknown fictitious amount was added to the legal debt of the national transportation fabric,[1] colossal fortunes were built up by complicated swindle and theft,[2] the public service was corrupted, and private control, maintenance and operation of railways in the United States finally collapsed as a consequence of wrong-doing. The existing system of ownership and control did not contain within itself, or at least did not display, the elements essential to its moral rehabilitation and so the Federal government finally found it necessary to step in and undertake, with respect to the railroads of the country, those functions which ordinarily pertain to the ownership and administration of a legitimate, honestly conducted business enterprise.

Development of the modern traffic system, at the close of the fifth decade, was not going ahead in accordance with any comprehensive plan based on a view of the whole country and its requirements, but was still largely dictated by neighborhood considerations. The day was passing in which growth of that broader sort could be planned in all its features as a coherent, well balanced, continental undertaking and carried out, in all its ramifications, as the chief national work. Local impulse had been the original or controlling factor in a considerable part of such advancement up to that time.[3] Too much had been done hastily; too many standards of construction had been used; too much rivalry and jealousy had entered as governing motives into the various projects; too narrow horizons

---

[1] Some approximate idea of the sum may perhaps be obtained, about ten years hence, through the Governmental investigation lately begun into the financial history and present physical value of the railroads of the country.

[2] In which process the manipulation of the stock market was doubtless the principal factor.

[3] Although by no means in all of it. Such enterprises as the National Road and the Erie Canal had a broader foundation than mere local needs or desires.

326.—The Ohio and Mississippi Railroad was finished between Cincinnati and St. Louis in 1857, thus bringing the great central river and St. Louis into uninterrupted rail communication with the Atlantic coast cities. The event was attended by general popular rejoicing in the Middle West. In Cincinnati the city's fire department assembled in Market Square, as here shown, and threw water into the air. St. Louis held a big torch-light procession and fired one hundred guns. The first west-bound train was greeted with enormous enthusiasm along the way.

had influenced their creation and limited their usefulness. The needs of the various parts of the country were too divergent, or else altered too swiftly, to make it possible for all the new highways of movement to act in substantial harmony or be promptly welded into an economic machine purposely designed to furnish a maximum of accommodation to the public. The result of these conditions, under which the modern transportation system of the country came into being, and by which it was for a time so unfortunately though inevitably influenced, was a hodge-podge of facilities originally created with no thought of their common action for the people's benefit,

1103

and whose coöperation, when it did exist, was at first usually compelled by popular demand rather than foreseen and voluntarily undertaken. After a few years of mad scramble in all sorts of construction, and of piecemeal and unrelated work it had become too late to alter the conditions brought about by such methods, and the consequences of them were deeply stamped for a long time on the national life.

The fight by which railroads overwhelmed the canals and destroyed many of them, instead of recognizing the ultimate value of the two highways to each other, was one outcome of the jealousy and shortsightedness engendered by those conditions under which the modern era in transportation began. So, also, was the similar hostility manifested for a time by the railroads—though less openly—to the improvement of wagon roads and to river traffic. To-day many of the railways are systematically, and at large monetary cost, educating the people in the value of better wagon roads and are even beginning to suggest the resuscitation of the canal system and its extension, after the method used by France, in those parts of the United States to which that process is adaptable.

Nor did the virtual disappearance of the stage-coach, the curtailment of the canal system and substantial abandonment of the rivers, mark the end of a period of jealousy and hostility. After the railways had become dominant among the country's highways they began to fight among themselves, and for nearly two generations failed to rightly gauge their real relationship to one another and to the national life of which they formed so important a part. It was not altogether unnatural that this should have happened, for the railroads were born in a time of fierce controversy, were compelled to fight for their own existence, fell prey to an arrogance born of their victories, and grew up to maturity during a period when fraud and trickery in business affairs were looked upon with more complaisance than is lately the case. Thus they drifted into the practise of doing unfair and dishonest things to one another and to the people on whose good-will their corporate existence and self-control depended. Many of the errors that they made and the wrongs they did were, to a considerable extent, the result of a legacy left to them, and were committed by men who lived and worked and schemed according to the standards of a time now outgrown.

The travel conditions that prevailed throughout the eastern and middle states from about 1840 to 1850 were confusing and chaotic to anyone who had not purchased his knowledge at the cost of experience. There were so many different methods of making any contemplated journey of length, and so many possible conditions to be encountered during its progress that the prospective traveller was often bewildered—despite the advice he received and the innumerable guide books he read—with regard to the most desirable plan to pursue in reaching his intended destination. Of public conveyances fiercely competing for his patronage he sometimes had the choice of steamboats, stage-coaches, canal boats and railways in half a dozen combinations; and the advisability of using any particular combination often depended on matters or distant circumstances which it was impossible for him to know in advance. He was only certain of one thing, namely, that the representative of each line declared without qualification that his company's vehicles were pre-eminently the most desirable, comfortable, expeditious, cheapest and safest. Furthermore, the extension of existing public travel routes of every sort was going ahead with such rapidity that no source of advance information to which an ordinary man might obtain access could safely be depended upon as an accurate picture of the situations which he would encounter on his proposed trip.

All those things combined to make possible the practise of deceptions and frauds on travellers, and the opportunities thus presented were in many cases seized by

327.—A revival of the old custom whereby taverns issued money. Sample of the script printed by a Cincinnati hotel for the convenience of travellers and the local population during the Civil War.

men who were in position to profit by such conduct. Many of the guide books issued for the information of travellers contained references to certain deceptions here outlined and warnings against them, but perhaps none was more outspoken concerning this phase of the travel conditions of the time than a little volume printed in Boston in 1851.[1] An extract from this book will give a glimpse at some of those former elements of travel that sprang from deceit and misrepresentation rather than from actual

[1] "The Irish Emigrant's Guide for the United States." By Rev. J. O'Hanlon.

328.—Bird's-eye view of Detroit showing the water-front and a railway terminal after the railroad era had assumed importance in the Middle West. An example of the effect, upon an interior city's growth, of the introduction of steam transportation.

physical discomfort. In discussing the subject its author said:

"Frauds of boarding-house keepers, however, are cast in the shade by the impositions of forwarding houses and the persons in their employ. The nature of this business consists in a contract entered upon between . . . these firms and the owners of steamboats, stage coaches, canal boats and railroad cars, in which the forwarding houses agree to receive the tickets of these agents at a stated price, and to transport the holders and their luggage to places along their route. It will be the object of the forwarding agents to make as much on the tickets as the purchasers will agree to pay. This, however, would be the least objectionable feature in the business, if in all cases other engagements were fulfilled. But such is seldom the case. Sometimes tickets being [are] furnished to passengers in New York which profess to run them through to their destination without further charge; these tickets are protested[1] at the first stage of their route, and various objections made, either as to the mode of conveyance or the distance agreed on. The headquarters of these swindling concerns are established at important cities in the interior; as, for instance, those in the state of New York are principally located at Albany. Before the Emigrant starts from New York for a Northern or Western destination, he receives a ticket neatly printed and headed by engravings of a steamboat, railroad cars or canal boats, with three horses attached. He is given to understand that on the payment of an exorbitant or a low price, as the case may be, at New York, this ticket will carry him through Albany to a place mentioned; whereas the ticket itself only procures a passage to this latter city, where it has to be presented to some agent or company on which it is drawn. If the holder be supposed to possess plenty of money he is obliged to pay his fare over again, which he will frequently do, rather than delay or return to New York to prefer a useless complaint, no evidence being obtained to substantiate it. . . .

"Sometimes passengers are promised passage on packet boats on the canal, and are sent by line boats instead, when [where] they are crowded together in the hold without comfort or convenience. The following is the manner in which this deception is practiced in Albany. . . . The passenger with whom the false engagement is made is transported from Albany to Schenectady by railroad, a distance of 17 miles, and at a cost of 50 cents. Once there, the passenger cannot obtain redress, and is obliged to take up with any means of conveyance offered."[2]

The practise of defrauding travellers by means of misrepresentation and extortion grew so rapidly in New York

---

[1] By the transportation companies.
[2] The traveller who was proceeding to Buffalo and the West by canal embarked on his boat at Schenectady. O'Hanlon's "Guide," pp. 53-59.

CHICAGO—*By Railroad and Steamboat.*

NEW-YORK to	Distance.	Time	Ex. Frt. pr. 100 lb.	FARE. Am. Cur.	FARE. En. Cur.	
		d. h.	cents.	$ c.	s.	D.
Albany,	145	12	18	50	2	1
Utica,	255	17	Free.	2 6	8	6
Syracuse,	316	1	Free.	2 92	12	6
Auburn,	365	1 2	Free.	3 36	14	0
Rochester,	415	1 2	Free.	4 61	19	4
Buffalo,	508	1 8	Free.	5 50	22	11
Erie,	600	2 12	39	7 50	31	3
Ashtabula,	650	2 12	39	7 50	31	3
Cleaveland,	700	3	39	8 00	33	4
Black River,	720	3	44	8 50	35	6
Huron,	740	3 6	44	8 50	35	6
Sandusky,	755	3 6	44	8 50	35	6
Maumee and Monroe,	780	3 12	44	8 50	35	
Detroit,	825	4	44	8 50	35	6
Sandwich, U. C.	820	4	44	8 50	35	6
Mackinaw and G. Bay,	1474	6	70	12 00	52	1
Milwaukee and Racine	1480	6 00	70	12 00	52	1
Chicago,	1520	6 12	70	12 50	52	1

By this route at least seven days are saved, as also the freight of baggage from Albany to Buffalo—100 pounds baggage free to Albany, and the same on the Lakes. Children under twelve years, half-price. Infants free. The above time can always be depended upon.

329.—Table giving the time occupied in travelling from New York by rail and steamboat, in 1848, to Cleveland, Detroit, Milwaukee and Chicago. Also the cost of tickets. From Warner's "Immigrant's Guide and Citizen's Manual: 1848."

during the decade beginning with the year 1841 that an investigation of the subject was finally undertaken by the legislature of the state in 1849. This investigation brought out the fact that all concerns called "forwarding houses"[1] employed men called "runners" whose business it was to induce prospective travellers to buy tickets over the lines they represented. The runner was either paid a stated salary or else was given any money that he could obtain in excess of the proper price which should have been paid by the traveller for his ticket. The effect of this system on the general public was exposed to the New York legislators by a witness who testified that the legitimate cost of a ticket from New York to Buffalo was two dollars and fifty cents; of which sum the river steamboat received fifty cents, the line canal boat one dollar and fifty cents, and the forwarding house fifty cents. He further stated that his "runners" represented the cost of the ticket at five dollars, and that for each ticket thus sold at double its proper value the runner himself received two dollars and fifty cents. "I pay the runners at the time the passenger pays his fare," the witness said. "The account stands thus: the passenger pays five dollars; from this deduct river fare, fifty cents; office in New York, fifty cents; canal fare, one dollar and fifty cents. The balance of two dollars and fifty cents goes to the runner."[2]

Another forwarding agent who testified during the New York investigation stated that he employed thirty-six runners whose salaries ranged from ten dollars to one hundred and sixty-five dollars a week.[3] His total payments to runners exceeded six hundred dollars a week,

[1] The name generally given to those establishments which made a business of seeking passengers for transportation lines, and which were paid on a commission basis for the passenger traffic they secured.
[2] O'Hanlon's "Guide," p. 55.
[3] Ibid., p. 55.

which amount, of course, represented the sum unduly obtained from travellers by his representatives. Early methods of this sort formed the foundation on which was later systematically erected the widespread plan of rate-making generally known as "charging all the traffic will bear."

The four principal travel conveyances of the time were described by O'Hanlon in his Guide as follows:

"First: Railroad cars.—The passengers that travel by the first-class carriages pay at least double or treble fares,[1] and are, in consequence, provided with more elegantly fitted cars, lined and cushioned; the higher grades of society take passage by them. The second-class carriages are further removed from the engine, but in other respects their accommodations are not so good, being unprovided with cushioned seats and exposed in summer to flying clouds of dust. . . . The railroad is a safe and most speedy mode of travel. . . . Sometimes danger is to be apprehended from a running off the track, which may be out of repair in places, but an accident seldom occurs through explosion.

"Second: Canal boats.—There are two classes of these, the packets and the line boats. The packets are elegantly furnished, and meals are served up on board by the owners, but the line boat is only used for transportation of freight and passengers who find themselves.

"If the latter desire dressed meals they will have to take on board a cooking stove and cooking utensils, as it will be found a matter of difficulty to procure use of the apparatus belonging to the boat. Most passengers, however, prefer the use of cold victuals, and are satisfied to put up with inconveniences for a few days. There are no berths or beds on the line boat, as on the packet, so that these necessaries have to be taken on board. Passengers sleep in the hold of the boat. Travelling by canal is the safest but slowest mode of conveyance in the United States; the packet boats, however, have a great advantage over the line boat in regard to speed. . . .

"Thirdly: Steamboats.—These have been termed 'flying palaces,' and many of them are fitted up in a style of great magnificence. But the comfort of travelling by them is confined to cabin passengers. Staterooms, accommodating two persons each, in separate berths, are appropriated for retirement by day and for rest at night; ladies and gentlemen have separate cabins, but dine at the same table, which is set out in the

[1] Hardly a proper way in which to state the proposition. The standard fare was the honest cost of a first class ticket; the cheaper tickets—often costing about half the standard rates—represented special ticket prices made to people who were departing from the East to settle in the interior, and which were only good for passage in cars or trains of inferior accommodation and quality.

'social hall,' and stocked with a variety of luxuries. . . . The deck passengers are immediately under the cabin, and in the hinder part of the boat. A few berths are fitted up for their reception without bedding. Provisions must be provided at their own expense, and also a mode of preparing them. Sometimes numbers are huddled together on board without having room to move, or stretch themselves out for rest; the inconveniences of this mode of travelling can hardly be appreciated without being experienced. It has been truly stated that more accidents by explosion, burning or sinking of steamboats occur annually in the United States, and more lives are [thus] lost, than in crossing the Atlantic. Travelling by steamboats is, therefore, not without its dangers.

"Fourthly: Stage coaches.—These are generally more expensive and incommodious means of conveyance, in proportion to distance travelled, than any other. . . . . The roads over which they mostly run are so bad that accidents often occur by upsetting, and the passengers are continually jolted against each other. On some of the remote western routes they are nothing more than covered cabs, and afford little protection against cold in winter."[1]

By the middle of the fifth decade after 1800 the skeleton of the now existing railroad system of the East had come into existence, and railway journeys between most of the principal cities and towns could be performed. The following summary will sufficiently outline the principal features of railroad travel as they existed in the East at that time.

The traveller who left Washington on his way to Boston was limited to one train a day. It traversed the forty miles between the national capital and Baltimore in two-and-a-half hours, for which distance the price of a ticket was one dollar and sixty cents. Half an hour after arriving in Baltimore he was enabled to take passage in another train which carried him to Philadelphia, ninety-seven miles farther on his way, in six more hours. The fare between Baltimore and Philadelphia was three dollars. He was compelled to spend an hour and a half in Philadelphia, from which city he might secure a train that

[1] O'Hanlon's "Guide," pp. 72-74.

conveyed him to New York—eighty-eight miles—in five hours. His ticket for this part of the trip cost him four dollars. Arriving in New York at half past ten at night he was compelled to wait until the next day before resuming his journey, which began at eight o'clock in the morning, and he finally arrived in Boston at half past six o'clock on the second afternoon of his journey, after spending thirty-five and a half hours on the road. The total of his transportation expenses was eleven dollars and sixty cents.

The Baltimore and Ohio Railroad was in operation from Baltimore to Cumberland, which town, one hundred and seventy-eight miles distant, might be reached from Baltimore in nine and a half hours at a cost of seven dollars. One daily passenger train ran each way over the road, leaving in the morning and arriving at its destination in the evening. If a west-bound traveller was desirous of continuing onward from Cumberland he there found a stage-coach awaiting him in which he might proceed to Brownsville, Pennsylvania, a further distance of seventy-two miles. At Brownsville he transferred from his stage-coach to a steamboat and by it eventually reached Pittsburgh. He had then advanced two hundred and ninety miles westward from Baltimore at a cost of ten dollars, and the trip had taken him but thirty-four hours. So he had travelled by railroad, stage-coach and steamboat at the rate of almost nine miles an hour. If he took the National Road on arriving at Cumberland, and journeyed west by stage-coach he reached Wheeling thirty-six hours after leaving Baltimore, having paid eleven dollars for a ticket which had entitled him to travel three hundred and eight miles.

If the traveller desired merely to go from Baltimore to Philadelphia, and proceed no farther, he had the

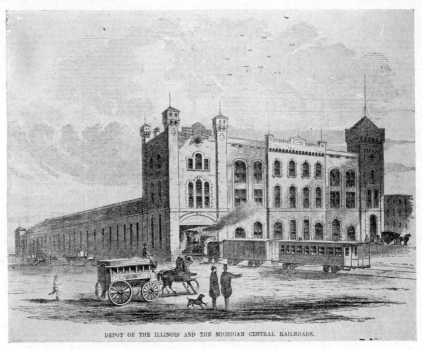

DEPOT OF THE ILLINOIS AND THE MICHIGAN CENTRAL RAILROADS.

330.—A train entering the Chicago railway station of the Illinois Central and Michigan Central roads. Date, 1857.

choice of two trains, one leaving at nine o'clock in the morning and the other at three o'clock in the afternoon. Either one would convey him to his destination in six hours. This was the daily service offered to the public by the Philadelphia, Wilmington and Baltimore Railroad, whose length was ninety-seven miles.

The journey from Philadelphia to Harrisburg, a distance of one hundred and seven miles, might be made in about seven hours at a cost of four dollars. To accomplish this trip the traveller used the Columbia and Philadelphia Railroad for seventy miles, and the Harrisburg and Lancaster Railroad for thirty-seven miles.

Passenger travel between New York City and the numerous near-by towns of New Jersey had increased to such an extent that several trains each day moved back and forth over the New Jersey routes. There were three daily trains between Jersey City and Paterson on the Paterson and Hudson Railroad, and the distance of seventeen miles between the two towns was frequently covered in less than one hour. A ticket cost fifty cents.

West-bound travellers leaving New York City for Newark, Elizabethtown, New Brunswick and Trenton had the choice of two daily trains, one departing at nine o'clock in the morning and the other at half past four in the afternoon. This rail route extended through to Philadelphia from Jersey City. It was composed of three lines, the first being the New Jersey Railroad, thirty miles long, between Jersey City and New Brunswick; the second being the New Brunswick and Trenton Railroad, twenty-nine miles in length; and the third being the Philadelphia and Trenton Railroad, which was twenty-eight miles long.

No less than eight passenger trains a day ran each way between New York and Newark, in New Jersey, and the price of a ticket between the two cities had been reduced to twenty-five cents. All those passengers between New York and the near-by New Jersey towns who bought their railroad tickets at the regular offices of the companies were presented, free of cost, with ferry tickets which entitled them to cross the Hudson River without extra charge.

The Erie Railroad, which still had to maintain its eastern terminus at a point on the Hudson River about twenty-four miles north of New York City, had been completed for seventy-seven miles of its length to the village of Middletown. A traveller desiring to use the Erie road embarked on a steamboat at New York, was conveyed to the eastern terminus of the road in an hour and three-quarters, and in three hours more he was in Middletown, a hundred miles from the big city where his journey had begun. His ticket had cost only one dollar and twenty-five cents.

If a traveller desired to journey northward from New York to Albany he had his choice of two stage-coach routes—one on each side of the Hudson River—or he could go up the river on a steamboat and reach Albany in about fourteen hours. He might then proceed still farther northward from Albany, by means of the Red Bird line of stage-coaches, which ran all the way to Montreal in Canada. The running time of the stage-coach between Albany and Montreal was forty hours, and the price of a ticket from New York to Montreal was sixteen dollars.

A through line of railroad no less than two hundred miles long[1] extended from Boston, in Massachusetts, to Albany, in New York, by means of which a man might be conveyed between the two cities in eleven or twelve hours, at a cost of five dollars. On this much travelled route two trains moved daily in each direction. One of them, however, stopped all night at Springfield, in Massachusetts, and passengers by it were about eight hours longer in making the trip than those who embarked on the cars that courageously refused to pause because of darkness.

The numerous little railroads which had been built with a generally east-and-west trend through central New

[1] Consisting of the Boston and Worcester Railroad, forty-four miles; the Western Railroad, one hundred and eighteen miles; and the Albany and West Stockbridge Railroad, thirty-eight miles.

331.—A bird's-eye view of Chicago just before extensive railway building began to alter a large town and favorable natural location into a world-center of population and economic consequence. The prediction of the unknown prophet of 1822 was in process of fulfillment within a generation.

York State had finally been physically united, and it was at last possible to go from Albany to Buffalo in railroad cars as well as by canal.

On the Erie Canal there were still two daily lines of packet-boats running between the same towns, on either of which a passenger might be carried the whole distance at a cost of five dollars and fifty cents. If he ate the meals furnished by the boat he paid two dollars in addition. The time between Albany and Buffalo by canal packet was about five days. On the Erie Canal line-boats the cost of travel was one cent, or a little more, a mile. But it should be borne in mind that when paying the cheaper of these two rates the traveller furnished his own provender and bedding.

A passenger on the Great Lakes was transported from Buffalo to Detroit for four dollars, and he was charged four dollars in addition for a cabin and his meals if he chose to avail himself of the bed and board furnished by the vessel. The lake boats made special rates to families, and five or six people moving as one party, together with all their domestic and household goods, could obtain passage from Buffalo to Detroit for twenty dollars.

On Ohio River steamboats—during favorable stages of water—the fare from Pittsburgh to Cincinnati was one dollar; to Louisville one dollar and a half; and to St. Louis, two dollars.

From Baltimore to Pittsburgh, by canal and railroad, the charge was about five dollars, with one hundred pounds of baggage free of cost. In journeying from Philadelphia to Pittsburgh the traveller paid from three to four cents a mile while on the canal and six cents a mile on the railroad.

The long trip from the eastern states to St. Louis by

way of the Erie Canal and the lakes cost about fifty dollars, including meals and all other necessary expenses. If the same journey was undertaken by means of line-boats on the canal, and without either cabin or meals while on the steamboats, it could be performed for twenty or twenty-five dollars. The passage by river from New Orleans to St. Louis, a distance of more than eleven hundred miles, cost about eighteen dollars.

The succeeding table will show the length, the means of conveyance and the cost of typical journeys through the Middle West and the South during the same years:[1]

THE JOURNEY FROM	Means of Conveyance	Distance in Miles	Cost
Philadelphia to Pittsburgh	Stage-coach	300	$15.00
Philadelphia to Baltimore	Stage-coach	128	3.00
Baltimore to Wheeling	Stage-coach	271	12.00
Pittsburgh to Wheeling	Stage-coach	59	4.00
Wheeling to Columbus	Stage-coach	140	8.00
Columbus to Cleveland	Stage-coach	177	10.50
Columbus to Cincinnati	Stage-coach	110	6.50
Cincinnati to Lexington, Ky	Stage-coach	76	4.50
Indianapolis to Madison, Ind	Stage-coach	86	4.00
Lexington to Louisville	Stage-coach	75	4.20
Louisville to St. Louis (Via Vincennes)	Stage-coach	276	15.50
Louisville to Nashville, Tenn	Stage-coach	180	12.00
Richmond, Va., to Knoxville, Tenn	Stage-coach	444	28.50
Baltimore to Richmond, Va	Steamboat	378	10.00
Nashville to Memphis	Stage-coach	224	15.00
Augusta to Montgomery	Stage-coach	300	18.50
Tuscaloosa to Mobile	Steamboat	676	12.00
Montgomery to Mobile	Stage-coach	180	12.00
Mobile to New Orleans	Stage-coach	160	12.00
St. Augustine to New Orleans	Stage-coach	600	35.00
Boston or New York to New Orleans (including meals)	Sailing packet		40.00 to 50.00

By the year 1848 the building of railroads had gone ahead to such an extent that their use—whenever such use was possible—had resulted in a material decrease in the time required in journeying from the East to the interior. The following table will indicate the advantage, in point of speed, derived through avail of those

[1] The tables are compiled from information contained in "The Immigrant's Guide and Citizen's Manual." By I. W. Warner. New York: 1848

railroads already extending toward the West or in operation there:

THE JOURNEY	Distance in Miles	Time by Steamboats and Canals	Time by Steamboats and Railroads	Cost by Steamboats and Canals	Cost by Steamboats and Railroads
New York to Utica............	255	2½ days	17 hours	$1.50	$2.06
New York to Buffalo	508	7¾ "	32 "	3.00	5.50
New York to Cleveland........	700	9 "	3 days	5.50	8.00
New York to Zanesville, O....	867	11¼ "	5½ "	7.62	9.75
New York to Portsmouth, O...1,010		13 "	7 "	8.75	11.50
New York to Detroit.........	825	10 "	4 "	5.75	8.50
New York to Milwaukee 1,480		14 "	6 "	9.00	12.00
New York to Chicago 1,520		14½ "	6½ "	9.00	12.50
New York to Pittsburgh	480	7½ "	6½ "	....	8.50
New York to Cincinnati	937	15 "	8½ "	8.25	12.00
New York to Louisville 1,068		....	9¼ "	....	13.00
New York to St. Louis 1,620		....	12½ "	....	14.50
New York to Dubuque, Ia....2,051		....	14¾ "	....	16.00

By means of steamboats, railroads and the Wabash and Erie Canal, the traveller could reach Toledo in four days from New York; Fort Wayne, Indiana, in five and a half days; and Lafayette, Indiana, in seven and a half days. The price of his ticket to Lafayette was twelve dollars and fifty cents. But if he went by way of the Erie Canal, then by steamboat from Buffalo to Toledo and continued thence on the Wabash and Erie Canal he had to pay only eight dollars and twenty-five cents, although he was fifteen days on the way.

In the South the revolution in travel facilities had not gone ahead quite so fast as in the North, but there was nevertheless a vast improvement visible over the circumstances which had confronted the pilgrim only ten or a dozen years before. Additional short railroads were springing into existence, the land roads were multiplying in number and improving in quality, the stagecoaches of the region were making better time than ever before and the steamboats on the rivers, though smaller in

THE GREAT THROUGH LINE
From New York via Baltimore

TO
St. Louis and the Southwest,
Is formed by the following
FIRST CLASS ROADS:

1.—New Jersey, and Camden & Amboy,
From NEW YORK to PHILADELPHIA—87 miles.

2.—Philadelphia, Wilmington & Baltimore,
From PHILADELPHIA to BALTIMORE—98 miles.

3.—The Baltimore & Ohio,
375 miles from BALTIMORE and 396 from WASHINGTON
CITY to BENWOOD JUNCTION; (379 to Wheeling Terminus,) or 383 from BALTIMORE to PARKERSBURG, on the
Ohio River, 96 miles below Wheeling.

4.—The Central Ohio,
From BELLAIRE (opposite Benwood Junction) to COLUM-
BUS—137 miles; or by *MARIETTA ROAD* from Marietta,
(12 miles above Parkersburg,)—200 miles to CINCINNATI.

5.—The Little Miami,
From COLUMBUS to CINCINNATI—119 miles.

6.—Ohio & Mississippi, (Broad Guage,)
From CINCINNATI to ST. LOUIS—340 miles.

☞ In the following pages will be found the details of these several Roads, prepared by their officers respectively.

332.—The joint advertisement of six railways, in 1857, announcing that by their
combined routes, over a distance of 1,156 miles, rail communication had
finally been established between New York City and St. Louis.

size than many of those in the North, often rivalled them in the matter of their appointments.

The man who desired to journey from Baltimore to New Orleans[1] in the most expeditious manner went by rail to Richmond, in Virginia, which he reached in ten and a half hours at a cost of six dollars and sixty cents, after a trip of one hundred and sixty-eight miles. Thence he proceeded, also by a series of railroads, to Wilmington in North Carolina, where he arrived twenty-one hours after departing from Richmond, having left two hundred and fifty more miles behind him. The fare for this part of his expedition was eight dollars and forty cents. He next embarked on a steamboat on which he reached Charleston, in South Carolina, one hundred and seventy-five miles farther on his way, after sixteen additional hours of travel. His steamboat ticket had cost him six dollars. He travelled from Charleston to Augusta, in Georgia, by railroads, thus advancing one hundred and thirty-seven miles in eight hours, and at a further cost of six dollars. Another railroad trip conveyed him over the one hundred and seventy-two miles between Augusta and Atlanta, demanded six dollars and fifty cents more of his money, and twelve hours more of his time. At Atlanta he deserted the railroad for a stage-coach in which he finally attained the town of Chehaw, in Alabama. His fare in the stage-coach was twelve dollars and the time he spent in the same vehicle was twenty-four hours. On reaching Chehaw he shifted back to a railroad again and so came to Montgomery, in Alabama, after a short ride of about three hours, for which he paid two dollars. Again he was compelled to change his method of con-

[1] The information on which the itinerary here outlined is based is to be found in "A Guide between Washington, Baltimore, Philadelphia, New York and Boston, etc., etc." New York: Published by J. Disturnell; June, 1846.

veyance, since the long jaunt of two hundred miles between Montgomery and Mobile still had to be made by means of stage-coach travel. He arrived at Mobile in thirty-six hours, somewhat shaken in the matter of his bones, and ten dollars poorer in pocket. Here he escaped the overland bouncing of railroad car and stage, exchanging them for the possibility of steamboat explosion while he voyaged by water over the one hundred and seventy-five miles that still separated him from the big city on the Mississippi. He reached New Orleans at last after an additional outlay of five dollars, and sixteen hours spent on the boat.

The total distance he had traversed in going from Baltimore to New Orleans was some one thousand four hundred and sixty miles, and his expenditure in transportation charges was sixty-two dollars and fifty cents. The time which had elapsed since he left Baltimore was about seven days. A man who made the trip here outlined, during the year 1846, was compelled to use five railroads, two steamboats and two stage-coaches. His average rate of progress by means of all the nine conveyances required in carrying him to his destination, during the week he spent on the way, was about eight and three-quarter miles an hour.

By the year 1845 the states of the Middle West were rapidly becoming dotted with numerous little railroads, and by the first years after 1850 the facilities for railroad travel in that region closely resembled the similar opportunities that had existed in the eastern states some ten or fifteen years before. In other words it was then possible, in western Pennsylvania, Ohio, Indiana, Illinois, Michigan, Kentucky, Tennessee, and other near-by states, to move between some of the principal cities and towns by means of the new system of transportation. The following compilation[1] will somewhat indicate the degree of advancement which had been reached in the commonwealths mentioned with regard to the possibilities for railroad and other travel. These journeys could then be made at the costs of time and money indicated:

FROM	Distance in Miles	Approximate Time Consumed	Cost of Journey
Cincinnati to Cleveland[2]	254	11 hours	$7.00
Cincinnati to Chicago[3]	571	30 hours	11.00
Cincinnati to Indianapolis	177	9 hours	4.00
Cincinnati to Springfield, Ill.[4]	394	about 30 hours	14.00
Cincinnati to Charleston, S. C.[5]	919	5 or 6 days	35.20
Chicago to St. Louis	407	24 hours	7.00
Indianapolis to Cleveland	431	about 30 hours	11.00
Louisville to St. Louis	570	by steamboat	18.00
Louisville to Chicago	977	3 days	17.00
Nashville, Tenn., to Chicago	844	3½ days	17.00
Lafayette to Indianapolis	63	4 hours	3.85
Detroit to Chicago	277	12 hours	7.00
Atlanta to Chattanooga	140	10 hours	4.20
Macon, Ga., to Atlanta	101	8 hours	4.00
Savannah, Ga., to Macon	191	16 hours	5.75

Such—broadly speaking—were the facilities for human intercourse between separated communities east of the Mississippi just before the memorable days of 1848 and 1849. Pioneer life and crude national conditions in that part of the land were forever gone, to be there supplanted by another and no less absorbing phase of history having to do with the groping of its people through the pioneer experiences of a newer and more complex social life. And now we turn our gaze to observe those few final years—so crowded with cyclopean themes—wherein were encompassed the remaining events that completed the conquest of the continent.

[1] Based on information to be found in "James' Rail-Road and Route Book for the Western and Southern States." Compiled by J. Griswold. Cincinnati: 1853.
[2] By means of the Little Miami Railroad, length 64 miles; the Columbus and Xenia Railroad, length 55 miles; and the Columbus and Cleveland Railroad, length 135 miles.
[3] Price of ticket by way of the Lakes, $6.50.
[4] From Terre Haute, Ind., to Springfield, the traveller went by stage-coach.
[5] By river, stage-coach and railroad.

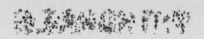